Bringing the Curriculum to Life

Bringing the Curriculum to Life

Engaging Learners in the English Education System

Edited by Janice Wearmouth and Karen Lindley

Open University Press

Open University Press
McGraw Hill
8th Floor, 338 Euston Road
London
England
NW1 3BH

email: enquiries@openup.co.uk
world wide web: www.openup.co.uk

First edition published 2021

A catalogue record of this book is available from the British Library

ISBN-13: 9780335249879
ISBN-10: 0335249876
eISBN: 9780335249886

Library of Congress Cataloging-in-Publication Data
CIP data applied for

Typeset by Transforma Pvt. Ltd., Chennai, India

Praise page

This is a terrific text which examines a wide range of contemporary issues in Education. The intrinsic value of the book is that it seeks to illuminate the discussions surrounding the issues identified, from differing and alternative perspectives in education. The text is clearly and logically structured and will be an essential read to all those involved in education, who genuinely seek to bring the curriculum to life in a real life *context, and where the learner is central and fully involved in their own learning.*
> Dr Barry Paraskeva Costas, Senior Lecturer in Physical Education,
> University of Hertfordshire, UK

Bringing the Curriculum to life delivers exactly what it promises on the cover. A highly engaging and refreshing look at how a diverse range of learners might be immersed in their learning, this book provides an imaginative and thought-provoking consideration of creative curricula to involve and inspire learners. Each chapter offers a reflective look at specific aspects of transformative learning which will be of interest to practitioners and academics alike.
> Julie Wharton, Senior Lecturer, University of Winchester, UK

'Curriculum' as an object of academic interest has been in relative decline in recent years in relation to other aspects of learning and teaching and assessment and pedagogy. Yet curriculum is a highly contested issue and as the contributors to this book explore, a hotly debated political topic. In this sense, this edited work is very timely, offering a scholarly and innovative counter-point to recent political attempts to conceive curriculum in very narrow ways. The contributions in this book show curriculum for what it is – challenging, innovative and at its heart a means to support divergent learners. This book does an excellent job of drawing together a wide range of contributions and contexts that collectively put the challenges and opportunities of curriculum centre stage. This is an excellent and detailed account of why curriculum matters so much.
> Dr Warren Kidd, School of Education and Communities,
> University of East London, UK

Contents

Introduction

Janice Wearmouth and Amber Fensham-Smith

The focus of this book is acknowledgement of the importance of creating curricula that engage learners in their studies at all stages of formal education, if they are to achieve levels of which they are capable, and, hence, leave school or college with enhanced future life chances. The rich and diverse collection of contributions made in this book reflect a range of values, assumptions and ideas about how and in what ways different groups and communities may construct, enact and imaginatively extend curriculum within (and sometimes outside of) state-maintained schools at different levels and in different areas of the curriculum. A core intention of this book is to offer its readership a wider lens through which to revisit and reflect on some of the assumptions that inform the design and delivery of curriculum in practice. Some of the overarching questions and ideas raised foreground the implicit tensions and opportunities connected to the rights of learners, the role of parents, the state and other stakeholders.

In some national contexts there are mandated national curricula that may, or may not, be overly prescriptive and/or sufficiently flexible to enable teachers to respond to the interests and strengths of their young people. Such is the case in England, for example. Prior to the advent of the National Curriculum in England in 1988, it was teachers who usually decided what and how to teach. The content of textbooks or examination syllabuses often guided decision-making, although the then Schools Council introduced a number of innovative curriculum development projects, for example, the Schools Council History Project; the Humanities Curriculum Project (HCP); and Nuffield Science, whose influence on curriculum and pedagogy is still discernible. However, there were politicians in all parties who were becoming critical of what they saw as the take-over of the curriculum by the educational establishment, that is, the teaching profession and the universities.

In 1976, the Labour prime minister, James Callaghan, initiated a 'great debate' on curriculum, followed by moves made by the Conservative prime minister Margaret Thatcher and her Secretary of State, Kenneth Baker, who brought in fundamental changes to education in England and Wales through the Education Reform Act of 1988 when the organization of education changed dramatically. The introduction of the Education Reform Act made wide-scale changes to the organization of education at primary, secondary and tertiary levels, including the introduction of a National Curriculum, and was the most significant piece of legislation since 1944. Norwich (1990) explains how a pre-occupation with the demonstration of accountability for improvement in the standard of pupil learning led to the formulation of an assessment-based curriculum (Lawton and Chitty, 1988) rather than an emphasis on engagement with the complex process of curriculum design to achieve educational aims. He notes, for example, how targets in the curriculum are identified with the primary aim of focusing on the assessment of attainment. There is less emphasis on curriculum design and development and the translation of broad intentions into increasingly more specific intentions at various levels in the education system:

> The focus on attainment targets and assessment derives mainly from the government's wish to raise national educational attainment levels. It is based on the belief that the wider use of assessment information by those with a stake in schools will increase accountability and raise standards.
>
> (Norwich, 1990, p. 160)

In expressed pursuit of raising standards in a post-industrial economy, Mrs Thatcher's favoured promotion of a free market in education viewed a common curriculum, and associated testing arrangements, as the way to evaluate schools and hold them accountable for their pupils' achievements, or lack thereof. The first National Curriculum (NC) comprised three core subjects (English, mathematics and science) and seven foundation, at both primary and secondary levels. However, it became clear that the curriculum was virtually unmanageable, so, in 1993, the first of a number of reviews and revisions was begun. Several reviews and revisions later, Michael Gove, Secretary of State in the new Conservative/Liberal Democrat coalition that came into power in 2010, initiated another review that eventually led to the current NC. A dominant concern of Michael Gove and his school standards minister, Nick Gibb, in commissioning this review appears to have been a belief that there was both a 'lack of attention to "knowledge" in the curriculum' and a 'dominance of progressivist pedagogy' (James, 2018).

In 2013, the government published the NC that is now in force. Despite Gove's promise to reduce the amount of curricular prescription, the primary curriculum gives 85 pages of statutory requirements and non-statutory guidance for English, 44 pages for mathematics, 31 pages for science, and two pages each for eight foundation subjects. Criticizing the narrowness of the government's approach, Alexander (2012) commented that what this represents is a proposal for three subjects only, not for a balanced curriculum. Attempts to conceptualize the curriculum as a whole by various educators, including the Expert Panel and the Cambridge Primary Review, and to address issues of balance and scope associated with economic, cultural and individual need

> have been rejected in favour of the assumption that if the inherited 'core' subjects are prescribed in detail the rest can sort itself out. Past evidence

shows that in relation to what happens in many schools this assumption is optimistic.

Although in the secondary curriculum there is less prescription, Amanda Spielman, Chief Inspector for the Office for Standards in Education (Ofsted), is reported in the *Times Educational Supplement* (Hazell, 2018), as being seriously concerned about secondary schools being encouraged by school examination boards to teach children to the tests from the age of 11, with the result that children have reduced experience of a full curriculum. Such a narrow approach reinforces a view that exposure to a rich curriculum is less important than pre-set targets relating to examination outcomes. In the same article, a mathematics teacher is quoted as concerned that narrow prescription and over-emphasis on testing and assessment risk pupil disaffection and disengagement from school studies.

A further article in the *TES* reporting on its analysis of Department for Education data over a period of eight years, from 2011 (Ward, 2018), revealed changes to the balance of the hours spent teaching subjects in secondary schools, with less time devoted to music, art and drama, and increasing numbers of hours spent on English, mathematics and science.

James (2018) notes a number of recurring themes throughout the last 30 years of the National Curriculum. Included in these are the balance between the NC and a school curriculum designed to address local interests, between the development of knowledge of facts, and of skills/processes, and the appropriate degree of prescription to avoid curriculum overload. The authors of chapters in the proposed publication acknowledge these themes, but would argue that there are further matters to be taken into account: proper consideration in the school curriculum of the issue of pupil engagement, immediate relevance to pupils' lives and personal interests, and the issue of rights and entitlements to education in the first place.

In terms of engagement and relevance, research has demonstrated that engaging students in the learning process increases their attention and focus, motivates them to practise higher-level critical thinking skills and promotes meaningful learning experiences (Schiefele *et al.*, 1992). One might quote from Ted Wragg's work as he reflected on the apparent straitjacket of the National Curriculum: 'One important element of the craft skills of teaching … is the ability to pick ways through a curriculum, even a prescribed one, via as imaginative and challenging routes as possible' (Wragg *et al.*, 1998, p. 23).

With regard to the right to education, compulsory education provision and implications for rights-respecting curriculum design and delivery fall across a collection of statutes, common law precedents, unwritten conventions and international treaties. In schedule 1, Article 2 of the Human Rights Act 1998 declares:

No person shall be denied the right to education. In the exercise of any functions which it assumes in relation to education and to teaching, the State shall respect the right of parents to ensure such education and teaching in conformity with their own religious and philosophical convictions.

Alongside the right to education, the Human Rights Bill 2010 sets out the right 'to respect for private and family life, his home and his correspondence'. Within this part of the statute, interference from a public authority in private lives and the home can only be made on the grounds of: 'the protection of health or morals, or for the protection of the rights and freedoms of others. Individuals also have the right to freedom of thought, conscience and religion and freedom of expression' (Articles 9 and 10). While education is compulsory, schooling is not. Section 7 of the 1996 Education Act states that:

> The parent of every child of compulsory school age shall cause him to receive efficient full-time education suitable—
>
> (a) to his age, ability and aptitude, and
> (b) to any special educational needs he may have,
>
> either by regular attendance at school or otherwise.

The ways in which the National Curriculum serves to prioritize, extend, or deny aspects of children's rights is a complex, multi-faceted field of study. Teaching of human rights, although broad in its inception, is mostly narrowly confined to citizenship education and PSHE (personal, social, health and economic) education, which is a compulsory subject from Key Stage 1, 2, but not in Key Stages 3, 4. However, the non-statutory KS4 curriculum now explicitly mentions human rights, within the context of personal health and ecological issues.

Human rights-centred education and, more recently, the number of schools that explicitly follow UNICEF's Rights Respecting framework (and are awarded status) have increased. UNICEF, for instance, has explicitly mapped the new personal development of judgement, spiritual, moral and social and cultural behaviour and attitudes to a rights-respecting set of criteria:

- Children and young people are included and valued as individuals.
- Children and young people value education and are involved in the decisions about their learning.
- Children's social and emotional well-being is a priority.
- Children know that their views are being taken seriously.
- Relationships are positive and founded on dignity and mutual respect.
- All children and young people have taken action to uphold their rights and the rights of other locally and globally.

Much of the research and case studies of best practice in Rights Respecting Schools initiatives, have highlighted the importance of pedagogic approaches, in addition to merely content teaching related to human rights, that serve to promote democracy, citizenship and a deeper awareness of children's rights within and across education and society. Within the field of RRS initiatives, Webb's (2017) work speaks to the need to foster and reignite 'critical' sensibilities within the context of taken-for-granted discourses of children's rights (p. 2).

Importantly, this work and others have shown the tension between translating rights into the content and pedagogic approaches used across schools. With its emphasis on returning to basics and a somewhat reductive lens on 'essential knowledge', spaces for creativity, innovation and learner-centred curriculum design seem to have shrunk within the context of English policy.

Research in practice has shown that relational approaches that align themselves to children's rights are often positioned as a transformative learner motivation, engagement, belonging and sense of self. It is beyond the scope of this book to consider the complexities of enacting rights-based approaches in practice, from the position of rights-centred or rights-respecting education. Instead, we are encouraged to question the degree to which learners and their communities are afforded opportunities actively to influence what, how and where they learn. We take the view that offering learners opportunities to develop modes of enquiry and problem-solving skills that transcend the acquisition of neatly packaged subject-specific skills speaks to some of the ways in which novel, flexible and evolving strategies might be used to build opportunities for young people to develop deeper and more meaningful connections to the co-constructed worlds they inhabit. This speaks to the importance of transformative learning that encourages pupils to see the value and relevance of education to their everyday lives.

Structure of the book

Part 1: Current curriculum context at national level

The editors have taken the view that it is important first to discuss the constraining influences in the national context in England so that the significance of what is discussed in various chapters of this book can better be understood. The opening two chapters, Chapters 1 and 2, therefore outline a brief history of the development and changes in the government's education inspection arm in England, the Office for Standards in Education, that keeps the national curricular requirements on schools in place. They go on to consider the importance of teacher autonomy for successful relationships between teacher, learner and the curriculum they are exploring together and the damage that may be done by the privileging of particular views of curriculum by policy-makers and central government more widely.

Part 2: Alternative/bespoke education

Subsequently, Chapters 3 and 4, in Part 2, turn to issues of alternative or bespoke education: elective home education (EHE) and curriculum provision for learners with profound and multiple learning difficulties (PMLD). They discuss the rise of EHE and the voices of EHE children commenting on experiences and needs, and offer an overview of the right of learners with profound and multiple learning difficulties to access a curriculum that is meaningful to them and explores research around how curricula can support their needs.

Part 3: Creative engagement in the curriculum

Chapters 5 and 6, in Part 3, focus on literacy learning, and how to bring this aspect of the school curriculum to life. They discuss moving away from the rather formulaic and GCSE-dominated approaches that have taken hold in recent years and moving back to being a curriculum area focused on celebrating the best that the discipline of English has to offer. They argue that, even within the tight prescription of the National Curriculum framework, there can be room for a degree of flexibility to enable cultural responsiveness and sensitive engagement with students' own views, aimed at addressing literacy difficulties. In chapters 7 and 8, the authors focus specifically on the power of student voice in bringing the curriculum to life, and suggest the potential of dialogic group work in enhancing student engagement across the English National Curriculum. In Chapter 8, there is a case study of effective personalized provision made for one rather disaffected young man that used the concept of his hobby, pigeon racing, to rekindle his engagement with literacy learning and achievement. The theme of student engagement is continued in Chapters 9 and 10 with, first, a challenge to the oft-cited notion that contemporary teaching practices are better and more innovative than their historical counterparts, using the example of Physical Education (PE) and the historical legacy of both Rudolf Laban (Dance) and Kurt Hahn (outdoor learning and adventure education) (OAA). Then there is a further focus on the physical education curriculum and a plea for a broad and balanced curriculum offer, where all children and young people are challenged, engaged, included and inspired to achieve.

Part 4: Making it real

Part 4 moves on to consider the benefits of experiencing subject content with real-life examples in a variety of contexts and discusses the limitations to understanding when 'perfect' situations are used, in Chapter 11. It continues the theme of authenticity in Chapter 12 by considering the role and purpose a quality Forest School education has within the National Curriculum. Next, there is a focus on authentic teaching of modern foreign languages using strategy-based instruction in Chapter 13, but within a social constructivist understanding of learning through collaboration, to provide generalist teachers with the skills necessary to develop their multilingual awareness and promote multilingual literacies.

Part 5: Learning environment: teacher trainers', early years teachers' and child and adult learners' perspectives

The final Part first takes the important issue of pupil behaviour and its relationship to the wider curriculum, and in Chapter 14 discusses ways of helping new teachers, teaching assistants and other adults who work in schools to understand the 'bigger picture' within which behaviour occurs. Chapter 15 moves to the early years to consider how, for the authors, teaching in two contrasting environments for early years education (England and Tanzania) led to them reflecting on the connections between learning environments and teaching pedagogies. The next chapter, Chapter 16, discusses culturally responsive approaches for children with English as an Additional Language (EAL). The volume concludes in Chapter 17 with a discussion of ways in which the content of the PSHE curriculum can be inclusive of all learners. It is written from the perspective of one of the authors on the theme of Personal, Social, Health, and Economic (PSHE) programmes. While such programmes may have a positive impact on both academic and non-academic outcomes for some pupils, lesson content may be potentially damaging to those who are disadvantaged in some way.

References

Alexander, R. (2012) 'Neither national nor a curriculum', *Forum*, 54(3): 369–83. Available at: https://cprtrust.org.uk/wp-content/uploads/2014/06/Neither-National-Nor-a-Curriculum.pdf (accessed 25 January 2021).

Hazell, W. (2018) 'Exclusive: Exam boards market GCSE-style tests for Year 7s', *TES*, 21 August. Available at: https://www.tes.com/news/exclusive-exam-boards-market-gcse-style-tests-year-7s (accessed 25 January 2021).

James, M. (2018) *National Curriculum in England: The First 30 years, part 1*. Available at https://www.bera.ac.uk/blog/national-curriculum-in-england-the-first-30-years-part-1 (accessed 28 January 2021).

Lawton, D. and Chitty, C. (1988) *The National Curriculum*, London: Kogan Page.

Norwich, B. (1990) *Reappraising Special Needs Education*, London: Cassell.

Schiefele, U., Krapp, A. and Winteler, A. (1992) 'Interest as a predictor of academic achievement: A meta-analysis of research', in K.A. Renninger, S. Hidi, and A. Krapp (eds), *The Role of Interest in Learning and Development*, Mahwah, NJ: Lawrence Erlbaum Associates, Inc., pp. 183–212.

Ward, H. (2018) 'Exclusive: Arts slashed as core subjects take over', *TES*, 31 August. Available at: https://www.tes.com/news/exclusive-arts-slashed-core-subjects-take-over (accessed 25 January 2021).

Webb, R. (2017) '"Being yourself": Everyday ways of doing and being gender in a "rights-respecting" primary school', *Gender and Education*, 31: 1–16.

Wragg, E.C., Wragg, C.M., Haynes, G.S. and Chamberlain, R.P. (1998) *Improving Literacy in the Primary School*, London: Routledge.

Part **1**

Current curriculum context at the national level

The editors have taken the view that, in a book focused on bringing the curriculum to life, it is important first to discuss the constraining influences in the national context in England so that the significance of what is discussed in various chapters of this book can better be understood. Chapter 1, therefore, opens the book by drawing on the UK context to outline a brief history of the development and changes in the government's education inspection arm, the Office for Standards in Education, that keeps the Department for Education's (DfE) curricular requirements on schools in place. Chapter 2 continues the theme of the curriculum and considers that teacher autonomy is crucial if there is to be a rich, successful relationship between teacher, learner and the curriculum they are exploring together. However, curricula are exercises in power. Chapter 2 suggests that the views of curriculum espoused by politicians, school regulators and other educational commentators are, frequently, manifestations of educational power relations. The privileging of particular views of curriculum by policy-makers and central government more widely has, in many ways, damaged the development of the teacher-learner-curriculum relationship and what theoretical ideas about curriculum can offer as a way to support the best teaching and learning. It concludes with a plea for practitioners and policy-makers to think more widely about theoretical conceptions of curriculum and their relationship to practice.

Part 1

Current curriculum context at the national level

1 The Office for Standards in Education (Ofsted) and the curriculum

Oliver Belas

Major questions addressed in this chapter are:

- How has Ofsted developed since its inception in the late 1980s, and how has this influenced curriculum 'delivery'?
- In what ways is Ofsted part of a broader – and 'longer' – educational history, in which curricula, culture, and the role of the state are all contested?
- In what ways does Ofsted 'shape' schools' curriculum planning and 'delivery'?

Abstract

This chapter offers an overview and critique of the Office for Standards in Education, Children's Services and Skills, better known as Ofsted. While Ofsted does not write the curriculum, it does assess the efficacy and quality of schools' curricular provision; and because schools in England stand or fall by Ofsted's judgements, often their curricular provision will be a function of their 'Ofsted-readiness' plans (something Ofsted has tried to address in recent years through revised inspection frameworks and 'myth-busting' exercises). This chapter aims to sketch the ways – both covert and overt – in which Ofsted exerts pressure on schools' curricular provision.

Introduction

The aim of this chapter is to offer, with an eventual focus on curricular matters, an overview and critique of the non-ministerial wing of England's national government known as Ofsted – originally the Office for Standards in Education; more recently the Office for Standards in Education, Children's Services and

Skills. This task brings with it the obvious difficulty of writing about a 'living' entity subject to change, something not yet fixed in and consigned to the past. The familiar story of the relationship between Ofsted and schools is one of antagonism, of a relationship characterized by growing reciprocal distrust.[1] Unsurprising perhaps, as one can hardly imagine a perfectly balanced, mutually beneficial symbiosis catching the headlines. But this story of discord is not mere caricature: journalistic and academic accounts alike consistently tell tales of educators demoralized, deprofessionalized, and sometimes made unwell, not only by the lived reality of Ofsted inspections, but also by having to exist in a constant state of panoptic Ofsted-readiness. (Doubtless some will dismiss tales of the haunting effects of Ofsted as shabby dime-store horrors spun by 'the New Enemies of Promise' (as a former Education Secretary once characterized his opponents) (Gove, 2013), and will offer a counternarrative of rising standards in teaching and learning outcomes (e.g. Wilshaw, 2016).). Despite this all too familiar and overwhelmingly negative popular narrative, there are commentators (other than politicians and Ofsted directors, managers and inspectors) who recognize the need for – and potential good of – if not Ofsted *per se*, then some state-run mechanism for school accountability and improvement. Frank Coffield (2017), for example, while being highly critical of Ofsted in its current form, has proposed an alternative model of inspection and accountability – one, he believes, that would recognize the expertise of educators and would be founded upon equitable, constructive yet critical dialogue.

England's education system is relatively unusual for having a National Curriculum tightly controlled by central government. While Ofsted does not write the curriculum, it does assess, among other criteria, the efficacy and quality of schools' curricular provision, one indicator of which, for the inspectorate, is external results data which record student progress and the proportion of students crossing benchmark attainment thresholds. Because, as some readers will know, schools in England stand or fall by Ofsted's judgements of their overall efficacy, and because final outcomes are a key indicator, in many cases schools' curricular provision is a function of their strategies for 'Ofsted-readiness' – something Ofsted (2018b) has tried to address in recent years through revised inspection frameworks and 'myth-busting' exercises. Via brief considerations of Ofsted's role and processes, two of its more prominent Chief Inspectors, and the longer cultural history of educational and cultural politics in which it is inscribed, this chapter aims to sketch the ways – both covert and overt – that Ofsted exerts pressure on schools' curricula provision.

Ofsted: A brief overview[2]

Role and inspection framework

Ofsted's educational role is the monitoring, reporting on and driving of school improvement (primarily but not exclusively in the state sector) through systematic inspection. In the organization's own words, 'Ofsted exists to be a force for improvement through intelligent, responsible and focused inspection and regulation' (Ofsted, 2019, p. 4). It was the product of the 1992 Education Act, and by 1998 all state primary and secondary schools in England had been inspected at least once (Scanlon, 1999). Schools' performances are assessed against an inspection framework, which undergoes periodic revision (significant changes were made in 2005, 2012 and 2014). In 2019, Ofsted published a draft of its next inspection framework, in which the key areas for judging schools' overall effectiveness are quality of education; behaviour and attitudes (of both staff and students); personal development; leadership and management. In the previous framework (Ofsted, 2015, p. 11), the key areas were: effectiveness of leadership and management; quality of teaching, learning and assessment; personal development, behaviour and welfare; outcomes for children and learners. In the 2005 framework for inspection (Ofsted, 2005, pp. 18–21), other than overall effectiveness, the key areas were: achievement and standards; the quality of provision; leadership and management. There is some consistency between the key areas as stated in the most recent inspection framework and earlier iterations, *though note the changes both in the language and sequencing of the areas.*

Her Majesty's Chief Inspector (HMCI)

Ofsted is headed up by Her Majesty's Chief Inspector (HMCI), of which there have been nine to date, and of which the best known are Sir Chris Woodhead (appointed in 1992 under a Conservative government, and kept on by 1997's incoming New Labour government), and Sir Michael Wilshaw (HMCI from 2012 until 2016). Divisive figures both, they are remembered for their pugilistic styles and are closely associated with the steady souring of Ofsted/educator relationships over the years.

Certainly, neither Woodhead nor Wilshaw seemed concerned to court the favours of educators. Upon his appointment in 1994, Woodhead called for incompetent teachers to be sacked, and he went on to claim, the following year, that there were 15,000 such teachers in England (Beckett, 1999; Smithers, 2015). Newspapers reported parties erupting in schools upon the news of Woodhead's resignation in 2000 (Chrisafis, 2000), yet another indication of the historically poor relations between Ofsted and schools. Ethical question-marks hang over Woodhead's record as HMCI. In 2005, *The Guardian* unearthed evidence that in 1997 Woodhead had personally overruled the judgement of two inspection teams which had passed Islington Green, and had declared the school to be failing (Smithers, 2005). Woodhead's public fall from grace must surely have delegitimized Ofsted for many, though certainly not all, educators (Chrisafis, 2000).

Wilshaw is an equally divisive figure. In 2012 – before he had officially taken office – he declared: 'If anyone says to you that "staff morale is at an all-time low", you know you are doing something right.' He attacked 'lazy' teachers, thus fuelling a pernicious stereotype not supported by research, though he later defended his words as 'shorthand for saying "take performance management seriously'" (Britland, 2012; Whittaker, 2018). Wilshaw has been criticized for what some see as an over-emphasis on leadership at the expense of teachers and pupils (Coffield, 2017, Chapter 1) – note again the ordering of the key areas for judgement in the 2015 Ofsted framework – although his exact position on this issue is hard to discern: pendulum-like, he appears to swing between vilification and valorization of teachers, schools and parents (*Guardian/Press Association*, 2014; Wilshaw, 2016). It was under Wilshaw's leadership that the overall judgement 'Satisfactory' was replaced with 'Requires Improvement' (though his predecessor, Christine Gilbert, had insisted that being merely satisfactory was not satisfactory); that light-touch inspections for 'Outstanding' and 'Good' schools, and a general slimming down and clarifying of guidance for schools, were introduced; and that inspectors' training was brought in-house and their freedoms for private enterprise (such as hiring themselves to schools for Ofsted support) were curtailed. In short, Wilshaw's legacy, as Laura McInerney (2016) noted upon his retirement, is mixed: where he once likened himself to Clint Eastwood's anti-hero 'Dirty' Harry Callahan, McInerney suggests that *The Good, the Bad, and the Ugly* provides a better point of comparison.

Inspections and outcomes

Following inspection, a written report is supplied to the school, and is subsequently made available to the public online. Schools judged as either 'Requires Improvement' or 'Inadequate' may be placed under Special Measures; failure to demonstrate sufficient, timely improvement can lead to forced academization[3] or even closure. While full inspections are scheduled on a roughly four-yearly cycle, 'Outstanding' schools are exempt from routine inspection and 'Good' schools may receive one-day 'light-touch' inspections carried out by a single inspector or reduced team (though the validity of these has been called into question (NFER, 2019)).

Educators' trust in Ofsted is often low (Hopkins *et al.*, 2016). Parental trust, however, tends to be high (von Stumm *et al.*, 2020). Research suggests that Ofsted reports and final judgements are key factors for parents choosing schools for their children; but the same research also suggests that Ofsted's impact on students' academic attainment and well-being is negligible (ibid.). Von Stumm *et al.* (ibid., p. 2) report that, while a 'survey of 1,000 parents in the United Kingdom found that Ofsted ratings were the third most important factor to parents when choosing a school, after location and suitability to the child's needs',

> Ofsted ratings of school quality predicted <1% of the observed differences in GCSE examination grades. This finding suggests that even the small benefits of school quality for students' individual outcomes can be largely attributed to schools' selection of student intake, not to their added value.
>
> (ibid., p. 6)

In order to be judged outstanding overall, a school must be judged outstanding for quality of teaching, learning and assessment (Ofsted, 2018a, p. 41); usually, the school will be judged outstanding in all other key areas, though '[i]n exceptional circumstances one of the key judgements may be good, as long as there is convincing evidence that the school is improving this area rapidly and securely towards outstanding' (ibid.). The most recent inspection framework attempts to address, implicitly and somewhat abstractly, the matter of schools narrowing their curricula in order to improve final outcomes – the section dealing with personal development states that inspectors will look for a school curriculum that 'extends beyond the academic, technical, or vocational' and 'provides for learners' broader development' (Ofsted, 2019, p. 11). However, given the requirements of the 'Outstanding' judgement, and the implications of the priority accorded to teaching, learning, and *assessment* – the only recognized measure of which is external data – it is hardly clear that the pressure on outcomes has been reduced either *de facto* or *de jure*.

The extent to which a school's overall judgement depends upon examination results has received a good deal of attention and criticism (Coffield, 2017, p. 732; de Waal, 2008), with some commentators considering, from an international, comparative perspective, the possible merits of decoupling certification from accountability measures (Harlen, 2005). Clearly, such emphasis upon final outcomes will have curricular implications (on which more below).

The Ofsted experience

Unfortunately, many of the reports of educators' Ofsted experiences paint a bleak picture. Frank Coffield claims that a common feeling among educators is that school inspections are an adversarial and punitive process 'done *to* them, not done *with* them in the joint search for improvement' (2017, p. 981). That educators often speak of being 'Ofsteded' perhaps bears out Coffield's claim – nothing indicates notoriety and cultural influence quite like antonomasia (the substitution of a proper noun for a more general concept). Certainly, Coffield is supported by the empirical, qualitative research that punctuates Ofsted's history: repeatedly, we hear of educators feeling demoralized, disempowered, deprofessionalized – and sometimes made ill – by the Ofsted process (Coffield, 2017; Hopkins *et al.*, 2016; Scanlon, 1999; von Stumm, 2020).

Questions have also been raised over the extent to which socio-economic factors pre-determine Ofsted judgements of schools. In a 2016 empirical report on the efficacy and equitability of Ofsted inspections, Hutchinson (2016, p. 25) came to the following three linked conclusions: first, that 'the least disadvantaged schools are most likely to be judged "good" or "outstanding," and that notable proportions of "good" and "outstanding" schools are not down-graded following a substantial deterioration in their academic performance'; second, 'if schools were rated according to levels of pupil progress, we would expect many fewer "outstanding" schools with very low proportions of pupils eligible for free school meals, or low prior attainment when they join the school'; and third, based on measures of pupil progress, 'it is also likely that there would be more "outstanding" schools in disadvantaged areas, which could provide more system leaders in these areas, and would reward and recognise able school leaders who take on the most challenging schools.'

Neither Hutchinson nor Coffield is politically radical, arguing, *pace* Illich, for example, for the dismantling of the school system and cognate state apparatuses.[4] Hutchinson's report is designed to identify 'room for improvements' in Ofsted. Coffield, it is true, delivers a searing critique of Ofsted; he does, however, acknowledge some positives, and factors these into his blueprint for an alternative and, in his view, more humane inspection model. The challenge that Hutchinson and Coffield, among others, have raised in their research is critically important, for such work shows us that the in-built biases (especially socio-economic) of Ofsted and the collateral damage caused by the Ofsted inspection process hamper rather than enable the very improvements with which the organization is charged. This must be a concern to anyone with an interest in education and its systematization; but it is particularly germane to the present volume, as Ofsted's primary focus, since Wilshaw's departure, has been the curriculum (Spielman, 2017).

State education and the politics of culture

Although it was established by the Education Act of 1992, Ofsted can also be read into a longer political history. Ofsted largely replaced Her Majesty's Inspectorate, established in 1839, though a version of this older body survives in the form of the HMCI and a number of Her Majesty's Inspectors (HMIs), who carry out supervisory and training functions and are sometimes involved in Ofsted inspections. In an institutional sense, Ofsted continues a tradition of political technology that reaches into the pre-history of England's state education (timelines for which often take the 1870 Forster Act as a convenient starting point), and which operates on the constantly shifting and contested grounds of national culture.

Perhaps the best-remembered HMI of the nineteenth century is the poet and critic Matthew Arnold, whose definition – so-called – of culture as 'the best which has been thought and said in the world' is regularly cited by educational policy-makers (Arnold, 1869, p. viii). As Shadow Education Secretary, in a speech which augured the reforms to come, Michael Gove (2009) spoke of every child's right 'to be introduced to the best that has been thought, and written' (p. 3); and Arnold remains alive, if not exactly well, in the National Curriculum, which aims to 'introduc[e] pupils to the best that has been thought and said' (DfE, 2014, p. 6).

While Arnold's words have often been used in the service of a narrowly conceived, culturally monochrome curriculum (see, e.g., Belas and Hopkins, 2019), the philosopher Kwame Anthony Appiah points out that Arnold should be read not as a rallying cry for English cultural conservatism, based upon 'anything as narrow as class-bound connoisseurship', but as pointing the way to cosmopolitanism (albeit cosmopolitanism circumscribed by the racialism typical of the day): the best that has been thought and said *in the world*.[5] Arnold was a member of the Taunton Commission, appointed in 1864 to report on the state of middle-class education; his *Schools and Universities on the Continent* is his version of the report he wrote for the Commission. If Arnold's view was not a cosmopolitanism in Appiah's truly global and intersectional sense, certainly his views on education – its importance as a mechanism of cultural transmission and national character-formation; the need, therefore, for a strictly ordered system of political administration – were informed by his direct observations of the systems operating in Europe, to which, he felt, England's secondary education compared poorly (Arnold, 1864).

At a time when there was no truly *national system* of education, Arnold advocated for a dedicated education department, headed by a secretary of state. He believed that England's middle classes in particular were among the least educated and cultured, and the most parochially minded, in Europe, and that the only way to correct this was a rigorous system of centrally administered and monitored education (Connell, [1950] 2002, Chapter V). Ian Hunter's seminal work on the political dynamics of literary education begins with the example of Arnold and his belief in the superiority of state over private education. Arnold considers two letters, each written by a child to a family member; the author of one has been educated privately, the other in a state school. Comparing the letters' qualities, Arnold finds in favour of the state-educated child and thus of state education, for here the 'stamp of plainness and the freedom from charlatanism' are assured by the benign oversight of 'impartial educated persons' (Arnold, quoted in Hunter, 1988, p. 2). 'The "impartial educated persons" are, of course,' writes Hunter, 'the inspectorate and the new educational bureaucracy. And the remarkable thing is that Arnold attributes sincerity and "freedom from charlatanism" of the state-educated child's letter 'to the fact that it was produced in a governmental apparatus organized by a certain supervisory function' (Hunter, 1988, p. 2).

It may be tempting, given the strength of control now exercised by central government, to think of Arnold as anticipating the current state of educational play in England, and thus, depending on one's views of the current situation, to vilify or lionize him. To be sure, if he seems to imagine state agencies in the role of Platonic philosopher kings, as the guardians and gatekeepers of culture, then those who incant the Arnoldian cultural maxim seem only too happy to assume that mantle. It is likely, however, that he would have disapproved of the course of educational events since 1988. One might think, for example, that 'performance-related' pay for teachers is a recent idea, one of the many neo-liberal reforms introduced by New Labour (Ball, 2017, 2674–2760); a version of this, however, was proposed in the Revised Code of 1861, which Arnold vociferously opposed. Arnold's opposition to such interventions anticipates and is echoed by more recent calls to decouple pupil outcomes from accountability measures and judgements of school efficacy (mentioned above) (Connell, [1950] 2002; Harlen, 2005).

More obviously relevant to the aims of this chapter and the overall focus of the book is Arnold's proposal of a High Council of Education, a body comprised of the country's best educationalists, whose duty it would be to advise the secretary of state; the secretary of state, for their part, would be obliged to follow the council's advice (Connell, [1950] 2002). Arnold was by no means opposed to the idea of expert arbiters of culture; certainly, he was not averse to what seemed to him the exercise of enlightened authority (Arnold, 1869). But his arbiters of culture should not be the same persons also vying for political power. The role of his High Council would be to protect both culture (that most agile term of art which appears to refer to virtually every- and any-thing while specifying nothing) and its heirs from overweening governmental interference. And the anarchy for which, according to Arnold, culture is the antidote is not class-bound (to draw once more on Appiah); it pervades all tiers of English society and is the result of nothing less than self-interest running rife in the working, middle, and aristocratic classes; the principle of inviolable personal liberty degraded to merely and selfishly 'doing as one likes' (ibid., p. 88, *passim*).

Arnold's proposal for a High Council of Education would hardly have guaranteed against curricular incursions from government, of course. The idea that any organ of the state can be a reliable arbiter of culture and morality is fraught with problems: politics and aesthetics, as Amiri Baraka (Jones, [1963] 2010) and Jacques Rancière (2013) have argued (from very different perspectives), cannot be hermetically sealed off from one another; they are co-implicating – especially so, once 'culture' becomes a site of political contestation. And there are obvious and easy means by which non-executive wings of government can be clipped: ministerial intervention and pressure (direct or indirect); strategic appointments.[6] What we have seen in England, since the Education Reform Act of 1988, is a dual restructuring of power and responsibility: control over the scope of education and schooling has been drawn to the centre, while accountability has been devolved (Ball, 2017, Chapters 1, 2). It is a nice irony that Arnold's polemic against anarchy is a polemic against mechanicalism – as both over-reliance on technology and non-critical, automaton-like behaviour (a lack of enlightened thought) – and that his proposed antidote is more complex mechanisms of government.

Such irony aside, Arnold would surely disapprove of the extent to which he has been misquoted and traduced, especially by policy-makers. For culture is *not* the best which has been thought and said in the world. It is, rather, autopoiesis through engagement with those culture products; it is transformation, not unquestioning acceptance. Here is the sentence, in full, from which the Arnoldian maxim is taken:

> The whole scope of the essay is to recommend culture as the great help out of our present difficulties; culture being a pursuit of our total perfection by means of getting to know, on all the matters which most concern us, the best which has been thought and said in the world, and, through this knowledge, turning a stream of fresh and free thought upon our stock notions and habits,

which we now follow staunchly but mechanically, vainly imagining that there is a virtue in following them staunchly which makes up for the mischief of following them mechanically.

(Arnold, 1869, p. viii)

There is a tension in Arnold, between culture as imposition and emancipation and culture as a mechanism potentially of control or liberation. This tension is not uncharacteristic of philosophical liberalism in general; certainly, it is a familiar feature of nineteenth-century political debate on education, which often found itself caught between the moral obligation to improve the lot of the masses and the need to control them on two fronts: an expanding working class at home and colonial subjects abroad (see Belas and Hopkins, 2019). But such tensions notwithstanding, it is striking that culture, for Arnold, involves grappling with thought; it is not, as policy-makers sometimes suggest by poorly ventriloquizing and traducing Arnold, the passive reception of the past's 'great' culture products and acceptance of their 'greatness'.

Ofsted and the curriculum

One of the ways Ofsted assesses the efficacy of teaching and learning is by examining schools' assessment data, which can be set in local, regional, and national contexts with relative ease due to England's system of national exams. In recent years, the emphasis has shifted from final outcomes (the proportion of students passing a minimum threshold) to rates and levels of progress. Amanda Spielman, HMCI at the time of writing, has acknowledged that previous metrics and accountability measures were in part to blame for schools designing – often narrowing – their curricula around target outcomes; she has said of Attainment 8 and Progress 8 – the government measures of, respectively, pupil and whole-school progress – that these offer 'a fuller picture of pupils' learning' than previous mechanisms; and she has been keen to turn attention away from final outcomes to pupils' educational experiences and the curriculum (Spielman, 2017).

Early in her tenure, Spielman acknowledged that while teaching hours in England were 'close to the international average', teachers also 'spend significantly more time on planning, marking and administration', and that 'unnecessary preparation for inspection plays a major part' in this. To make a recentring of the curriculum feasible, Ofsted published some 'myth-busting' guidance, the aim of which was to make schools and teachers aware of the reduced inspection burden (Ofsted, 2018b).[7] In the speech cited above, Spielman (2017) gives an example of Ofsted's new focus on curriculum provision over and above final outcomes:

Only this week I spoke to an HMI who explained how he'd recently come to judge outcomes in a school to be outstanding. Published progress data was broadly average. But he recognised that the leadership had stuck to its guns, continued to insist on modern foreign languages for all pupils, including in its sixth form, and provided an exceptional curriculum. Those 'average progress points' were hard won by a courageous leadership team, who, by the way, were also judged outstanding as a result.

No doubt this story, coupled with Ofsted's demythologizing, will be welcomed by many. But we must still set this story in the secondary-educational context within which Ofsted works.

It is true that Attainment 8 and Progress 8 measure final outcomes as indications of progress or development. But it is also the case that, in these mechanisms, subjects are placed into one or more of three groups; that subjects are differentially weighted; and that the subjects given priority are the so-called 'Ebacc' (English Baccalaureate) subjects: English, Mathematics, the Sciences, History or Geography, Modern Foreign Languages. The subject groups have become known among educators as 'buckets' – an apt name, for each subsequent bucket is able to take the overflow of the former. In the first are English and Mathematics, which are double-weighted (they contribute twice as much to a school's progress score than other subjects); in the second are all Bucket 1 subjects, as well as the remaining EBacc subjects (the Sciences, History or Geography, Modern Foreign Languages); in Bucket 3 are all EBacc subjects (that is, Buckets 1 and 2), and any remaining subjects on the Department for Education's approved list.

The emergence of the so-called EBacc roster of subjects was part of a government response to schools' supposed gaming of performance measures by entering students into 'soft' GCSE or even point-carrying non-GCSE subjects (Jin *et al.*, 2011). EBacc and Progress 8 were introduced, we are told, 'to encourage schools to offer a broad and balanced curriculum with a focus on an academic core at key stage 4' (DfE, 2016, p. 2). But if 'balance' suggests some sort of equality or equivalence, then one can only conclude that while all subjects are equal, some are more equal than others. The performing and expressive arts, sports, and the various forms of craft and design subjects are among the unnamed soup of Bucket 3 subjects, and are absent from EBacc (though the marginalization of the arts in education is a concern that predates the most recent waves of curriculum and Ofsted reform, and is not a uniquely English concern; Abbs, 1987; Greene, 2001; Nussbaum, 2010). This has led to concerns that arts subjects will become, even more than before the inventions of Progress 8 and EBacc, the preserve of affluent schools and pupils (primarily those in the independent sector) (Belas, 2019). And while results alone are not the sole determinant of a school's overall Ofsted grading, it seems to remain the case, as mentioned above, that schools cannot be judged outstanding overall if they are not so judged in the area of student outcomes. On this score, there seems to be some inconsistency between Spielman's anecdote and Ofsted's guidance.

As well as the twinned contexts of accountability and performance, Ofsted's training and accompanying guidance may also exert a pressure on the ways in which schools interpret and enact the National Curriculum. There is no space for forensic detail here; and it must be said that many of the changes ushered in since 2016 have been welcomed (Coffield, 2017; McCallum, 2019a; 2019b; NFER, 2019). Nevertheless, there are concerns that a lack of understanding, on Ofsted's part, of different subjects and disciplines might negatively impact judgements on schools. This is not the place for a philosophical digression on the epistemic framing of disciplinary knowledges. For now, it is enough to recognize that different subjects consist of different recognized disciplinary practices. Accepting this, it's desirable that Ofsted understand 'subject knowledge' flexibly enough that the various practices of the various subject areas can be recognized and appreciated. The English and Media Centre (EMC), however, while welcoming Ofsted's new direction, has raised questions over the way English and literacy, both implicitly and explicitly, have been framed by Ofsted. They have spelt out their concerns in careful detail (McCallum, 2019a; 2019b). In brief, though, EMC is worried that knowledge in English – and by extension all subjects – is being modelled primarily on mathematical and scientific knowledge (understood in procedural or formalistic terms); that the evidence-base for such modelling is narrow (and may not take into consideration subject-specific research); and that the research Ofsted does consider does not in fact support the conclusions it draws regarding learning and knowledge. Two illustrative examples: Ofsted remains, in the opinion of EMC, overly concerned with spelling, punctuation, and grammar, as well as abstract vocabulary teaching, rather than whole-language learning; it also fails to distinguish between oracy (the deliberate adapting of one's speech depending on context) and talk for learning (dialogic inquiry), in which style or register are relatively unrestricted.

It remains to be seen, then, the extent to which the most recent set of accountability measures, performance metrics, inspection guidelines, and smattering of learning theory will achieve Ofsted's desired shift away from outcomes-oriented schooling. As things stand – with curricula designed and their 'implementation' monitored by government; and with school performance and accountability measures still directly tied to outcomes – we are a long way from the Arnoldian ideal of culture as and thorough education.

Postscript

The Covid-19 crisis, which became a global emergency in 2020, interrupted normal educational processes of teaching, learning and assessment. Such interruptions are especially problematic in England, where we have a centrally controlled system of national qualifications based primarily upon terminal examinations. (Some readers may be aware of – may, perhaps, even remember – the reforms of 2012, led by then Education Secretary Michael Gove, which all but ended modular assessment.) These examinations, upon which, as discussed above, Ofsted relies for much of the data it uses to determine a school's efficacy, were temporarily suspended after England's schools were closed in late March 2020; because of this, Ofsted halted all school inspections. In early July 2020, Spielman announced Ofsted's plans for autumn 2020, as schools prepared to return in September. As this chapter is being written, most schools in England have been open since September 1 – some for staff-only training, while others are open to students and have resumed teaching. Ofsted does not plan to resume graded inspections until January 2021; between October and December 2020, they will carry out visits, the aims of which are to ascertain 'how schools and colleges are getting pupils back up to speed after so long at home' (Spielman, 2020); these visits will be piloted with volunteer schools for the month of September (ibid.). Ofsted 'will help [schools and colleges] though collaborative conversation, without passing judgement – this isn't inspection by stealth. We'll use our visits to listen to school leaders' experiences and plans, and to provide constructive challenge.' Spielman continues:

> The visits will not be graded. We'll publish the outcomes of our discussions with leaders in a short letter so that parents can understand what steps are being taken to help children back into full-time education. And we will use what we learn from our visits to report on the picture across England ... I would stress again that this is about a constructive conversation – we're not trying to catch schools out. After all, we share the same aim: helping this generation of children and young people make up for lost time and get the high-quality education they deserve.
>
> (ibid.)

If they are carried out on the basis Spielman suggests, the stories we hear in the near future about schools' experiences of these visits may be more positive than they have generally been before; research suggests that it is the nature of Ofsted feedback that has the greatest impact on school improvement, with schools responding best (unsurprisingly) to collaborative and open dialogue (Ehren and Visscher, 2008). But even as that tentative suggestion is made, John Roberts reports in the *Times Educational Supplement* that Ofsted *will* have the power to turn these visits into formal inspections, and of educators' calls for a longer suspension of inspections, post-lockdown (Roberts, 2020a, 2020b; 2020c).

With the mass return to school, however, come complexities and pressures. Concerns over the loss of learning and the widening of the learning and attainment 'gap' between the most and least deprived students have led to government promises of a 'massive catch-up operation', though the fine details of this operation are as yet unknown. While the plan does involve funding for additional tuition, the national tutoring programme is unlikely to start until October or November 2020 – around two months into England's school year. The tuition funding is offered at a flat rate on a per-pupil basis, meaning that schools in more economically deprived areas will receive the same funding, per pupil, as those based in relatively affluent areas, despite the former and its pupils being worse affected by lockdown measures. Questions have also been raised over where the additional funding offered to schools has come from. It is not yet clear, for example, whether government has simply redirected funds, rather than increase them. The difference is critical for schools—many of which have lost substantial income usually generated by summer rental of their sites and buildings—trying to budget for the coming year and beyond.[8] This, of course, has curricular implications. Teaching and learning resources cost money. Before the Covid-19 crisis, it was not uncommon to hear of schools supplementing their incomes through parental donations, and here is yet another indicator of educational inequality: schools judged inadequate by Ofsted raised, on average, 'almost 97 per cent less [through parental donation] than their "outstanding" peers' (Allen-Kinross, 2018; see also Ferguson and McIntyre, 2019; McIntyre and Adams, 2019).

Conclusion

This chapter has been written in a time of uncertainty. We end, then, with a series of questions for there are numerous other curricular matters, emerging from or exacerbated by Covid-19, in which Ofsted is implicated. How to budget for the curricular impact of the lockdown? What form or shape will the 'massive catch-up operation' take? (Additional time on certain 'core' subjects, on top of or at the expense of other subjects? How to address the demands of reducing the learning and attainment 'gap', while also offering a 'broad and balanced curriculum' (the semantic vagaries of that term notwithstanding), while also aiming for acceptable levels of progress (which are not the same as outcomes but are measured by them), especially in the ever-scrutinized, priority areas of mathematics and English? How to offer, once again, a 'broad and balanced curriculum' at a time when the possibility of reducing the number of subjects some students might study is being mooted, and when syllabi for some subjects are being reduced in order to ensure national exams can run in 2021 (surely a case, when curricula are tailored to the 'needs' of examinations, of the tail wagging the dog) (Ofqual, 2020; Santry, 2020; Weale, 2020)?

And how to respond to emergent and resurgent calls for curriculum reform? During the period of school closure, some attention was given to the call for a 'Recovery Curriculum', responsive to children's needs post lockdown, and which places sociality first (Carpenter and Carpenter, 2020). This Recovery Curriculum is based upon '5 Levers': relationships; community; a transparent, co-constructed curriculum; metacognition; and conceptual or emotional space. Though developed in response to the pandemic, doubtless some will read this, for both good and ill, as classic Deweyan progressivism. How can schools possibly square the recommendations of the Recovery Curriculum with the demands of Operation Catch-Up, and the looming possibility of visits that may or may not become inspections?

A second example: for some time now, schools, colleges and universities have been under pressure to decolonize their curricula. The murders in the United States of America of Breonna Taylor and George Floyd by white police officers have drawn, for now, mainstream attention back to centuries-old systemic racism and to the Black Lives Matter movement, and also to the decolonize movement. Arnoldian 'culture' is, in fact, a sufficiently vague and abstract notion that it can be marshalled to arguments both for and against decolonized curricula – though Arnold and the decolonize movement are aligned to the extent that both ask us to challenge and revise taken-for-granted, received wisdom. Rewriting curricula, and thus the models of culture and knowledge they presuppose, is more easily addressed in universities – where academics have *relative* freedom over curricula – and schools and colleges with money enough to replace and revise teaching materials. The capacity to change does not, of course, guarantee it.

Notes

1 See, for example, Coffield (2017), de Waal (2008), Hopkins *et al.* (2016), and Scanlon (1999).
2 Thomas (1998) offers a useful pre- and early history of Ofsted. Coffield (2017) is a useful critical source.
3 Readers unfamiliar with the English academy system can consult the government's list of brief definitions (Gov.UK, n.d.).
4 For a recent post-Illichian critique of mass formal schooling, see Bojesen (2020).
5 Appiah (2018, p. 190). Appiah's book is based on his 2016 BBC Reith Lectures. In the discussion following the lecture which corresponds to the last chapter of his book, Appiah re-emphasizes the global reach of Arnold's so-called definition (which is in fact no definition at all) (Appiah, 2016, p. 12).
6 For recent examples of this in England, see Conn (2020) and Dickens (2020d).
7 The guidance, though still accessible online, has been officially withdrawn since the publication of the new inspection framework.
8 On the impact of the school closures on different socio-economic groups, see EEF (2020); on the (at this time) unfolding story of Operation Catch-Up, see Dickens's reports in *Schools Week* (e.g. Dickens, 2020a; 2020b; 2020c).

References

Abbs, P. (ed.) (1987) *Living Powers: The Arts in Education*, London: Falmer Press.
Allen-Kinross, P. (2018) 'Top-rated schools and grammars pocket the most in parental donations', *Schools Week*, 7 December. Available at: https://schoolsweek.co.uk/top-rated-schools-and-grammars-pocket-the-most-parental-donations/ (accessed 23 August 2020).
Appiah, K.A. (2016) Lecture 4: 'Culture'. [Transcript.] 'Mistaken identities: creed, colour, country, culture', BBC Reith Lectures. Recording available at: https://www.bbc.co.uk/programmes/b081lkkj (accessed 13 August 2020).
Appiah, K.A. (2018) *The Lies that Bind: Rethinking Identity: Creed, Country, Colour, Class, Culture*, London: Profile Books.

Arnold, M. (1864) *A French Eton; or, Middle Class Education and the State*, London: Macmillan.

Arnold, M. (1868) *Schools and Universities on the Continent*, London: Macmillan.

Arnold, M. (1869) *Culture and Anarchy: An Essay in Political and Social Criticism*, E-text based upon 1st ed. Available at: http://www.gutenberg.org/cache/epub/4212/pg4212-images.html (accessed 29 August 2020).

Ball, S. (2017) *The Education Debate*. 3rd ed., Bristol: Policy Press.

Beckett, F. (1999) 'The Real Chris Woodhead scandal', *The New Statesman*, 26 April. Available at: https://www.newstatesman.com/node/192892 (accessed 30 August 2020).

Belas, O. (2019) 'Knowledge, the curriculum, and democratic education: The curious case of school English', *Research in Education*, 103(1). 49–67. DOI: https://doi.org/10.1177/0034523719839095

Belas, O. and Hopkins, N. (2019) 'Subject English as citizenship education', *British Journal of Research Education*, 45(2). 320–39. DOI: https://doi.org/10.1002/berj.3500

Bojesen, E. (2020) *Forms of Education: Rethinking Educational Experience Against and Outside the Humanist Legacy*, Abingdon: Routledge.

Britland, M. (2012) 'Teachers who leave school at 3pm shouldn't be branded as lazy', *Guardian*, 27 September. Available at: https://www.theguardian.com/teacher-network/2012/sep/27/teachers-leave-school-not-lazy (accessed 7 July 2020).

Carpenter, B. and Carpenter, M. (2020) 'A Recovery curriculum: Loss and life for our children and schools post pandemic', *Evidence for Learning*. Available at: https://www.evidenceforlearning.net/recoverycurriculum/ (accessed 13 August 2020).

Chrisafis, A. (2000) 'Chris Woodhead's resignation day', *Guardian*, 7 November. Available at: https://www.theguardian.com/education/2000/nov/07/schools.ofsted (accessed 30 July 2020).

Coffield, F. (2017) *Will the Leopard Change Its Spots? A New Model of Ofsted Inspection*, [E-text.] London: UCL IOE Press.

Conn, D. (2020) 'Firm linked to Gove and Cummings hired to work with Ofqual on A-Levels', *Guardian*, 20 August. Available at: https://www.theguardian.com/education/2020/aug/20/firm-linked-to-gove-and-cummings-hired-to-work-with-ofqual-on-a-levels (accessed 23 August 2020).

Connell, W.F. ([1950] 2002) *The Educational Thought and Influence of Matthew Arnold*, London: Routledge.

de Waal, A. (ed.) (2008) *Inspecting the Inspectorate: Ofsted Under Scrutiny*, London: Civitas.

DfE (2014) *The National Curriculum in England*. Available at: https://www.gov.uk/government/publications/national-curriculum-in-england-framework-for-key-stages-1-to-4 (accessed 23 July 2020).

DfE (2016) 'Progress 8: How Progress 8 and Attainment 8 are calculated'. Available at: https://www.gov.uk/government/publications/progress-8-school-performance-measure (accessed 3 August 2020).

Dickens, J. (2020a) 'Boris Johnson promises "massive catch-up operation" for pupils be announced next week', *Schools Week*, 10 June. Available at: https://schoolsweek.co.uk/boris-johnson-promises-huge-amount-of-catch-up-for-pupils-to-be-announced-next-week/ (accessed 7 July).

Dickens, J. (2020b) 'DfE refuses to confirm in £1bn catch-up is cash new funding', *Schools Week*, 25 June. Available at: https://schoolsweek.co.uk/dfe-refuses-to-confirm-if-1bn-catch-up-cash-is-new-funding/ (accessed 3 July 2020).

Dickens, J. (2020c) '"Badly targeted" £80 per-pupil catch-up cash "unlikely" to stop learning gap widening', *Schools Week*, 20 July. Available at: https://schoolsweek.co.uk/badly-targeted-80-per-pupil-catch-up-cash-unlikely-to-prevent-widening-of-learning-gap/ (accessed 27 July 2020).

Dickens, J. (2020d) 'Teach First graduate and Conservative Teachers founder to be new schools policy adviser', *Schools Week*, 23 July. Available at: https://schoolsweek.co.uk/teach-first-graduate-and-conservative-teachers-founder-to-be-new-schools-policy-adviser/ (accessed 23 July 2020).

Education Endowment Foundation (EEF) (2020) 'Best evidence on impact of school closures on the attainment gap', updated 2–3 June 2020. Full report and summary available at: https://educationendowmentfoundation.org.uk/covid-19-resources/best-evidence-on-impact-of-school-closures-on-the-attainment-gap/ (accessed 37 July 2020).

Ehren, M.C.M. and Visscher, A.J. (2008) 'The relationships between school inspections, school characteristics and school improvement', *British Journal of Education Studies* 56(2). 205–27. DOI: https://doi.org/10.1111/j.1467-8527.2008.00400.x.

Ferguson, D. and McIntyre, N. (2019) 'Tale of two schools: "We're paying for a mother to bring her child to school out of PTA funds – and from my pocket,"' *Guardian*, 14 July. Available at: https://www.theguardian.com/education/2019/jul/14/schools-education-funding-parents-children (accessed 7 July 2020).

Gov.UK (n.d.) Types of school. Available at: https://www.gov.uk/types-of-school (accessed 7 August 2020).

Gove, M. (2009) 'What is education for?' [Speech.] RSA. Available at: https://www.gov.uk/government/publications/national-curriculum-in-england-framework-for-key-stages-1-to-4 (accessed 31 August 2020).

Gove, M. (2013) 'I refuse to surrender to the Marxist teachers hell-bent on destroying our schools: Education Secretary berates "the new enemies of promise" for opposing his plans', *Mail Online*. 23 March. Available at: https://www.dailymail.co.uk/debate/article-2298146/I-refuse-surrender-Marxist-teachers-hell-bent-destroying-schools-Education-Secretary-berates-new-enemies-promise-opposing-plans.html (accessed 3 August 2020).

Greene, M. (2001) *Variations on a Blue Guitar: The Lincoln Center Institute Lectures on Aesthetic Education*, New York: Teachers College Press.

Guardian/Press Association (2014) 'Schools should fine "bad parents", says Ofsted chief', *Guardian*, 17 June. Available at: https://www.theguardian.com/education/2014/jun/17/schools-fine-parents-ofsted-michael-wilshaw (accessed 13 August 2020).

Harlen, W. (2005) 'Trusting teachers' judgement: Research evidence of the reliability and validity of teachers' assessment used for summative purposes', *Research Papers in Education*, 20(3), 245–70.

Hopkins, E., *et al.* (2016) 'Teachers' views of the impact of school evaluation and external inspection processes', *Improving Schools* 19(1). 52–61. DOI: https://doi.org/10.1177/1365480215627894.

Hunter, I. (1988) *Culture and Government: The Emergence of Literary Education*, London: Macmillan.

Hutchinson, J. (2016) 'School inspection in England: Is there room for improvement?', Education Policy Institute. Available at: https://epi.org.uk/publications-and-research/school-inspection-england-room-improve/ (accessed 17 July 2020).

Jin, W., *et al.* (2011) 'Subject and course choices at ages 14 and 16 amongst young people in England: Insights from behavioural economics', DfE. Available at: https://www.google.com/url?sa=t&rct=j&q=&esrc=s&source=web&cd=&ved=2ahUKEwit46ri7NHrAhWBy6QKHXQbDY4QFjABegQIBRAB&url=https%3A%2F%2Fassets.publishing.service.gov.uk%2Fgovernment%2Fuploads%2Fsystem%2Fuploads%2Fattachment_data%2Ffile%2F182677%2FDFE-RR160.pdf&usg=AOvVaw29pPk1_43vnT2yLOllypGI (accessed 27 August 2020).

Jones, L. [Baraka, A.] ([1963] 2010) 'Jazz and the white critic', *Black Music*. New York: Akashic Books, pp. 15–24.

McCallum, A. (2019a) 'Response to Ofsted curriculum workshop', EMC. 8 January. Available at: https://www.englishandmedia.co.uk/blog/response-to-ofsted-curriculum-workshop (accessed 13 July 2020).

McCallum, A. (2019b) 'EMC response to draft Ofsted framework and guidance materials', EMC. Available at: https://www.englishandmedia.co.uk/blog/emc-response-to-draft-ofsted-framework-and-guidance-materials (accessed 17 July 2020).

McInerney, L. (2016) 'Farewell, Sir Michael Wilshaw, the Dirty Harry of Ofsted', *Guardian*, 20 December. Available at: https://www.theguardian.com/education/2016/dec/20/michael-wilshaw-ofsted-chief-inspector-schools (accessed 17 August 2020).

McIntyre, N. and Adams, R. (2019) 'More than 1,000 English schools turn to online donations to raise funds', *Guardian*, 9 April. Available at: https://www.theguardian.com/education/2019/apr/09/cash-strapped-english-schools-turn-to-online-donations-to-close-funding-gap (accessed 3 August 2020).

NFER (2019) 'Education Inspection Framework 2019: NFER response', Available at: https://www.nfer.ac.uk/education-inspection-framework-2019-nfer-response/ (accessed 27 August 2020).

Nussbaum, M. (2010) *Not for Profit: Why Democracy Needs the Humanities*, Princeton, NJ: Princeton University Press.

Ofqual (2020) 'Proposed changes to the assessment of GCSEs, AS and A Level in 2021'. Available at: https://www.gov.uk/government/consultations/proposed-changes-to-the-assessment-of-gcses-as-and-a-levels-in-2021 (accessed 26 August 2020).

Ofsted (2005) 'The common inspection framework: Education, skills and early years'. Available at: https://www.google.com/url?sa=t&rct=j&q=&esrc=s&source=web&cd=&ved=2ahUKEwjQrJu95NHrAhWRCuwKHZVkBcsQFjAAegQIBBAB&url=https%3A%2F%2Fassets.publishing.service.gov.uk%2Fgovernment%2Fuploads%2Fsystem%2Fuploads%2Fattachment_data%2Ffile%2F828112%2FWithdrawn_common_inspection_framework.pdf&usg=AOvVaw11Loh5TUkBBC0VBYRVG04K (accessed 13 July 2020).

Ofsted (2015) 'Inspection Handbook'. Manchester: Ofsted. Available at: https://assets.publishing.service.gov.uk/government/uploads/system/uploads/attachment_data/file/390141/School_inspection_handbook.pdf (accessed 1 February 2021).

Ofsted (2018a) 'School inspection handbook'. Available at: https://www.gov.uk/government/publications/school-inspection-handbook-from-september-2015 (accessed 25 August 2020).

Ofsted (2018b) 'Ofsted inspection – clarification for schools'. Available at: https://www.gov.uk/government/publications/school-inspection-handbook-from-september-2015 (accessed 23 July 2020).

Ofsted (2019) 'The education inspection framework'. Available at: https://www.gov.uk/government/publications/education-inspection-framework (accessed 7 August 2020).

Rancière, J. (2013) *The Politics of Aesthetics*. Trans. Gabriel Rockhill. London: Bloomsbury.

Roberts, J. (2020a) 'Ofsted visits could become formal inspections', *TES*. Available at: https://www.tes.com/news/coronavirus-ofsted-visits-could-become-formal-inspections (accessed 5 September 2020).

Roberts, J. (2020b) 'Exclusive: Stop Ofsted for a year or more, say teachers', *TES*. Available at: https://www.tes.com/news/coronavirus-stop-ofsted-year-or-more-say-teachers (accessed 5 September 2020).

Roberts, J. (2020c) '"Dismayed" heads call for Ofsted "visits" rethink', *TES*. Available at: https://www.tes.com/news/back-to-school-dismayed-heads-call-ofsted-visits-rethink (accessed 5 September 2020).

Santry, C. (2020) 'Spielman: Dropping a GCSE "may make sense" for some', *TES*. 6 July. Available at: https://www.tes.com/news/coronavirus-ofsted-spielman-dropping-gcse-may-make-sense-some (accessed 7 July 2020).

Scanlon, M. (1999) 'The impact of Ofsted inspections', NFER/NUT. Available at: https://www.nfer.ac.uk/the-impact-of-ofsted-inspections (accessed 27 August 2020).

Smithers, R. (2005) 'Woodhead overrode inspectors to fail improving school', *Guardian*, 4 February. Available at: https://www.theguardian.com/uk/2005/feb/04/politics.freedomofinformation (accessed 31 July 2020).

Smithers, R. (2015) 'Sir Chris Woodhead obituary', *Guardian*, 23 June. Available at: https://www.theguardian.com/education/2015/jun/23/sir-chris-woodhead (accessed 30 July 2020).

Spielman, A. (2017) 'Amanda Spielman's speech at the 2017 ASCL annual conference'. Available at: https://www.gov.uk/government/speeches/amanda-spielmans-speech-at-the-ascl-annual-conference (accessed 30 July 2020).

Spielman, A. (2020) 'HMCI commentary: Our plans for the autumn', 6 July. Available at: https://www.gov.uk/government/speeches/hmci-commentary-our-plans-for-the-autumn (accessed 7 August 2020).

Thomas, G. (1998) 'A brief history of the genesis of the new schools' inspection system', *British Journal of Education Studies*, 46(4): 415–27.

von Stumm, S., et al. (2020) 'School quality ratings are weak predictors of students' achievements and well-being', *The Journal of Child Psychology*. DOI: https://doi.org/10.1111/jcpp.13276.

Weale, S. (2020) 'Pupils in England likely to face reduced GCSE courses and delayed exams', *Guardian*, 2 July. Available at: https://www.theguardian.com/world/2020/jul/02/pupils-in-england-likely-to-face-reduced-gcse-courses-and-delayed-exams (accessed 27 July August 2020).

Whittaker, F. (2018) '"Not all teachers do their best," and 7 others things Sir Michael Wilshaw said at the Festival of Education', *Schools Week*, 21 June. Available at: https://schoolsweek.co.uk/not-all-teachers-do-their-best-and-7-other-things-sir-michael-wilshaw-said-at-the-festival-of-education/ (accessed 13 July 2020).

Wilshaw, M. (2016) 'The power of education'. [Speech.] Available at: https://www.gov.uk/government/speeches/the-power-of-education (accessed 13 July 2020).

2

From curriculum theory to curriculum practice

Some observations on privilege, power and policy

Steve Connolly

Major questions addressed in this chapter are:

- What kinds of ideas about curriculum are translated into school practices?
- What kinds of ideas about curriculum have been most prevalent in the last ten years and where do these come from?
- What other kinds of thinking about curriculum might teachers and school leaders find useful that have not had very much exposure in the recent past?

Abstract

This chapter takes the view that teacher autonomy is crucial if there is to be a rich, successful relationship between the teacher, the learner and the curriculum they are exploring together. However, curricula are exercises in power. The views of curriculum espoused by politicians, school regulators and other educational commentators are, frequently, manifestations of educational power relations. In the UK at least, the privileging of particular views of curriculum by policy-makers and central government more widely has, in many ways, damaged the development of the teacher-learner-curriculum relationship and what theoretical ideas about curriculum can offer as a way to support the best teaching and learning. The chapter uses some recent and not so recent examples to exemplify this point. In a plea for practitioners and policy-makers to think more widely about theoretical conceptions of curriculum and their relationship to practice, it introduces the reader to the work of two curriculum theorists, Allan Luke and his contemporary Zongyi Deng, who have important contributions to make in teachers' search for bringing the curriculum to life for learners.

A practical example: 'cultural literacy', 'powerful knowledge' and curriculum reform in England

Discussions about the nature of curriculum and what it should consist of stretch back to ancient times. The Greek philosopher Plato put much thought, for example, into what kinds of subject would form the best education for young people. As Robert Brumbaugh notes, in addition to reading, writing and computation, Plato considered both music and physical education to be essential for all citizens as a basic requirement (Brumbaugh, 1987, p. 127). However, in recent history some distinct theoretical views about curriculum have developed which have begun to inform both policy and practice. The best examples of this in the curriculum in England have been in recent governments' reliance upon using the work of two academics in particular to justify their curriculum policy. The American academic E.D. Hirsch, whose work in the 1980s on an idea that he terms 'cultural literacy', became regularly name-checked by government ministers, such as Nick Gibb and Michael Gove, when they came to power in 2010. Hirsch's ideas about 'cultural literacy' rely upon teachers transmitting what he calls 'core' or 'commonly shared knowledge' (Hirsch, 1983). Hirsch is concerned about the state of literacy in America at the time of writing, and puts this state down to children having a lack of knowledge about things which give context to what children are reading. The logical conclusion of this view – to which the last 60 or so pages of the book *Cultural Literacy* are devoted – is to produce lists of this core knowledge which Hirsch thinks children need to be taught in order to become better readers. He characterizes this knowledge as 'intended to illustrate the character and range of knowledge that literate Americans tend to share' (Hirsch, 1987, p.146) and the lists themselves cover a wide range of terms, people and events, from the Biblical story of Abraham and Isaac to the Marshall Plan. These are, for Hirsch, the foundation stones not only of literacy, but education more generally.

Putting aside, for one moment, questions about what Hirsch means by 'literate Americans' – and who he thinks they might be – both issues that Donaldo Macedo (1994) critiques at some length, it is fascinating to consider how this sometime American literary theorist came to be an educational figurehead for British politicians. The lists which feature in the latter part of *Cultural Literacy* point to something fundamental in the way that governments of a particular type think about teaching and learning. With five thousand people, events and terms to transmit to young people, Hirsch becomes a model of curriculum which is both easily memorable and easily measurable, manifested in what the UK government and its inspectorate, Ofsted, term a 'knowledge-rich curriculum'. Concomitantly, this makes for easy reportage of successes and failures – 'pupil knowledge of X number of key terms has improved by Y percent'. This may seem facetious at first glance, but this is a really clear example of the theory/policy/practice nexus, particularly when one observes the long list of metalinguistic and grammatical terms which one sees in the 2014 iteration of the English National Curriculum for Key Stage 2 (KS2) (Upper Primary). The KS2 statutory test for this curriculum, or SAT, asks pupils to identify many of these terms and their meanings via a multiple choice test (e.g. DFE, 2019). This is a direct manifestation of Hirsch's ideas about curriculum which shape both education policy and teacher practice, with 'knowledge-rich' curricula being both inspected by England's Office for Standards in Education (Ofsted) (Spielman, 2019) and promoted by educational commentators and influencers, some of whom have never even been teachers, such as Toby Young (2014). In one sense, it is important to see politicians taking theoretical perspectives into account when talking about education as a positive move. However, in this particular instance, two significant observations must be made. First, as Bob Eaglestone has pointed out, Hirsch is likely to be favoured by politicians because he brings an easily measurable scientism to the curriculum (Eaglestone, 2020). Second, what is absent from the current situation is the kind of debate about theoretical perspectives that was such a feature of the development of the National Curriculum some 30 years ago. The DFE, Ofsted and those who claim to be champions of 'knowledge-rich curricula' often seem reluctant to debate some fairly essential questions which are raised by Hirsch's work, such as what they actually mean when they use the term 'knowledge' (e.g. Sherrington, 2018).

Running alongside this use of Hirsch's work has been UK policy-makers' tendency to fall back on the position of the sociologist Michael F.D. Young when challenged on the over-simplified nature of the cultural literacy model. Young, and his idea of 'powerful knowledge' have become influential with politicians (Gibb, 2018), school regulators (Spielman, 2019) and educational commentators (Didau, 2019; Myatt, 2018), who have taken some of the key arguments from both his book, *Bringing the Knowledge Back In* (Young, 2008), and the work of a number of sociologists of education who have followed in his wake (Maton, 2010; Moore; 2013; Rata, 2017). These academics are sometimes termed 'social realist' thinkers because they are categorizing knowledge as a social object and trying to describe how knowledge works in social contexts. Young's work has been discussed extensively (for a detailed critique, see White, 2018), but for teachers, four key ideas that he propounds can be summarized as follows:

1 Powerful knowledge is different from everyday knowledge. As Young himself comments, 'The curriculum cannot be based on everyday practical experience. Such a curriculum would only recycle that experience' (Young, 2008, p. 89). As a consequence, what the teacher does requires specialist knowledge and involves transmission of this to the student. Additionally, whatever knowledge or agency the student has in terms of the subject will always, by definition, be in some way inferior to that of the teacher.

2 Powerful knowledge is systematic, and in schools that system is constituted by distinct subjects. For Young and other social realist thinkers (e.g., Moore, 2000), discussion of interdisciplinary or thematic learning marks a

slide into a sort of epistemic relativism. For schools and teachers, then, there must be distinct subjects and the knowledge within these subjects must be fixed.

3 Implicit within point 2 is the idea that certain kinds of knowledge are canonical. Social realists like Karl Maton have attempted to suggest that canons are a necessary part of powerful knowledge and can be justified by describing them in terms of a 'knower structure' (Maton, 2010), in which the canon is constituted by all the knowers who contribute to it. This allows Maton to subtly avoid questions about canonical knowledge as an exercise in power in a subject like English or History. As the current author has written elsewhere, (Connolly, 2021), this tends to ignore people's lived experience of canons as a means of marginalization, but the implication for teachers is that canonical knowledge is a necessary part of subject knowledge that they will have to impart to their students.

4 There is also an implicit connection for both Young and the policy-makers who quote his work between powerful knowledge and 'cultural capital'. This latter term, which has its origins in the work of Pierre Bourdieu, has become a kind catch-all term for the kinds of powerful knowledge which are associated (often mistakenly, in the current author's view) with social mobility. The English schools inspectorate, Ofsted, uses the term in quite a confused way, connecting it to the Victorian religiosity of Matthew Arnold at one moment (Ofsted, 2019) and then a middle-class lamentation for the loss of the nursery rhyme at another (Spielman, 2020). For Bourdieu, cultural capital was really neither a good nor bad thing, but rather something that he used to indicate the stratification of social class (Bourdieu, 1979, pp. 114–15), but for teachers currently working in English schools, the term has become freighted with all sorts of expectations about particular types of cultural experience which they should be aiming to give students. It is these experiences that will, apparently, help to bestow powerful knowledge.

These features of Young's work, like those of Hirsch, have subtly found their way then, from the rarely read pages of academic journals into the policy papers, speeches and curriculum documents authored by civil servants and politicians. The regulators who enact these policies – in this case, Ofsted – will often find that this enacting will drive teacher and wider school behaviour (Perryman *et al.*, 2018), and so 'cultural literacy' and 'powerful knowledge' will become terms that head teachers use in staff briefings, run training sessions about and write into school policy documents. There is nothing inherently wrong with this; as suggested earlier, seeing the development of a praxis is generally a positive thing. However, what is absent here is a wider debate about a range of other, thoughtful and nuanced theoretical positions on curriculum which have generally not been presented in this way. At the time of writing, the twin challenges laid down by both the Covid-19 pandemic and the Black Lives Matter movement suggest that the early part of the 2020s will not be a time for fixed and non-negotiable ideas about curriculum. For example, calls to decolonize the curriculum do not sit particularly well alongside a theoretical model which frequently seeks to deny the agency and experience of the student. Developing a History curriculum which looks to acknowledge the influence of say, the Kingdom of Benin, or an English curriculum which incorporates a wider range of post-colonial authors will require curriculum models which are underpinned by more forward-looking thinking than Hirsch and Young offer.

Another way: the work of Allan Luke and Zongyi Deng

There is another way here; other views of curriculum are available, but the problem is the means by which teachers and school leaders become aware of them. The ideas of E.D. Hirsch and Michael Young have had a significant amount of exposure, both because of their connections to official government policy, but also because they have been put forward by groups of influential bloggers and commentators across the last ten years. The current author started this chapter by suggesting that its writing was a plea for broader thinking about curriculum and he wants to make that plea by talking about three sets of ideas that establish a means of doing so: (1) critical realist views of knowledge; (2) the German concepts of *Bildung* and *Didaktik*; and (3) the agency of both the individual learner and the teacher. These three sets of ideas are prominent in the work of two thinkers about curriculum who, to some extent, are not in vogue with teachers in the UK: Allan Luke and Zongyi Deng. Writing at different points across the last 20 years, sometimes individually, and sometimes in collaboration, they propose ways of thinking about curriculum which address the concerns about the status of knowledge raised by social realists, while at the same time producing rounded theoretical models which address the practical concerns of schools who wish to engage students in the curriculum. Luke's work and Deng's work are built on some distinct critical foundations. First, they are characterized by a much broader view of knowledge, informed by critical realist (CR) philosophers, such as Roy Bhaskar. It is true to say that social realists like Rob Moore (Moore, 2013) also used CR as the foundations of their thought, but as I have argued elsewhere, (Connolly, 2021), Moore's account of the way that CR and social realism are related is really quite selective in that it often seems to ignore a key tenet of Bhaskar's account of knowledge, which is the agency of the individual doing the knowing.

Second, the German concepts of *Didaktik* and *Bildung* also recur frequently in their work as ways of thinking about the intention of curriculum and the way it might be taught. *Bildung* is the German notion of self-cultivation or self-formation, which has implicit connections to knowledge, language and culture. As Sijlander *et al.* (2012) suggest, it is a term which sometimes seems imprecise, but in contemporary educational discourse, can be summarized as: (1) a creative process for the self-development of the individual and (2) through this process, advancement is achieved. The important thing to note here is the agency of the individual. *Bildung*-informed curricula should acknowledge that the student must have some power over what is being learnt. The pedagogical relation of *Bildung* is *Didaktik*. *Didaktik* embodies the notion that curriculum is part of teaching, and best occurs at the classroom (rather than the school or national) level (Westbury, 2000). This connects with that final set of ideas about agency, and as a consequence, both Deng and Luke use the term *Didaktik* to signify the autonomous role of the teacher in designing their own curriculum as it should best suit their students.

The question of how these critical perspectives might influence what teachers do in the classroom is at the forefront of Luke's and Deng's thinking. In the Introduction to *Curriculum, Syllabus Design and Equity* (Luke *et al.*, 2013), Allan Luke and his colleagues suggest that despite a good deal of theory being generated, there has actually been little attempt to connect this to curriculum practice. As Luke points out, there is almost no empirical proof of efficacy of one particular curriculum model over another, much less the way that such models might be informed by theory:

> Simply, there is little in the curriculum studies literature and research that actually makes the case for any particular technical form of curriculum. There has been little interest in or problematizing of the shape, format and form of the curriculum – beyond teachers' practical notions of use and ease of working with this frame or that.
>
> (Luke *et al.*, 2013, p. 8)

Deng takes up this theme in his most recent work, arguing that one of the problems with using something like powerful knowledge as a foundation for curriculum is that it is not really possible to build a school curriculum out of an epistemological theory. For him, the curriculum must make a concrete connection between knowledge, the needs of the learner and wider society and it is these connections which will constitute school subjects, rather than facts or knowledge in isolation. Deng also suggests that teachers and schools need to consider the wider purposes of schooling:

> Apart from the academic purpose (passing on disciplinary knowledge to future generations), schools are believed to serve three other purposes, the economic (preparing students for jobs), the cultural and social (socialising students into social and cultural orders), and the educational (fostering students' self-actualisation and flourishing). Each of these purposes calls for a different answer to what should be taught from the one provided by the social realist school.
>
> (Deng, 2020, p. 6)

However much teachers, school leaders and commentators might want to argue that knowledge is foundational to all learning (e.g., Blake, 2019), Deng reminds us that in order to do so, one must (1) have a reasonably broad definition of what knowledge is, and (2) accept that this is not entirely contained within school subjects. It is this desire to create a Freirean praxis that, the author would argue, allows their work to be located within the critical realist tradition. For Luke, all education policy, including that which governs curriculum, needs to avoid the scientism and measurability fostered by the kinds of argument that E.D. Hirsch makes about 'knowledge-rich' curricula, and it needs to avoid it because education is a very human activity – one that does not respond well when policy is guided by positivist instinct. What Luke calls 'the messy ecologies' of policy-making mean it is fairly pointless to try to pick out curriculum models that 'work', as they generally cannot be replicated through the 'intersubjective capacities and material social relations of communities, staffrooms and classrooms' (Luke, 2009, p. 174) and this is why critical realist views of both knowledge and learning should be helpful to teachers. In Roy Bhaskar's original work on critical realism in education, knowledge is agile, and has 'no endpoint or absolute rules' (Corson, 1991) and Luke's and Deng's views of curriculum can accommodate this. The bigger demands of both individual learners and society need the curriculum to cope with this agility, and acceptance of the human messiness of education is built into the way that this view of knowledge interacts with both the concept of *Bildung* and *Didaktik*.

For Zongyi Deng, the messiness and intersubjectivity of curriculum are at the heart of European traditions of a liberal education. Such traditions, which focus on the development of a range of capacities, ways of thinking and understanding the world, are in stark contrast to the recent attempts to see education as a science (Deans for Impact, 2015), which, in many cases originate in the Anglophone world. Deng's employment of what is termed '*Bildung*-centred *Didaktik*' is designed to make a theoretical link between views of knowledge, subject content and teaching, and he draws on the work of Steffan Hopmann (2007) and others to establish a model of curricular knowledge which allows not only the exploration and acquisition of knowledge but also the personal development of the student in other ways – the '*Bildung*' aspect of education.

Didaktik is really a different concept to the notion of 'curriculum', in that it does not set out a preferred curriculum structure for a subject, but rather relies upon understanding how the student encounters the world and how the teacher helps the student to negotiate that encounter. This negotiation involves what Steffan Hopmann calls *restrained teaching*, wherein the teacher thinks carefully about what kinds of intervention are required and when, in order to inform learning. In Germany, where *Didaktik* was first formalized towards the end of the nineteenth century, this view was allied to the idea of both 'pedagogical freedom' (Hopmann, 2007, p. 133) for the teacher and that of an actively learning student. *Didaktik* can be summarized as comprising three distinct features: (1) the focus on *Bildung*; (2) a teacher focus on the difference between matter (or content) and meaning; and (3) autonomy for both the teacher and the learner. These features are markedly different from the way that E.D. Hirsch characterizes knowledge and teaching, and emphasize both teacher and student interactions in a way that Young's powerful knowledge does not. As a consequence, they result in a different conception of curriculum.

Implications for curriculum design

The five-step model of instructional planning: *Bildung*-centred *Didaktik*, adapted from Klafki (2000) and Deng (2018)

Deng connects the concept of *Bildung*-centred *Didaktik* with the idea that educational 'content' (something subtly different from just 'knowledge') is what is important for curriculum. This content needs to be carefully selected by the teacher – so good subject knowledge pedagogy (Shulman, 1986) is vital – but the teacher also needs to know how this informs what Deng calls 'general human powers and capabilities' (Deng, 2018), as well as thinking about the best way for the student to encounter that knowledge. These connections are augmented by reference to Klafki's (2000) five-step model of instructional planning which gives teachers a clear way of thinking about *Didaktik* and the move from curriculum to teaching. These five steps, which are often formed by Deng and others (Luke and Deng, 2008) as questions for the teacher to ask themselves about the relationship between content knowledge and curriculum delivery, are aimed at helping the teacher plan an appropriate curriculum and subsequent lessons. The five questions are:

1 What sense of the world does this content exemplify?
2 What significance does this content already have in the minds of my students?
3 What constitutes the significance of the topic for the students' futures?
4 How should this content be structured?
5 In what ways can the particular nature of this content be made stimulating by the pedagogical work done by the teacher?

It is particularly important for the purposes of this chapter to note questions 2 and 3 in this model. Deng builds his argument on the idea that students will have some kinds of pre-existing knowledge of what they are being taught, and that content should be selected according to what students will need to know in the future, rather than what might have been significant in the past. These principles make a connection to Allan Luke's work with the New London Group (Cazden *et al.*, 1996) on both multiliteracies and curriculum, where knowledge and teaching are agile enough to cope with the demands made on them by new technologies. When Deng and Luke write collaboratively (e.g., Luke and Deng, 2008), they are keen to emphasize that knowledge in the school curriculum involves knowing about the application of what has been learnt through technology, and this is one of several reasons why they see *Didaktik* as a more satisfactory basis for a school curriculum than either cultural literacy or social realism. It also implies some agency for the learner, which is something that seems to be neglected by both E.D. Hirsch and Michael Young. Consideration of these types of questions is likely to result in a broader, more flexible and in some ways more *knowledgeable* curriculum than those proposed by the former two thinkers. It may well include many, or indeed all of those 'facts' that Hirsch considers important, but by the same measure, it allows a dialogue in which both teacher and student establish the usefulness of that knowledge.

Unfortunately, for reasons of space, only the briefest of introductions to the work of Allan Luke and Zongyi Deng has been possible here, but the intention of the last part of this chapter is really to suggest that this work presents us as teachers and educationalists with another view of how curricula might be theorized and practically conceived. Because of the privileged status which both 'cultural literacy' and 'powerful knowledge' have been accorded (at least in the UK), it is necessary to push back against the idea that they might be the only ways of thinking about curriculum. It would be fair to assume that Deng and Luke do not have 'all the answers' to issues of curriculum, but a consideration of their work by school leaders and teachers might mean a more pluralist approach to such issues in future.

Conclusion

These questions of policy, power and privilege are not merely academic; they have implications for the everyday practices of teachers and the young people that they work with. The influence of E.D. Hirsch's model of cultural literacy raises profound questions for teachers and school leaders about a whole range of issues that perhaps, have not been foregrounded for some time: the role of memory, the notion of what kinds of knowledge are most valuable to us as human beings; and whether or not learning lists of facts really is the basis for better learning. Similarly, for Michael Young, questions of power and powerful knowledge will always lead to his critics asking, 'Who gets to decide what is powerful and what is not?'. While Young and those who follow him often make subtle arguments for their view of knowledge and how it should constitute the school curriculum, it is too easy for politicians to subvert this view into something which is both prescriptive and exclusionary. This is why it is important for teachers to consider a wider range of views of curriculum and a wider range of content knowledge as proposed by the *Didaktik* model, and other critical realist views of learning. However, such consideration requires teachers to be given time, space and opportunities to discuss which theoretical views of curriculum might best support their work, and also perhaps to consider empirical support for these views (such as that collected by Allan Luke in his work on school science; Luke and Exley, 2009) or even doing their own empirical research to explore this. In turn, such opportunities rely upon a recognition that the teacher is an autonomous professional, capable of making these decisions and having the time to read, discuss and learn about them. While policy-makers privilege particular views of curriculum through both the inspectorate and government, while at the same time not giving teachers the opportunity to explore other models, such recognition is unlikely to be achieved.

References

Blake, J. (2019) 'Who decides what knowledge should be taught?' Available at: https:// arkonline.org/blog/who-decides-what-knowledge-should-be-taught (accessed 25 January 2021).

Bourdieu, P. (1979) *Distinction: A Social Critique of the Judgement of Taste*, London: Routledge.

Brumbaugh, R.S. (1987) 'Plato's ideal curriculum and contemporary philosophy of education', *Educational Theory*, 37(2): 169–77.

Cazden, C., Cope, B., Fairclough, N., Gee, J. *et al.* (1996) 'A pedagogy of multiliteracies: Designing social futures', *Harvard Educational Review*, 66(1): 60–92.

Connolly, S. (2021) *The Changing Role of Media in the English Curriculum 1988–2018: Returning to Nowhere*, London: Routledge. (in press).

Corson, D. (1991) 'Bhaskar's critical realism and educational knowledge', *British Journal of Sociology of Education*, 12(2): 223–41.

Deans for Impact (2015) *The Science of Learning*, Austin, TX: Deans for Impact.

Deng, Z. (2018) 'Pedagogical content knowledge reconceived: Bringing curriculum thinking into the conversation on teachers' content knowledge', *Teaching and Teacher Education*, 72: 155–64.

Deng, Z. (2020) *Knowledge, Content, Curriculum and Didaktik: Beyond Social Realism*, Abingdon. Routledge.

DFE (2019) 'Key Stage 2 tests: 2019 English grammar, punctuation and spelling test materials'. Available at: https://www.gov.uk/government/publications/key-stage-2-tests-2019-english-grammar-punctuation-and-spelling-test-materials (accessed 25 January 2021).

Didau, D. (2019) 'Where we're getting curriculum wrong: Part 2 – Powerful Knowledge'. Available at: https://learningspy.co.uk/curriculum/why-we-need-powerful-knowledge/ (accessed 25 January 2021).

Eaglestone, R. (2020) 'Ploughing the sea: Against "powerful knowledge" and "cultural literacy" for the study of English literature', PESGB Impact Pamphlet series. Salisbury: PESGB.

Gibb, N. (2018) 'Speech to the Research ED conference at Harris Secondary Academy, St Johns Wood'. Published 8 September 2018. Available at: https://www.gov.uk/government/speeches/school-standards-minister-at-researched (accessed 25 January 2021).

Hirsch, E.D. (1983) 'Cultural literacy', *The American Scholar* 52(2): 159–69.

Hirsch, E.D. (1987) *Cultural Literacy: What Every American Needs to Know*, Boston, MA. Houghton Mifflin.

Hopmann, S. (2007) 'Restrained teaching: The common cores of Didaktik', *European Educational Research Journal*, 6(2), 109–24.

Klafki, W. (2000) 'Didaktik analysis as the core of preparation', in I. Westbury, S. Hopmann, and K. Riquarts (eds), *Teaching as a Reflective Practice: The German Didaktik Tradition*, Mahwah, NJ: Erlbaum, pp. 139–59.

Luke, A. (2009) 'Critical realism, policy and education research', in K. Ercikan and W.M. Roth (eds), *Generalizing from Educational Research*, New York: Routledge, pp. 173–200.

Luke, A. and Deng, D. (2008) 'Subject matter: Defining and theorizing school subjects', in F.M. Connelly, M.F. He and J. Phillion (eds), *Sage Handbook of Curriculum and Instruction*, Thousand Oaks, CA: Sage, pp. 66–87.

Luke, A. and Exley, B. (2009) 'Uncritical framing: Lesson and knowledge structure in school science', in D. Cole and D.L. Pullen (eds), *Multiliteracies in Motion: Current Theory & Practice*, London: Routledge, pp. 17–41.

Luke, A., Woods, A. and Weir, K. (2013) 'Curriculum design, equity and the technical form of the curriculum', in A. Luke, A. Woods, and K. Weir (eds), *Curriculum, Syllabus Design, and Equity: A Primer and Model*, New York: Routledge, pp. 6–39.

Macedo, D.P. (1994) *Literacies of Power: What Americans Are Not Allowed to Know*, Boulder, CO: Westview Press.

Maton, K. (2010) 'Canons and progress in the arts and humanities: Knowers and gazes', in K. Maton and R. Moore (eds), *Social Realism, Knowledge and the Sociology of Education: Coalitions of the Mind*, London: Continuum, pp. 154–78.

Moore, R. (2000) 'The (re)organisation of knowledge and assessment for a learning society: the constraints on interdisciplinarity', *Studies in Continuing Education*, 22(2): 183–99.

Moore, R. (2013) 'Social realism and the problem of knowledge in the sociology of education', *British Journal of Sociology of Education*, 34(3): 333–53. doi: 10.1080/01425692.2012.714251

Myatt, M. (2018) *The Curriculum: Gallimaufry to Coherence*, Melton; John Catt Educational Ltd.

Ofsted (2019) *School Inspection Update: Special Edition*. Available at: https://assets.publishing.service.gov.uk/government/uploads/system/uploads/attachment_data/file/772056/School_inspection_update_-_January_2019_Special_Edition_180119.pdf (accessed 25 January 2021).

Perryman, J., Maguire, M., Braun, A. and Ball, S. (2018) 'Surveillance, governmentality and moving the goalposts: The influence of Ofsted on the work of schools in a post-panoptic era', *British Journal of Educational Studies*, 66(2): 145–63, doi:10.1080/00071005.2017.1372560

Rata, E. (2017) 'Knowledge and teaching', *British Educational Research Journal*, 43(5).

Sherrington, T. (2018) 'What is a knowledge-rich curriculum?' Available at: https://impact.chartered.college/article/what-is-a-knowledge-rich-curriculum/ (accessed 25 January 2021).

Shulman, L.S. (1986) 'Those who understand: Knowledge growth in teaching', *Educational Researcher*, 15(2): 4–14.

Siljander, P., Kivela, A. and Sutinen, A. (2012) *Theories of Bildung and Growth: Connections and Controversies Between Continental Educational Thinking and American Pragmatism*, Rotterdam: Sense Publications.

Spielman, A. (2019) 'Speech', given at the 'Wonder Years' curriculum conference. Available at: https://www.gov.uk/government/speeches/amanda-spielman-at-the-wonder-years-curriculum-conference (accessed 25 January 2021).

Spielman, A. (2020) 'Speech', given at the Royal Opera House. Available at: https://www.gov.uk/government/speeches/amanda-spielman-speaking-at-the-royal-opera-house (accessed 25 January 2021).

Westbury, I. (2000) 'Teaching as a reflective practice: What might Didaktik teach curriculum?' In I. Westbury, S. Hopmann and K. Riquarts (eds), *Teaching as a Reflective Practice: The German Didaktik Tradition*, Mahwah, NJ: Erlbaum. pp. 15–39.

White, J. (2018) 'The weakness of "powerful knowledge"', *London Review of Education*, 16(2): 325–35.

Young, M.F.D. (2008) *Bring Knowledge Back in: From Social Constructivism to Social Realism in the Sociology of Knowledge*, London: Routledge.

Young, T. (2014) *Prisoners of the Blob: Why Education Experts Are Wrong About Nearly Everything*, London. Civitas.

Part **2**

Alternative/Bespoke Education

In the search for ways to bring the curriculum to life, Part 2 turns to issues of alternative or bespoke education. Chapter 3 begins by discussing the rise of elective home education (EHE), what, where and why, and includes consideration of personalized learning and a flexible curriculum, grassroots communities and networks in EHE, the voice of EHE children: experiences and needs, and concludes with a deliberation on new frontiers and future avenues. Subsequently, Chapter 4 gives an overview of the right of learners with profound and multiple learning difficulties (PMLD) to access a curriculum that is meaningful to them, which has proven challenging for educators, and explores research on how curricula can support their needs.

3 Alternative education

The rise in elective home education: issues related to recognition, collaboration and successful partnerships

Amber Fensham-Smith

Major questions addressed in this chapter are:

- To what degree might the case of home education disrupt the notion of a broad and balanced National Curriculum?
- In what ways does curriculum within elective home education (EHE) extend, challenge and reinforce notions of parental participation and child-centred learning?

Abstract

This chapter aims to equip practitioners with a balanced and research-informed overview of the key trends, developments and examples of best practice in elective home education (EHE). Chapter sections include the rise of EHE: who, what, where and why; personalized learning and a flexible curriculum; grassroots communities and networks in EHE; the voice of EHE children: experiences and needs; new frontiers and future avenues. Broadly, it considers the case of home education through the alternate perspective of a highly permeable and changing landscape of division and change that considers the world in which we live and how we get there.

Introduction

In the UK, parents have a duty to ensure that their child of compulsory school age receives a suitable education, either by school attendance or 'otherwise'

(Section 7, 1996 Education Act). Home education, home schooling,[1] or elective home education (EHE) is a topic of growing interest (Kunzman and Gaither, 2020). In stepping away from the tightly bounded context of the National Curriculum, the practice of EHE reconfigures learning contexts and pedagogic relationships, and invokes new opportunities, challenges and controversy. Historically, EHE has also attracted misrecognition from stakeholders who are invested in supporting the welfare and educational success of pupils in mainstream formal education settings (Mukwamba-Sendell, 2019; Ryan, 2019).

This chapter presents a research-informed overview of the key trends, developments and examples of practice in EHE. It begins with addressing the legal basis for EHE, motivations and the framing of a 'suitable' and 'efficient' education. Existing and ongoing tensions surrounding the rights of parents, children and the role of state are presented. To extend learning beyond the home, examples are provided to illuminate some of the ways in which EHE families have pooled together to form online networks and Communities of Practice (CoPs) (Wenger, 1998) to deliver a community-orientated and personalized programme of learning for their children (Fensham-Smith, 2017). Here the author questions some of the taken-for-granted assumptions of freedom, learner choice and access embedded within some EHE pedagogic approaches. The voices of EHE children, their experiences and perceptions of themselves and others are used to reflect upon some of the implicit assumptions and values to underpin the intended purpose of a broad and balanced curriculum and the very notion of 'informal', 'non-formal' and 'formal' learning contexts. In weaving together various areas of debate, the author concludes by presenting a series of suggestions and future avenues that might broker mutual recognition and constructive dialogue between EHE and 'mainstream' practitioners' communities.

A note on methodology

As one of the few UK EHE researchers in an established HEI position, the author presents her own research alongside those of other key scholars in this field. The literature and case studies presented in this chapter derive from past and ongoing research and knowledge exchange projects that author has undertaken on the topic including a mixed-method UK-wide study with 242 EHE families (Fensham-Smith, 2017).[2] Original data extracts from the 2017 study are synthesized alongside other key studies to illuminate discussion.

While she is not an active campaigner (advocate) of EHE, nor was she home-educated, the author is sensitive towards the struggles and misrecognition[3] that accompany a choice that is sometimes presented as 'sub-par' or inferior to the normalcy of an education via school. There are ideas, concepts and questions presented in this chapter that are designed to elicit debate and reflection from multiple groups both within and outside of EHE.

Legality and policy developments

In the UK, education is compulsory, school attendance is not. Under Section 7 of the 1996 Education Act, the parent/carer of every child of a compulsory school age must 'cause him' [sic] to receive an efficient and full-time education that is suitable and efficient to the age, ability, aptitude and any special educational need they may have, either by school attendance or 'otherwise'. Legally, EHE families are not required to provide a broad and balanced curriculum, nor are EHE learners required to sit national tests and/or observe school day working patterns. The non-statutory guidance for parents, LAs and schools differs between England, Scotland, Wales and Northern Island. This section focuses on the contemporary English EHE context (DfE, 2019a).

There are two routes to EHE: deregistration, or EHE from the outset (start of statutory school age).[4] In both cases, parents are not required to seek permission and/or notify their local authority (LA) of their decision to home educate.[5] At present, LAs do not have any statutory duties with respect to monitoring the 'quality' of EHE provision.[6]

On behalf of the government, the then Secretary of State, Ed Balls, commissioned Graham Badman to conduct an independent review of EHE in England between 2008 and 2009. Among the 18 recommendations made, was the early and compulsory registration of EHE children and increased powers for LAs to legally enter homes and interview children without parents being present (Badman, 2009). Following an independent inquiry, the Badman recommendations and proposed changes to clauses contained in the Children and Families Bill 2010 were quashed (Stafford, 2012).

A decade after the Badman (2009) Review, the Department for Education (DfE) issued new non-statutory guidance for LAs and parents (DfE, 2019a; 2019b). This was published alongside the government's response to the 2018 call for evidence that covered: existing voluntary registration schemes operated by some LAs; monitoring and support for EHE families (DfE, 2019c). Following this, a public consultation ran between March and June 2019 to seek responses to establish a compulsory registration system for children who do not attend state-funded or registered independent schools.

The current proposals would necessitate changes to the law in the next few years. A key shift in the balance of responsibility lies in the proposed duty of LAs to provide support to EHE families – if such support is requested by families (DfE, 2019a). Currently, parents/careers assume sole responsibility for all costs associated with the provision of resources and materials associated with EHE. In the absence of national guidelines, each LA follows their own set of highly individualized guidelines and models of support (Bhopal and Myers, 2015). The implications of this for equity and children's rights are covered further in the proceeding discussion.

A suitable and efficient education?

To begin to scaffold ways in which EHE might disrupt notions of a broad and balanced curriculum necessitates delving deeper into the implications of S7 of the 1996 Education Act. Arguably, the context of curricula objectives, ways of doing things and the expectations of role holders (teachers and pupils) is clearly demarcated within the context of formal schooling (Davies, 2015). However, no definitive and/or homogeneous definition of what constitutes a suitable and efficient education exists in English statute (DfE, 2019a), nor is there a unanimous account of the purpose and methods appropriate for a suitable education. One limited example of case law provided in Badman's (2009) review depicts a suitable education as one that '1) achieves what it sets out to achieve and 2) equips a child for life in the community they are part of and does not foreclose options in later years to adopt some other life form' (2009, p. 3).[7] Davies (2015) encourages us to widen the conceptual space within which to judge a suitable and efficient education. Rather than focusing on 'forms' of knowledge (Hirst, 1974) to be fostered, he urges practitioners to consider methods that build in opportunities to reflect on the dispositions that a suitable education is intended to develop. A broader vision might include a greater focus on learner agency and development of self-actualization across broader educative experiences.

Within the context of EHE, the degree to which parents, children and the state currently do, or should, play a greater or lesser role in actively defining and monitoring a suitable and efficient education is heavily contested (Monk, 2015). Article 2 of Protocol 1 of the European Convention of Human Rights sets out that the 'state shall respect the rights of parents to ensure such education and teaching is in conformity with their own religious and philosophical convictions'.[8] Yet the ways in which different role holders interpret a suitable and efficient education has unique implications for working relationships with EHE families (Sperling, 2015).[9] Historically, the ways in which some LAs have interpreted their role, EHE methods, styles and approaches have been described as a clash of paradigms. In one of the few studies to research this area, Mukwamba-Sendell (2019) found that as ex-teachers, several Education Officers (EOs) in her study initiated contact with EHE families, expecting to see timetables and formal schemes of work as evidence of a suitable and efficient education.[10] Yet, as it will be shown later, this is only one of many methods and approaches used in EHE. The number of anecdotal accounts online, alongside a limited pool of research that illustrates LAs and EHEs families not working together, sometimes overshadows authentic examples of brokering and relationship building.

Badman (2009) presented three LAs to exemplify 'good practice' in terms of their commitment and ingenuity in supporting EHE families within the present legislative framework.[11] Underpinning these relationships, Badman asserts were: 'mutual respect, regular information and the celebration of EHE achievements' (ibid., p. 15). Across these case studies the following forms of engagement and approaches were advocated:

- Regular 'drop-in' days: whereby parents and children could meet profession-als from the LA, to discuss issues and to ask for advice. Parents provided feedback which was used to tailor the planning of the next session/s.
- LA websites and EHE published booklets: presented in a supportive, respect-ful tone that demonstrated a deeper understanding of the variations of EHE; styles, methods and approaches.
- Subsidy towards the cost of examinations (GCSEs) for families who have been practising EHE for 1 year or more.
- A regional forum for multiple LAs to share and shape consistent practice. EHE representatives should be encouraged to attend.

An example of a LA which has established successful partnerships with EHE families is Hampshire County Council. Within this LA, the Inclusion Support Service leads for the Council in working with EHE families. This LA is reported to regularly consult with EHE families and provides some financial subsidy towards the cost of examinations. The Council signposts new EHE families to existing community groups including the 'Faregos Home Education Exam Cen-tre'– a fully registered exam centre 'run by a group of current and past home educating parents with the aim of organising exams for students from all over Hampshire and beyond' (Hampshire County Council, 2020).

Anecdotal accounts suggest that this LA subsidy towards the cost of public examinations is not widespread practice. The implications of this for equity among different groups in EHE are complex. Moreover, very little is known about the extent to which, following deregistration, children who require addi-tional forms of specialized support (as part of an Education Health and Care Plan) continue to receive this. Under current arrangements, the degree to which LAs have sufficient resources to engage in further training and to engi-neer opportunities to review and harmonize good practice for EHE is also unclear (Mukwamba-Sendell, 2019).

EHE: who, what, where and why?

The exact number of children currently receiving EHE across England is not precisely known, according to the ADCS[12] (ADCS, 2019). However, the impres-sion is that numbers have risen over the past two decades and are continuing to grow. The single representative study that exists sampled 6,000 households using the Opinions and Lifestyle Survey (Smith and Nelson, 2015). Their find-ings projected that 1 per cent of all families in England 'with dependent chil-dren have home-educated either on a full- or part-time basis' (p.1). EHE provision was 'episodic', which reflects the fluidity of EHE practice. The authors concluded that EHE families are likely to be a small and diverse social group. Thus, EHE families are not confined to a family type, occupational class, professional background or ethnic group.

More recently, ADCS (2019) surveyed all LAs in England (n = 132) to better understand the size and characteristics of a cohort of children and young people 'known to receive EHE'. It was estimated that 54,959 children and young people were home-educated across 152 LAs. A year-on-year increase by an average of 20 per cent has been observed over the past five years.

However, despite the suggested heterogeneity, D'Arcy (2014) notes that as a group, Gypsy and Travellers parents are not perceived as proper 'home-educators' and disregarded in 'mainstream' UK home-education research. Equally, few studies have explored experiences of Muslim EHE families (Fensham-Smith, 2014; Myers and Bhopal, 2018).

Motivations

Reasons for home education are highly multifaceted and often vary greatly, depending on the needs and experiences of children within and across the EHE population. Reasons also evolve and change depending on whether EHE is a temporary, medium or longer-term part of a child's education provision (Rothermel, 2002). While the ideas and positions of EHE families change, there are two relatively distinct starting points associated with deregistration versus EHE from the outset. Families at the first point, so-called positive 'first choice' families, usually do so for philosophical and/or ideological reasons and/or wanting to provide an alternative way of life and learning for their family (Morton, 2010). In contrast, the reactive decision-making linked to deregistration is often connected to children's declining social and emotional well-being in school and/or SEN provision – the so-called 'last resort' families.[13] The impression is that the proportion of families entering EHE from this position has largely fuelled the overall increase in numbers.[14]

In Fensham-Smith's (2017) study, among the 607 children within the 242 families surveyed, children's special educational needs, mental health conditions and other general health problems of home were a prominent theme. Just over a third of the 140 qualitative responses mentioned conditions, most commonly including: 'autism/Asperger's syndrome', 'sensory processing problems', 'attention deficit hyperactivity disorder', 'dyspraxia' and 'dyslexia' while just under a quarter cited experiences linked to social and emotional well-being including 'anxiety' and 'depression', 'stress' and 'unhappiness'.

While decision-making and familial circumstances are highly individualized, the decision to home educate is often framed as a difficult choice. It necessitates significant changes to parental working patterns and family life. Though there are exceptions, mothers often assume primary responsibility for facilitating, managing and organizing their everyday practice of EHE. Balancing the dual role of acting as parent and educator through EHE necessitates a great deal of emotion work and social support (Lees, 2013). In cases of deregistration, this can sometimes follow a distressing breakdown in relationships and trust between parents and the school.

Grassroots communities and networks in EHE

> Many more children and parents are unhappy with school and they're finding out through online groups and social media that there is an alternative which the schools don't advertise, and the government doesn't advertise... (Kim home-educator)
>
> (Fensham-Smith, 2017, p. 199)

Over the past decade, hundreds of online networks and offline communities have been created, managed and run by new and experienced EHE parents to support the social, emotional and educational needs of EHE families on a national, regional and local level.[15] Some of these communities are 'online only' and are intended to primarily to support parents. Others correspond to offline local and regional EHE Communities of Practice (Safran, 2008). Many of these groups are private and are only open to EHE families or those seriously considering it (Fensham-Smith, 2017). Some of EHE groups are loosely organized, while others are formally timetabled with a pre-arranged programme of educational activities regularly offline. Co-operative-style groups, for example, require regular commitment to and engagement in the shared practice of the group (ibid.). Online, titles and domain pages function as markers to manage the boundaries between illegitimate and legitimate peripheral participation (Wenger, 1998). In researching this landscape, Fensham-Smith (2017) found that as the social and emotional needs and interests of both parents and children change, EHE families leave groups, join others and/or form new communities of their own. Fensham-Smith argues that some of these groups are likely to be self-selecting by being open only to specialized specific styles, methods, ideologies and/or family types. The extent to which some of the EHE groups who meet offline are parent-led or child-initiated, depended on the nature, ethos and intended purpose of the group.

Vignette: 'Green', a co-operative support group for families

One EHE parent in Fensham-Smith's (2017) study set up and ran a co-operative group called *green* in a local community centre for 15 families in the south-west of England (parents and children attended). Families who joined were required to agree to be responsible for organizing at least one of the activity days every 4 weeks for the rest of the families who attended. Activities were broad and wide-ranging, including museum trips, science experiments and a book club. The group met twice weekly and this participation was viewed as substantial part of their EHE family practice. In this group, parents and children shared a 'strong' sense of *green* identity. One the other end of the spectrum, one home-educated father in Fensham-Smith's (2017) study set up a community called *tribe*. The only rule of the group was that 'no one in the group could tell you what to do'. Children arrived, some with their parents and some without, and decided how to use their 5 hours of time. Some parents joined *tribe* and then left because they felt 'uncomfortable' with how unstructured the activities offered in this group were.

There are many other examples that might be cited of EHE groups also.

Vignette: The 'Cabin', a self-directed learning community

As an example of just one of many varied EHE groups, at a public BERA Alternative Education event organized by the author of the current chapter in 2019, an EHE parent, and co-director and co-founder of the 'Cabin' described how they set up a self-directed learning community for educated children in the East of England. The group meets twice a week during term-time:

> I co-founded a self-directed, consent and rights-based education setting called the Cabin, as a space to realize children's rights in the here and now, and model this new way of being to enable others to make the change. To our knowledge it is the first explicitly consent-based education setting for children in the UK, and also the first to identify itself as Ed Positive – a transdisciplinary education philosophy that breaks down traditional subject silos, hierarchy and gatekeeping, and instead is curiosity-driven, problem-oriented, critical, and an open access approach rooted in children's rights.

> The organized activities will be a combination of things instigated by the children and facilitators, on a rolling basis. Throughout the day the children can, if they want, choose to be entirely independent in what they do, and not participate in the organized activities – they design their own day ...

> For children who attend the Cabin, their day is orientated around a flexible rhythm that 'evolves over time in response to the needs, views and interests of the group'.

> The launch rhythm will be:

> 10am: arrive, settle in, and opening circle.
> Morning: opportunity to participate in an organized activity, plus free access to the The Cabin resources and outside area.
> 12–1pm: Lunch
> Afternoon: opportunity to participate in an organized activity, plus free access to The Cabin resources and outside area.
> 2.30–2.45: Clearing up time
> 2.45–3pm: Closing circle and collection.

The Cabin will be set up and resourced with the following which can be freely accessed.

1) The Library: a comfy and cosy corner with books and audio books.
2) Role Play Area: set up with dressing up and props for those theatrical moments!
3) Maker Space: a project space with writing, art and craft equipment.
4) Games Chest: puzzles, board and card games galore.
5) Building Zone: Lego and other building kits to turn ideas into reality.
6) Discussion Circle: a place to share ideas and experiences.
7) Show and Tell Table: bring something in from home that you would like to share!
8) The Outside Box: filled with equipment that you might want to use in the outside play area.
9) Cooking and Gardening: We will be equipt for cooking and growing.

We are so happy to have a large, enclosed grassy outdoor space to use, including a roly poly hill!

(Source: downatthecabin.com)

Arguably, the pedagogic approaches, styles, and curriculum built within this delicate eco-system of EHE networks and offline communities somewhat blur the perceived boundaries presupposed to exist between 'formal', 'informal', 'non-formal' learning contexts (Jones, 2013).

Evidentially, with the help of the internet, some EHE parents have harnessed the forms of cultural and social capital (Bourdieu, 1986) needed to grow and extend highly personalized learning contexts for their children. However, the parents in Fensham-Smith's (2017) study were largely white, highly educated and middle class. In their study involving 12 Gypsy and Traveller families, Bhopal and Myer's (2015) findings surfaced numerous barriers experienced by families in arranging extra-curricular activities due to transportation issues. The extent to which regular participation in a variety of EHE groups is a widespread form of practice is unknown.

With the growth of highly individualized communities in the EHE context, critics might question the extent to which this form of provision sufficiently prepares learners to participate and engage with a broader set of communities of different faiths, cultures and beliefs and/or restricts learners from adopting a range of perspectives and values. More broadly, others might argue that socialization towards individualization signals a withering away of the 'common' good (Lubienski, 2000). However, it also could be argued that, in interacting with EHE families and groups, some children might have the opportunity to experience a broader range of interactions with adults and children of different ages based on shared interests. Conversely, Ryan (2019) contemplates that such contexts might promote and/or support collaborative relationships that more closely resemble those found in higher education and/or the workplace.

Personalized learning and a flexible curriculum

The educational philosophies approaches, styles and curricula utilized in EHE are highly personalized to the ages, individual needs and interests of children and the beliefs and values of parents. While some families follow a more formal routine and structure with use of the National Curriculum, others do not. Even within families the approach, curricula and styles taken for one child might differ from that of their sibling/s. In Fensham-Smith's (2017) study, nearly half (123) of the 242 survey respondents indicated that their EHE practice was influenced by educational philosophies, methods and or/approaches (including unschooling, autonomous and child-led learning), while the remaining 47 per cent (114) suggested that it was more of a 'pick and mix' semi-structured approach; with some parent-initiated, timetabled sit-down lessons at home alongside child-initiated family projects and EHE local community activities.

Across a spectrum of practice, and one that departs substantially from the formalities of pre-planned curricula, objectives and distinct 'subject domains', is 'unschooling'. Inspired by the writings of John Holt (1977; 1984), unschooling is a philosophy of repositioning life, family relationships and learning to respond to children's interests and needs without predetermined curriculum or syllabus. Within these approaches, there is a tacit interrelation between a child's personal, social and educational development and this can make it difficult to identify these, not least name them (Ryan, 2019). The purpose of child-led and/ or autonomous methods could be likened to the search for 'self-acualization' whereby, as Davies (2015) asserts: 'there are no specific dispositions to be fostered in advance, only a context within which the individual becomes who they want to be' (p. 23).

Central to autonomous and child-led approaches are the reconfigured relationships that children have with their parents. Qualitative and tacit forms of assessment happen through the mutual exchanges and observations between parents and children in the context of shared everyday experiences in the home and their respective communities (Thomas and Pattison, 2013). Unschooling advocates often herald this as an inherently liberating and freeing form of education for children. While the EHE context affords parents greater opportunities to extend positive support and encouragement to learners, it may also extend their power relations and control (Jones, 2013). Drawing on Bernstein's (1975) code theory and the notion of 'invisible' pedagogies, one of Fensham-Smith's (2017) findings was that while children have greater control of the sequence and pace of their learning, through tacit and continuous parental surveillance, relations of power and control between the EHE parent and child are reconfigured, rather than non-existent.

What is interesting to note here is the ways in which EHE both challenges and reinforces notions of parental participation. Within the context of the National Curriculum, the involvement of parents and their children – including the provision of curricular and co-curricular support – is seen as a vital part of promoting effective learning within school. Studying together at home and initiatives that serve to strengthen home-school partnerships have been found to have a positive effect on children's motivation and engagement (Jones, 2013). While not overlooking the opportunities and tensions of parental participation in the EHE context, when reflecting on what this means within mainstream settings, perhaps one might ask where and how there might be further scope to build in opportunities for pupils to play a greater role in designing and managing their own programme of learning. Additionally, wider research suggests that incidental learning opportunities and capacity for pupils to have a greater and more varied choice impact positively upon learning engagement. Moreover, one might pause to reflect on the degree to which local communities can, and/or should, also be involved in these decisions.

EHE transitions: formal curriculum

Very little is known about the educational transitions of EHE children and young people towards the latter stages of their educational journey. There is some, albeit limited, evidence that EHE children transition to more formal modes of learning as they get older. In Fensham-Smith's (2017) study, over 65 per cent over the ages of 16 were reported to be receiving 'mixed' and or 'state-school provision,' rather than EHE.

One of the challenges facing some EHE learners who wish to return to formal curriculum, is in securing the funding and places necessary to sit examinations as private candidates. It is unclear how many EHE children undertake formal qualifications, but there are some online networks and local parent-led groups, who work with LAs, schools and/or exam boards to support tuition. The Hampshire LA example, cited earlier, provides a small subsidy towards the cost of one GCSE and EHE parents have set up and registered their own exam centre. One example of a successful partnership between a school, local authority and a community of home educators is PLACE (parent-led community-based education).

Partnership and collaboration: PLACE, East of England, UK

PLACE is a novel education programme that is best described as 'a home-education community affiliated to a mainstream school'. It was originally set up in 2003 through a partnership between an EHE community and a head teacher of a local school in the East of England. PLACE 'has evolved from operating informally at the fringe of mainstream education to approved "alternative provider" status, under the auspices of the Local Education Authority' (PLACE.org, 2020) PLACE children remain on the register of the partnered school. The characteristic of PLACE are:

- The family as a focus for learning: home is the 'basecamp' for independent learning.
- Parent-led provision: a parent committee and parent volunteers drive and shape the curriculum, depending on their philosophical standpoint, this may be child-led or parent-led.

- Multiple pedagogic approaches and project-based, inquiry-driven learning.
- Extended learning relationships: each child accesses a unique constellation of learning opportunities and experiences depending on their needs, want and philosophies of learning.
- Families decide who will support their learning: this group may include parents, siblings' peers, trained teachers and tutors.
- The role parents play in PLACE most closely resembles the one that parents play in early childhood learning.

(PLACE.org, 2020, p. 34)

Since it was developed, PLACE is reported to have supported hundreds of EHE learners to obtain formal GCSE qualifications. Among the perspectives of some of the parents whose family participated in the scheme, there was the recognition that:

> [W]hen entering qualifications, a significant amount of flexibility is lost, as the whole family cannot attend and content becomes driven by the qualification rather than by the child's interests. A compromise must be made, and through PLACE the family can access the best bits of home education and necessary elements of school education

(ibid., p. 36)

Within the context of a process-driven curriculum that values quantitative assessments of learning, a provocative question is whether qualifications should be a necessary part of a 'suitable' and 'efficient' education within EHE, if we interpret a suitable and efficient education as one that 'does not foreclose options in later years to adopt some other life form'. It could be legitimate, therefore, to argue that obtaining GCSE qualifications in English, Mathematics and Science might be an essential precursor to extending employment opportunities and/or entry in to further and higher education and employment later in life. Considering the rights of the child, it is perhaps reasonable to question whether more flexible pathways to free access to these qualifications (e.g. IGCSEs) and relevant tuition should be made available to learners in the EHE rather than being left to the discretion of some LAs and/or the individual resources of parents. Conversely, some EHE parents might argue that fostering the sensibilities of 'self-confidence', self-determination and deeper 'critical thinking' skills might ultimately better equip EHE young people to succeed in securing alternative routes and pathways to meaningful employment and a happy and enriching life. In reflecting on their family's EHE journey, parents/facilitators were keen to emphasize that no one size fits all and that there were benefits to a childhood free from the constraints of high stakes testing in a supportive and enriching environment (Ryan, 2019).

Yet very little is known about how EHE children have come to make sense of their own experiences and future needs. Many EHE empirical studies implicitly prioritize the voices, motivations, attitudes, beliefs and experiences of EHE parents. There are only a handful of UK EHE empirical studies that incorporate the participation of children and young people, to varying degrees, as a central feature within their research design (de Carvalho and Skipper, 2019; Fensham-Smith, 2017; Jones, 2013; Nelson; 2014; Ryan, 2019). The following section presents key trends and prioritizes extracts of original data from the voices of EHE children and young people to enrich the discussion.

The voice of EHE children: experiences and needs

While representative longitudinal data on the 'hard' outcomes of EHE in terms of qualification levels achieved, employment, etc. does not exist, some studies have represented EHE children's and young people's expressions of 'self and identity'. Common themes include:

- a strong awareness and perception of sense of self: 'confident'; 'well rounded'; 'self-assured'; 'free thinking'; 'determined'; 'imaginative';
- an awareness of 'the other' in relation to their own EHE experiences and 'schooled' children; 'special'; 'unique'; 'privileged; 'better';
- a perception of wider society and future pathways; 'positive world view'; 'motivated'; 'forward thinking'.

In Fensham-Smith's study across the several interviews, home-educated young people reiterated that their EHE experience had cultivated a vital skillset that was perceived to be absent in school (2017, pp. 219–22). For example:

> I am free thinking. You don't necessarily need GCSEs to be successful. If you are imaginative you can do things ...
>
> (Tristan, a home-educated young person)

> I think for me the main thing is, that because I got to choose what I learned about, I don't have an aversion to education because I think it's all boring. Whereas at school you are forced to do subjects you don't like, with teachers you don't get on with, for many hours a day ... It's much better I think, having the opportunity to learn yourself. I actually like the stuff I do and I'm excited to start college ...
>
> (Billie, a home-educated young person)

At the same time, however, these learners also developed a strong sense of the 'other', namely, being different from their schooled peers. For instance:

> I think I have become a better person for being home-educated than I would have been had I gone to school ... I have a more rounded view of the world. It's just a good viewpoint ...
>
> (Stephanie, a home-educated young person)

In Ryan's (2019) study, this strong sense of self was connected to a sense of purpose. The sense of self in relation to the 'schooled' other was also identified by Jones (2013, p. 113):

> Conversations with some of the children also suggest that they saw themselves as different to school children and to some extent in a more privileged position to school children. Ryan, reflecting on his experience of school, commented that 'I didn't feel like I slotted in very well there'. Charlotte described school children as 'the proper people'.

Both Jones (2013) and Fensham-Smith (2017) found explicit connections between these expressions of identity and the degree to which EHE learners had experienced educational contexts marked by varying degrees of 'choice', enthusiasm and engagement through child-initiated learning.

In her reflection, Jones (2013) considers what educators in mainstream settings might take away from these accounts. She questions the degree to which curricula, in most instances, needs to be so rigidly pre-planned. Equally, she asserted that children need supportive and encouraging relationships and learning contexts in order to develop self-regulated styles of motivation. Collaborative learning environments that allow children a greater balance between 'external regulation' and self-determined regulation are likely to increase learner engagement. She concludes that the practice of EHE might help to give practitioners who work with children who are experiencing disaffection from school, a deeper awareness of the sorts of collaborative relationships between peers and teachers that support reengagement.

Challenges and needs

One study which focused on the role of the educational psychologist in supporting EHE young people's transitions into a further education college in Wales, included interviews with four EHE children, two of whom had never attended school. Among several of the key findings was the issue of LA relationships and misrecognition (discussed earlier) as a barrier towards identifying EHE community needs and multi-agency partnerships. This included a breakdown in relationships and a lack of clarity in terms of EHE community needs (Ryan, 2019, p. 81).

In experiencing this transition, 15-year-old AJ (participant) was accustomed to being able to study alone at home at her own pace, and found the adjustment challenging:

> For AJ, who had never previously attended school, her unfamiliarity with school procedures, such as timetabling and navigating educational sites, was particularly challenging: 'They were like, "There isn't a lesson until period 3", and I was like, "'I don't know what that means"'.
>
> (Ryan, 2019, p. 69)

In Fensham-Smith's study, the transition to more formal modes of learning was not always a positive or straightforward experience for EHE learners (2017, p. 221). For example, Stephanie recalls accidentally self-teaching herself the incorrect syllabus for a Maths GCSE:

> Freedom is a gift and a bit of a curse, because you can just end up not doing stuff for a very long time ... My mum is starting a new career and she was really busy, so I've had to teach a lot of my GCSEs to myself, which is really quite difficult. I've had to read books, write down everything that I know about it, looking at questions on the internet and reading past papers ... all from scratch ... the problem was that I ended up learning the wrong tier for my Maths, so I had to revise it all again ...
>
> (Stephanie, a home-educated young person)

Moreover, Andrew articulated that at 16 years old, he felt that he had 'missed the boat' with regards to sitting GCSEs exams. At 14, he recalled 'not doing well':

> I was supposed to be doing GCSEs, although I am a bit late for them. Most of the people my age finished them by now. I did three GCSEs from the ages of 11 to 13. I didn't do very well ... Now I'd like to do an ancient history course on Coursera ...
>
> (Andrew, home-educated teenager)

Interestingly Dylan explained that as the child of single parent household, his mother could not afford to pay for GCSEs. Wanting to attending college, but without any formal qualifications, Dylan made use of a free Massively Open Online Course (MOOC) hosted on a platform called Coursera.[16] Having completed the course and gained a certificate, Dylan used this to apply for an ICT course at a local college:

> The internet is a massive tool; the amount of free resources you can get was helpful ... I also managed to get into college doing ICT without having to sit any GCSEs ... I finished a computer science course this year through Harvard University, it's the same course that they were offering their first-year university students but it was free ... With the course, itself, you log in and there are lectures, with it being computer stuff you also get problem sets every week, you complete those and it goes on a database ... I completed it, got a certificate and that was a big part of me being able to get into college ...
>
> (Dylan, home educated young person)

Reflecting on this example, we can question the extent to which the increasing availability of 'micro-credentials' and the possible wider recognition of alternative forms of prior learning might disrupt dominant ideas of progression, entry and access to further and higher education. It seems important to point out, that most undergraduate courses at the Open University, for example, do not require formal qualifications as a prerequisite for entry.[17] This is predicated on the assumption of access. The potential existence of a digital divide within and across EHE children's experiences is unknown (Fensham-Smith, 2019). Further work in the area of alternative routes, including barriers to access and post-16 transitions is sorely needed to develop a more balanced picture of future EHE community needs.

Conclusion: new frontiers and future avenues

In presenting the rise of EHE policy developments, motivations and new learning, this chapter has illustrated the myriad of ways in which the rise of EHE disrupts, extends and reconfigures notions of a broad and balanced curriculum, parental participation and child-centred learning.

The ways in which some families have extended new community contexts for children question the degree to which the standardized curriculum is fundamentally designed in consultation with the needs, interests and values of local communities. At its core, a broad and balanced curriculum rests on the presumption of a suitable and efficient education. Evidentially, the purpose and methods of how to facilitate such provision can and should be discussed and debated in principle and in practice. EHE perhaps represents the very antithesis of a process-driven and standardized model of curriculum (and comprehensive schooling). It perhaps encourages practitioners in mainstream settings to question how and to what degree such levels of prescription are needed to foster a range of educational, social and developmental outcomes.

The extent to which socialization towards individualization, as an expression of a liberal society, is inherently withering away the 'common' good is a much bigger debate that I am not able to address here. However, what EHE perhaps illustrates is the degree to which community learning contexts should play a greater role in where and how curriculum is both constructed and delivered.

Moreover, the degree to which pupils have agency in deciding what, where and how they learn, within a context that is meaningful to them, is important for fostering self-regularized motivation and engagement. It might be legitimate to reimagine a curriculum that offered a greater degree of flexibility and agency to suit a range of learner needs and interests. Equally, within the existing constraints, there might be further scope to identify further opportunities for establishing connections between the artificial divisions between discrete subject domains. One might ask, where and across the 'whole school' community context there might be room to build in greater opportunities to promote incidental learning – without pre-planned objectives, curricula and outcomes.

While no one size fits all, for EHE learners who do require additional support for their needs and in the provision of examination funding, there are important and ongoing questions with respect to equity and inequality of opportunity. The evidence base which LAs and policy-makers have to draw upon is substantially limited. However, future relationship building, irrespective of legislative changes, must build upon the premise of mutual recognition and openness to consider curriculum and education in their broadest sense. This also necessitates a willingness by EHE communities to acknowledge some of difficulties and shortcomings that can and do exist within the wider EHE population. Future work needs to build upon and showcase areas of good practice.

Notes

1 Home schooling is used primarily to refer to this form of provision in the US context. While I am critical of the limitations of the concept, elective home education (EHE) is a term that is used most in UK policy.

2 This research was funded by the Economic and Social Research Council, grant number: 1228036.

3 The author is referring to 'misrecognition' within the context of Fraser's (1999) framing of identity politics and social justice.

4 EHE differs from 'flexi-schooling'. Flexi-schooling is a form of provision, agreed at the discretion of a head teacher, whereby provision is partly divided between learning at home and attending school. In these arrangements, children continue to stay on the school roll and the school continues to attract full funding for said pupil/s (Bhopal and Myers, 2015).

5 Notifying the relevant LA is described as 'sensible', but this is currently an optional choice. Parents seeking to remove their child from the school roll are required to write and submit a short notice of deregistration to the head teacher or proprietor of the school (DfE, 2019b).

6 Under S437 (1), if an LA has reasonable grounds to believe that child is not receiving a suitable and efficient education, they have the power to issue a school attendance order.

7 The author recognizes that there are other limited examples and alternative case law rulings that one could draw upon for emphasis.

8 While DfE (2019a) acknowledges the wishes of parents as 'relevant', they also assert that, from the state's viewpoint, 'it does not mean that parents are the sole arbiters of what constitutes a suitable education' (p. 24).

9 The DfE (2019a) guidelines set out the importance of consulting with EHE families.

10 Limited evidence of relationship building, trust and collaboration between LAs and EHE in Mukwamba-Sendell's (2019) thesis was presented, nor did the author reflect on the role that advocates play in exacerbating divisions and fuelling mistrust among new families via social media (see Fensham-Smith, 2019).

11 Including: North Yorkshire County Council, Somerset County Council, Staffordshire County Council and West Midlands.

12 The Association of Directors of Children's Services Ltd.

13 There is no evidence to suggest that so-called 'off rolling' and/or temporary EHE to secure a school place is a widespread practice (ADCS, 2019).

14 In the most recent ADCS (2019) survey, just under half of the LAs who responded reported that between 81–90 per cent of their local cohort had previously attended school (p. 5).

15 Education Otherwise (a large charitable organization) provides an extensive directory of local EHE groups, see https://www.educationotherwise.org/

16 Coursera (see: https://www.coursera.org/) is one of many MOOC platforms. Other platforms include: Future Learn (https://www.futurelearn.com/) and OpenLearn: (https://www.open.edu/openlearn/).

17 For an interesting discussion on selecting students by academic ability in higher education, see https://theconversation.com/why-british-universities-should-rethink-selecting-students-by-academic-ability-45473

References

ADCS (2019) 'Elective Home Education Survey 2019'. Available at: https://adcs.org.uk/assets/documentation/ADCS_Elective_Home_Education_Survey_Analysis_FINAL.pdf (accessed 1 January 2020).

Badman, G. (2009) *Review of Elective Home-education in England*, London: DCSF.

Bernstein, B. (1975) 'Class and pedagogies: Visible and invisible', *Education Studies*, 1(1): 23–41.

Bhopal, K. and Myers, M. (2015) 'Marginal groups in marginal times: Gypsy and Traveller parents and home education in England, UK', *British Educational Research Journal*, 42(1): 5–20.

Bourdieu, P. (1986) 'The forms of capital', in J.G. Richardson (ed.), *Handbook of Theory and Research for the Sociology of Education*, New York: Greenwood Press, pp. 241–58.

D'Arcy, K. (2014) 'Home-education, school, Travellers and educational inclusion', *British Journal of Sociology of Education*, 35(5): 818–35.

Davies, R. (2015) 'A suitable education?', *Other Education: The Journal of Educational Alternatives*, 4(1): 16–32.

de Carvalho, E. and Skipper, Y. (2019) '"We're not just sat at home in our pyjamas!": A thematic analysis of the social lives of home educated adolescents in the UK', *European Journal of Psychology of Education*, 34: 501–16.

DfE (Department for Education) (2019a) 'Elective home education: Departmental guidance for local authorities', 20 August. Available at: https://assets.publishing.service.gov.uk/government/uploads/system/uploads/attachment_data/file/791527/Elective_home_education_gudiance_for_LAv2.0.pdf (accessed 1 April 2020).

DfE (Department for Education) (2019b) 'Elective home education: Departmental guidance for parents', 20 August. Available at: https://assets.publishing.service.gov.uk/government/uploads/system/uploads/attachment_data/file/791528/EHE_guidance_for_parentsafterconsultationv2.2.pdf (accessed 1 April 2020).

DfE (Department for Education) (2019c) 'Elective home education: a call for evidence 2018: Government consultation response', April 2019. Available at:

https://assets.publishing.service.gov.uk/government/uploads/system/uploads/attach-ment_data/file/791552/EHECfEResponseDocumentv9.4.pdf (accessed 1 April 2020).

Fensham-Smith, A.J. (2014) 'Gypsy and Traveller education: Engaging families – a research Report', Welsh Government. Available at: http://gov.wales/docs/caecd/research/2014/141125-gypsy-traveller-education-engagingfamilies-en.pdf (accessed 1 December 2019).

Fensham-Smith, A.J. (2017) 'New technologies, knowledge, networks and communities in home-education', unpublished PhD thesis, Cardiff University.

Fensham-Smith, A.J. (2019) 'Becoming a home-educator in a networked world: towards the democratisation of education alternatives?' *Other Education: The Journal of Educational Alternatives*, 8(1): 12–35.

Fraser, N (1999) 'Social justice in the age of identity politics: Redistribution, recognition and participation', in L. Ray and A. Sayer (eds), *Culture and Economy after the Cultural Turn*, Thousand Oaks, CA: Sage, pp. 25–52.

Hampshire County Council (2020) 'Elective home education'. Available at: https://www.hants.gov.uk/educationandlearning/educationinclusionservice/electivehomeeducation (accessed 1 June 2020).

Hirst, P.H. (1974) *Knowledge and the Curriculum*. London: Routledge and Kegan Paul.

Holt, J. (1977) *Instead of Education*. Harmondsworth: Penguin.

Holt, J. (1984) *How Children Fail*. New York: Delacorte Press.

Jones, T. (2013) 'Through the lens of home-educated children: Engagement in education', *Educational Psychology in Practice*, 29(2): 107–12.

Kunzman, R. and Gaither, M. (2020) 'Homeschooling: An updated comprehensive survey of the research', *Other Education: The Journal of Educational Alternatives*, 9(1): 253–336.

Lees, H.E. (2013) *Education Without Schools: Discovering Alternatives*, Bristol: Policy Press.

Lubienski, C. (2000) 'Whither the common good? A critique of home-schooling', *Peabody Journal of Education*, 75(1&2): 207–32.

Monk, D. (2015) 'Home-education: A human right?', in P. Rothermel (ed.), *International Perspectives on Home-education: Do We Still Need Schools?* London: Palgrave Macmillan, pp. 166–78.

Morton, R. (2010) 'Home-education: Constructions of choice', *International Electronic Journal of Elementary Education*, 3(1): 46–56.

Mukwamba-Sendell, F. (2019) 'Policy interpreted: The effect of local authority administration and officer perception and practice on national-education policy implementation', unpublished doctoral thesis, Lancaster University.

Myers, M. and Bhopal, K. (2018) 'Muslims, home education and risk in British society', *British Journal of Sociology of Education*, 39(2): 212–26.

Nelson, J. (2014) 'Home education: Exploring the views of parents, children and young people', unpublished doctoral thesis, University of Birmingham.

PLACE.org (2020) 'PLACE: a case study Building a Learning Community without Going to School, Innovation Unit report'. Available at: https://place-programme.org/wp-content/uploads/2014/06/PLACE-Programme-Case-Study.pdf (accessed 10 August 2020).

Rothermel, P.J. (2002) 'Home-education: Rationales, practices and outcomes', PhD thesis, University of Durham.

Ryan, L. (2019) 'Elective home education in Wales: Post-16 transition and the role of the educational psychologist', unpublished doctorate in Educational Research (DedPsy), Cardiff University.

Safran, B.L. (2008) 'Exploring identity change and communities of practice among long term home-educating parents', unpublished PhD thesis, the Open University.

Smith, E. and Nelson, J. (2015) 'Using the Opinions and Lifestyle Survey to examine the prevalence and characteristics of families who home-educate in the UK', *Educational Studies*, 41(3): 312–25.

Sperling, J. (2015) 'Home-education and the European Convention on Human Rights', in P. Rothermel (ed.), *International Perspectives on Home-education: Do We Still Need Schools?* London: Palgrave Macmillan, pp. 179–88.

Stafford, B. (2012) 'Bad evidence: The curious case of the government-commissioned review of elective home-education in England and how parents exposed its weaknesses', *Evidence & Policy*, 8(3): 361–81.

Thomas, A. and Pattison, H. (2013) 'Informal home-education: Philosophical aspirations put into practice', *Studies in Philosophy and Education*, 32(2): 141–54.

Wenger, E. (1998) *Communities of Practice: Learning, Meaning and Identity*, Cambridge: Cambridge University Press.

4 Exploring accessible curricula for learners with PMLD

Cathal Butler

Major questions addressed in this chapter are:

- How does government policy inform how the curriculum is delivered for learners with profound and multiple learning difficulties?
- How can teachers meaningfully engage with learners with profound and multiple learning difficulties?

Abstract

Continuing advances in medicine mean that children with complex, rare and often life-limiting conditions are living longer, and are accessing education. The organization of the curriculum in England means that these learners are classified as being below Key Stage 1 of the National Curriculum. However, rather than using the Early Years Framework and curriculum, this group of learners, until recently followed the P Scales. The Rochford Review (Rochford, 2016) has recommended substantial reform in this area, focusing more on the developing cognitive capacities of these learners. This chapter explores the cognitive, social and emotional development of learners with profound and multiple learning difficulties (PMLD), and research on how curricula can support this. It will focus in particular on the difficulties in distinguishing between assessment and curriculum. Finally, it will focus on a specific piece of research, looking at the extent to which curriculum guidance developed in Northern Ireland (Quest for Learning), based on Welsh materials (Routes for Learning), can be applied to support the learning of students with PMLD. Specific examples of practice, drawn from research, will be used to demonstrate how the skills required to access the National Curriculum can be taught.

Introduction

The right of learners with profound and multiple learning difficulties (PMLD) to access a curriculum that is meaningful to them has proven challenging for educators. Continuing advances in medicine mean that children with complex, rare and often life-limiting conditions are living longer, and are accessing education. The organization of the curriculum in England means that these learners are classified as being below Key Stage 1 of the National Curriculum. However, rather than using the Early Years Framework and curriculum, this group of learners until recently followed the P Scales (Rochford, 2016). The Rochford report (Rochford, 2016) has recommended substantial reform in this area, focusing more on the developing cognitive capacities of these learners. This chapter explores in detail the cognitive, social, and emotional development of learners with PMLD, and research on how curricula can support this. It focuses in particular on the difficulties in distinguishing between assessment and curriculum. Broader elements of the whole school curriculum, particularly social interaction, are explored, before focusing on recent and current policy in the UK which informs the assessment and curriculum made available to this group of learners. It discusses a specific piece of research (Butler, 2018), looking at the extent to which curriculum guidance developed in Northern Ireland (Quest for Learning; Council for the Curriculum and Examinations, 2012), based on Welsh materials (Routes for Learning; Welsh Assembly Government, 2006), can be applied to support the learning of students with PMLD. Specific examples of practice drawn from research are used to demonstrate how the skills required to access the National Curriculum can be taught. A brief case study of an individual child is included that highlights the different teaching strategies, activities and resources used to support her in developing the skills to engage in social communication.

Rights to access education for learners with PMLD

The issue of what this group of learners should be taught, and indeed whether they should be taught, has historically been an issue, as this group of pupils were deemed ineducable prior to 1970 in the UK (Male and Rayner, 2007). Even though there is now access to education, questions remain about what expectations and opportunities there are for this group of learners (Gray and Chasey, 2006). In spite of rising numbers of learners classified as having PMLD in full-time education in the UK (Pinney, 2017), it remains the case that the majority of these learners access specialist rather than mainstream provision, globally (Lyons and Arthur-Kelly, 2014). Learners with PMLD 'are entitled to access a curriculum and assessment framework which is fit for purpose and meets their specific needs – there is little benefit or increase in entitlement if they are included in structures that fail to do this' (Qualifications and Curriculum Group, 2006, p. 46).

Imray and Hinchclife (2012) summarize some of the debates that have arisen around what type of curriculum meets the needs of learners with PMLD and severe learning difficulties (SLD), highlighting some of the negative impacts (Barber and Goldbart, 1998; Ware and Healy, 1994) of the National Curriculum on teaching and learning for learners with PMLD. In addition, they challenge the work of Lewis and Norwich (2000) on whether specialist pedagogy is required for learners with special educational needs. Imray and Hinchcliffe (2012, p. 151) state: 'We contend that pupils with profound and multiple learning difficulties are highly unlikely to learn to communicate, eat, reach out, make choices, proactively engage with others, and so on, effectively unless "distinct kinds of teaching" are used.' We return to this point later in this chapter.

The label used in this chapter, PMLD, is not universally understood or applied. Ware (2005) and Bellamy, Croot, Bush, Berry and Smith (2010) highlight a lack of consensus over the terminology to be used, noting that while the term PMLD is in common usage in the UK, other terms, such as Profound Intellectual and Multiple Disability (PIMD), and complex needs, are also used. Gittins and Rose (2008) provide a helpful summary of a variety of the ways that different researchers define this category. They cite for example the World Health Organization, which notes in relation to profound mental retardation, that the intelligence quotient (IQ) is estimated as under 20. This means that, in practical terms, individuals experience great difficulty in their ability:

> [to] comply with requests or instructions. Most such individuals are immobile or severely restricted in mobility, incontinent, and capable at most of only very rudimentary forms of non-verbal communication. They possess little or no ability to care for their own basic needs, and require constant help.
>
> (World Health Organization (1992),
> cited in Gittins and Rose, 2008, p. 40)

A number of researchers (Gittins and Rose, 2008; Ware, 1996) state that learners with PMLD typically have learning difficulties so severe that they are typically functioning at a developmental level of less than 2 years of age. An important aspect that must be highlighted is that PMLD involves more than one disability (Dee, 2002; Lacey, 1998). Beyond the physical disabilities associated with this category of need, researchers have highlighted a variety of ways in which having profound and multiple learning difficulties can impact on different capacities (Carpenter, 2007). Hughes, Redley and Ring (2011) for example state that learners with PMLD can be characterized as being pre-intentional, with little or no ability to purposefully engage with the world. Similarly, Poppes, van der Putten, ten Brug, and Vlaskamp (2016a) note that communication is a major difficulty for these learners, with many relying on non-symbolic forms of communication. Other researchers (Bellamy, Croot, Bush, Berry and Smith, 2010; Samuel and Pritchard, 2001) highlight the delays in social development experienced by these learners. Poppes et al. (2016b) highlight the sensory difficulties which are common to this group of learners, while Rees (2017) highlights the health and mobility needs of this group of learners, with Gittins and Rose (2008) identifying epilepsy, and respiratory problems in particular, as having a high probability of occurring for this group.

Generally speaking, the needs of learners with PMLD are very diverse (Simmons and Bayliss, 2007), with Rees (2017) in particular noting that PMLD is a very heterogeneous category or grouping. The population of learners with PMLD tend to display very 'spiky' cognitive profiles, as the abilities of these learners are varied, and do not necessarily follow any recognized linear developmental pathway, a point that will be returned to when discussing assessment. Given this, it is not surprising that the value of the term PMLD has been subject to criticism (Vorhaus, 2017) with Goldbart, Chadwick and Buell (2014) noting that PMLD 'is a description rather than a diagnostic category' (p. 68). A final key critique of these definitions, raised by Simmons and Watson (2015), is that they focus entirely on deficits, rather than looking at the capacities of these learners.

Curriculum challenges in addressing difficulties in social interaction

This discussion around how to describe and define the needs of this group of learners serves to highlight the complex and multiple issues that researchers and practitioners must address in order to understand and support this group of learners, and to perhaps pre-empt some of the difficulties faced by educators when trying to understand and support their learning.

Learners with profound and multiple learning difficulties typically have limited communicative abilities. Porter, Ouvry, Morgan and Downs (2001) note that these learners have little access to spoken language, while Nijs, Vlaskamp and Maes (2016) highlight difficulties in relation to symbolic communication. They highlight that communication, which is at a pre-symbolic or protosymbolic level, creates a barrier to others accessing and understanding them. Jones, Pring and Grove (2002) similarly note that intentional communication develops slowly for this group of learners. This can leave a relatively limited range of ways for these learners to communicate – through body movement (which can be very limited depending on their level of physical impairment), through vocalizations (Hostyn and Maes, 2009), as well as through facial expression and eye gaze (Francis, 2011). These forms of communication are termed idiosyncratic (Porter, Ouvry, Morgan, and Downs, 2001), and likely to vary greatly across a population of learners. This can leave limited or ambiguous channels for learners with PMLD to convey messages to people in the environment (Griffiths and Smith, 2016). This means that whatever these learners try to communicate may well be misinterpreted or missed.

Being able to communicate is identified as a key tool to support individual development and Social Development (Rayner, Bradley, Johnson, Mrozik, Appiah and Nagra, 2016). Green and Reid (1999) provide an example of how the behaviour of these learners is explored using an 'index of happiness', as a broad means to measure quality of life. Simmons and Watson (2015) describe happiness in this instance as facial expressions or vocalizations that would typically be considered to communicate happiness in learners without disability (e.g. smiling, laughing). Simmons and Watson (2015) describe how a range of research using indices of happiness show increased indications of happiness when preferred stimuli are presented. This provides evidence of these learners being able to communicate a preference. However, Jones, Pring and Grove (2002) highlight that the progress towards intentional communication is very slow in learners with PMLD. A Mencap report (1999, p. 7) states that:

> Parents often understand their sons and daughters intuitively but find it difficult to put their instincts into words. To the outsider little is evident, but often a parent will say, 'She's really enjoying that' when apparently nothing is happening. An eye flicker or a twitch of the mouth can actually be rich in communication.

Similarly, Nijs, Vlaskamp and Maes (2016) provide a positive report on the nature of interaction between learners with PIMD and siblings, with Nijs *et al.* noting that interactions with siblings are 'in all likelihood motivating and encouraging' (p. 28).

Unfortunately, despite these positive findings, research also covers a range of negative findings, many of which focus on staff in schools. Porter *et al.* (2001) note that staff can find it difficult to comprehend the communication of learners with PMLD, and the resulting difficulties in sustaining interaction can lead to staff giving up. Munde and Vlaskamp's (2015) findings indicate that support staff may react too quickly when trying to interact with this group, rather than giving learners sufficient time to react to an activity/behaviour. Simmons and Bayliss (2007) report that staff would like to understand the learners with PMLD that they are supporting. Sadly, however, they cite a frequent lack of time and training to support their development in this area. To further highlight a potential lack of understanding of these students, a study focusing on perceptions of challenging behaviour of this group learners (Poppes *et al.*, 2016a), which as they note is relatively high (Poppes, van der Putten and Vlaskamp, 2010), highlighted that the most common attribution (out of a range of options) to explain challenging behaviour is a biomedical one, i.e., it is the condition that is the cause, with environmental factors playing presumably little or no role. Poppes, van der Putten, ten Brug and Vlaskamp (2016) cite further findings from their own previous research that challenging behaviour is seen as having 'minor consequences' for these individuals. In spite of major barriers, researchers have attempted to capture the 'voice' of learners with a wide range of needs, including those with PMLD (Hill, Croydon, Greathead, Kenny, Yates, and Pellicano, 2016; Jones, Pring and Grove, 2002). Similarly, there is some positive work setting out guidelines to support interaction (Hostyn and Maes, 2009), which focuses on factors such as sensitive responsiveness, joint attention, co-regulation, and an emotional component, which can support successful interaction. Hostyn and Maes (2009), in reviewing the small body of literature focusing on interaction between people with PIMD and their partners, described four components important in interactions: sensitive responsiveness, joint attention, co-regulation and an emotional component.

Simmons and Watson (2015) have also helped to widen the debate around the awareness of others in learners with PMLD. They discuss 'intersubjectivity', which captures broadly the developing awareness that these learners have of other people as subjective beings, and how this can be seen during interactions. Brigg, Schuitema and Vorhaus (2016) also look at the ability of learners with PMLD to experience and share enjoyment through humour as evidence of the ability of these learners to express themselves, and to be seen as 'fellow human beings' (p. 1175).

Vorhaus (2017, p. 65) highlights the complexities in trying to understand what these learners may be capable of, stating:

> One and the same pupil may be capable of subtle reciprocity in personal relations whilst not able to utter a single word; or she is able to notice and laugh at the incongruity evident in using a large broom as a paint brush, but cannot be left alone for a moment.

Curriculum provision for learners with PMLD in England

Policy on assessment plays a key role in focusing curriculum provision for these learners (Aird, n.d.). From 1998 (Imray and Hinchcliffe, 2012) until 2017, the P Scales set out a range of 'performance attainment targets' (DfE, 2017, p. 3) for learners who were working below National Curriculum Levels. The P Scales are numbered 1 through 8, with subdivisions (e.g. P1i and P1ii) used in P1 through P3 (see Table 4.1). The P Scales are divided into a range of standard curriculum areas; however, it is worth noting that the levels are fairly generic from P1 to P3 (see Table 4.1), with distinctions in P Scale descriptors across curriculum subjects emerging at P4.

Table 4.1 P1–P3 Scales

P Scale level	Descriptor
P1 (i)	Pupils encounter activities and experiences
P1 (ii)	Pupils show emerging awareness of activities and experiences
P2 (i)	Pupils begin to respond consistently to familiar people, events and objects
P2 (ii)	Pupils begin to be proactive in their interactions
P3 (i)	Pupils begin to communicate intentionally
P3 (ii)	Pupils use emerging conventional communication

Source: DFE (2017).

Imray and Hinchcliffe (2014) cite a range of authors who note that P Scales (and alternative measures such as Pivots and B Squared) as a linear system, aligned with eventual academic subjects, are inappropriate. They are not in any way aligned, as Smith, Critten, and Vardill (2020) note, with the provision made available to those within mainstream early years provision, who would also be working below National Curriculum levels.

McDermott and Atkinson cite Donnelly (2005), who highlighted that the highly academic subject-driven nature of the P Scales might detract from a focus on more important areas of learning and developmental targets, as they 'were seen as less important than attempting to measure "experiences" loosely linked to curriculum subjects which were unlikely to move learners on' (McDermott and Atkinson, 2016, p. 10). McDermott and Atkinson also cite Martin (2006), who notes that P Scales do not prove helpful in looking at progress at any degree of granularity, as they are best set up to measure progress across a Key Stage, rather than on a yearly basis. Making a similar point, Barber and Goldbart (1998, p. 113) comment:

> for those individuals who consistently fail to show measurable progress on conventional assessments, a different model of progress is required. It is not that these individuals cannot make progress, but we would argue that the instruments by which progress is measured do not suit the people whose abilities are being measured.

Smith, Critten and Vardill (2020) note that progress for this group of learners is often lateral, rather than linear.

Until 2017, schools in England have been legally bound to report student attainment in the form of P Scale data. In 2015, a review was announced to explore statutory assessment arrangements for pupils working below the National Curriculum (Rochford, 2016). This specifically criticizes how assessment tools such as the P Scales had 'come to be used as a curriculum restricting the kind of creativity and innovation that should be used to engage these pupils and to tailor teaching and learning to their unique needs' (ibid., p. 3). The obligation for schools to use and report progress on P Scales was therefore removed. The Rochford Report suggested a replacement:

> Creating a statutory duty to assess pupils who are not yet engaged in subject-specific learning against the 7 areas of engagement (responsiveness, curiosity, discovery, anticipation, persistence, initiation and investigation) will ensure schools give appropriate attention to the development of concepts and skills that are pre-requisites for progressing on to subject-specific learning.
>
> (ibid., p. 6)

In addition to this, ten recommendations were produced, covering the need for training and continuing professional development (CPD), collaboration between schools, and the removal of the requirement to submit assessment data for these learners to the DfE. The seven areas of engagement, identified in the previous quote, are based on the work of Carpenter *et al.* (2011), who argued that engagement was a multidimensional ability, which was essential for all learning. He worked to develop indicators based on the seven areas of engagement. Assessment materials based on these areas of engagement have been piloted (Standards and Testing Agency, 2018). The Rochford Report (2016, p. 20) noted that schools should be able to 'demonstrate every kind of progress made by a pupil, be it linear, lateral or consolidation'. The schools taking part in the piloting of the engagement profile viewed it as being useful for formative, rather than summative assessment (Standards and Testing Agency, 2018).

Aird (n.d.) notes that even with the P Scales no longer being statutory, many schools continue to use them. He implies that this is due to concerns that P Scale data is required/expected by Ofsted inspectors, to be able to demonstrate the quality of provision, and the progress being made by students. Another explanation offered by Smith, Critten and Vardill (2020) is that schools and teachers will continue to use these assessment methods until clearer guidance emerges from the government.

Teachers and the curriculum

The key role of teachers in informing what and how these learners are taught has been highlighted in the literature. Aird (n.d.) notes that the majority of the education learners with PMLD experience is through one-to-one support from a teacher, assistant, or other professional. It is no surprise therefore that teachers supporting these learners need to develop their own pedagogy and curricula for learners with PMLD (Carpenter, 2007; Salt, 2010). Ayer (1998) recommended a more sensory-focused curriculum for these learners. Rayner (2010) highlights the narrow range of activities that learners with PMLD experience: in the UK, it is entirely possible that the use of P Scales (critiqued above) contributes to this. McNicholas (2000, p. 151) reported a great deal of variety of practice in curriculum being used by teachers of learners with PMLD, and in particular highlighted a 'need to balance the developmental and therapeutic curricula with the National Curriculum'.

What teachers actually do in the classroom is difficult to interpret, and may even remain purposefully unrecorded, based on the literature. Rayner and Male (2013) claim that this is not surprising, as classroom practice is likely to be very individual, depending on the specific needs and interests of the learners in that classroom, and not driven by a focus on academic progress as school leadership might require. The pedagogies that these teachers adopt are very distinct from mainstream approaches (Colley, 2018), and teachers often approach meeting the needs of learners in a very creative way (Stewart and Walker-Gleaves, 2020), continually reflecting on their perceptions of how engaged their learners are (Jones and Riley, 2017).

Alternatives to P Scales: Routes for Learning and Quest for Learning

In the last decade, initiatives in Wales (Routes for Learning) and Northern Ireland (Quest for Learning) have provided assessment tools which are more exact than what is otherwise currently used in schools in the UK (e.g., the P Scales).

Routes for Learning

Routes for Learning was developed by academics and a working group of teachers, in conjunction with the Welsh Qualifications and Curriculum group of the Department for Education, Lifelong Learning and Skills in Cardiff (Welsh Assembly Government, 2006). A fundamental premise of Routes for Learning is that learners with PMLD, being a heterogeneous group, will follow a range of different developmental pathways. This group of learners, who display atypical development, require a flexible assessment model to capture the different rates and routes by which this group of learners may attain typical developmental goals (see Figure 4.1). Lacey (2009) notes that Routes for Learning focuses on the major developmental milestones to capture developments in the first year of life for typically developing infants, and does not necessarily capture some that may be identified below or beyond the 45 milestones set out in Routes for Learning (e.g., Uzgiris and Hunt, 1975). Major characteristics of Routes for Learning (Welsh Assembly Government, 2006) are:

- A set of key developmental milestones (yellow boxes: notices stimuli, responds consistently to one stimulus, contingency responding, contingency awareness, object permanence, selects from two or more items, initiates actions to achieve desired result[exerting autonomy in variety of contexts]). These are supported by more discrete milestones.
- Different pathways that might represent common trajectories of development, focusing on different aspects: a main cognitive route, main communication route, and two alternative routes. While there are different pathways, it is expected that learners should all achieve the key developmental milestones set out in the previous point.
- Although the route map is set out in a broadly linear way, with simpler milestones at the top, and given lower numbers, compared to more complex, higher numbered milestones at the bottom of the page, it is recognized that there is not one route: one does not, for example, move from milestone 3 to milestone 4 (with alternative routes to milestones 6 and 9 suggested).

The Routes for Learning materials also include a range of guidance on strategies and teaching approaches, both generally, and to support the development of particular milestones.

Figure 4.1 Routes for Learning Routemap
Source: Welsh Assembly Government (2019).

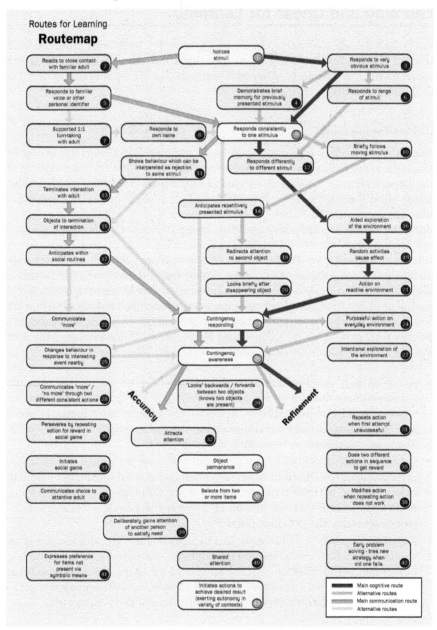

Quest for Learning

Quest for Learning was developed in Northern Ireland by the Council for the Curriculum Examinations and Assessment (CCEA) (Council for the Curriculum and Examinations, 2012). They directly acknowledge the major influence of Routes for Learning in the design of Quest for Learning. Indeed, in PMLD link, it is noted that 'Penny Lacey describes Quest as derivative but more finely honed' (Ashdown, 2014, p. 4.), when compared to Routes for Learning. The goal of Quest for Learning is framed in very positive terms, as it involves: 'Acknowledging and celebrating the different abilities and achievements of those learners with the most complex needs, rather than trying to fit them into an existing framework not developed with these needs in mind' (CCEA, 2012, p. 3).

Like Routes for Learning, Quest for Learning identifies a series of developmental milestones, 43 in this case. Quest for Learning identifies seven major developmental milestones, starting with the ability to notice stimuli, the ability to respond consistently to stimuli, through to contingency responding and awareness, object permanence, and the ability to select between two items. Alongside these major milestones, Quest for Learning identifies other milestones related to early cognitive development, to social interaction, and to communication (for details, see Council for the Curriculum and Examinations, 2012). Again, like Routes for Learning, it is not expected that learners will progress along these in a simple, linear manner.

When discussing observing learners to assess particular milestones, the Quest for Learning guidance (ibid., p. 40.) notes the high degree of skill needed to identify 'small variations in performance' and that observers need deep levels of concentration for long periods of time. Effective observation therefore requires knowing the learner so that the observer can differentiate between:

- an intentional response;
- a reflexive response;
- seizure activity;
- stereotyped movements.

The guidance also suggests that observers should:

- clearly plan and structure your observations;
- make sense of learners' responses;
- ensure all adults working with the learner contribute to the observation process.

A final note to highlight in relation to Quest for Learning is that it specifically states that: 'Quest is an assessment tool, and not the curriculum' (ibid., p. 10). This is important as Martin (2006), when discussing P Scales, commented on the danger of a blurring occurring between curriculum and assessment.

Vignette: Using Quest for Learning to support the needs of an individual learner with PMLD

This vignette describes the needs of a particular learner with PMLD, who was part of a piece of research undertaken in a special school in England (Butler, 2018), to assess Quest for Learning as an instrument for assessment, and for informing the curriculum used by teachers. In this piece of research, the researcher and staff in a classroom for learners with PMLD identified a range of lessons and activities designed to assess and develop capacities of learners, against the milestones set out in Quest for Learning. The student selected, Alice (pseudonym), is registered as blind and has cerebral palsy. Her school day tends to be quite varied, including:

- physio activities such as stretching exercises on a physio wedge, to address stiffness, exercises to support her head control, and to help with breathing, rebound therapy on a trampoline, and swimming;
- use of eye gaze technology, often during lunchtime while other students are eating. She engages with a range of tasks with this technology including choosing colours and painting, shape and colour matching, and matching and memory games;
- Tacpac, as well as a communication book, similar to PECs-based books, which allows her to share and request what she would like to do;
- sensory stories, and in particular messy play, which staff note she enjoys and finds particularly motivating;
- switch-based activities, particularly when using resources from helpkidz learn.com and activities
- a parachute game that involves staff singing, and the student joining in, while a parachute is covering and moving over the student.

The research (ibid.) involved recording videos of between 2 and 10 minutes of a lesson or activity the learner was involved in. This allowed the researcher, alongside staff, to independently code the child's behaviour against the developmental milestones in Quest for Learning. In spite of her limited physical capacities, Alice demonstrated a broad, spiky range of the developmental milestones in Quest for Learning. She was able to demonstrate preferences (milestone 11: shows behaviour which can be interpreted as rejection of stimuli), shows interest in exploring the environment (milestone 16), and perhaps most strikingly demonstrated changes in behaviour in response to an interesting event nearby (milestone 25): there were a number of occasions where Alice clearly focused on activities being undertaken by other learners and staff in the classroom, demonstrating awareness and engagement with the environment. The videos demonstrate a happy and engaged learner, who enjoys company and laughter.

Conclusion

The vignette above provides an example of the extent to which Quest for Learning materials are useful in the classroom (see Butler, 2018, for more details).

Quest for Learning materials provide formative guidance by indicating common developmental pathways, highlighting where new and developing skills can be built. They also provide a more helpful, and complex overview of the abilities of the child, compared to the entirely linear format of the P Scale. The set of 43 milestones can be used to identify progress in a much more fine-grained manner (Martin, 2006) than P Scales levels, and indeed the new engagement profile (Standards and Testing Agency, 2018). The research (Butler, 2018) identified that the range of milestones set out in Quest for Learning could be identified across all learners, with the individual learner profiles demonstrating the variety and spikiness cited by other researchers (e.g., Rees, 2017; Simmons and Bayliss, 2007). These provided a real, in-depth overview of the capacities of the learners – highlighting gaps, but also abilities. The Quest for Learning materials can provide a non-linear pathway that can provide staff with guidance on which targets each of these learners could potentially be in line to develop and demonstrate, given their current capacities. This could support teachers to identify creative ways to meet learning needs (Stewart and Walker-Gleaves, 2020), in line with the examples given in the vignette, and inform curriculum choices.

References

Aird, R. (n.d.) 'Reflections on the review of assessment for pupils working below the standard of national curriculum tests (The Rochford Review) with particular regard to pupils with special educational needs and disabilities'. Available at: http://thesendhub.co.uk/wp-content/uploads/2017/01/reflections-on-the-rochford-review-recommendations-2016.pdf (accessed 18 September 2020).

Ashdown, R. (2014) 'Teaching thinking', *PMLD Link*, 226(1): 2–5.

Ayer, S. (1998) 'Use of multi-sensory rooms for children with profound and multiple learning disabilities', *Journal of Learning Disabilities for Nursing, Health, and Social Care*, 2(2): 89–97.

Barber, M. and Goldbart, J. (1998) 'Accounting for learning and failure to learn in people with profound and multiple learning disabilities', in P. Lacey and C. Ouvry (eds), *People with Profound and Multiple Learning Disabilities*, London: David Fulton, pp. 102–16.

Bellamy, G., Croot, L., Bush, A., Berry, H. and Smith, A. (2010) 'A study to define: profound and multiple learning disabilities (PMLD)', *Journal of Intellectual Disabilities*, 14(3): 221–35.

Brigg, G., Schuitema, K. and Vorhaus, J. (2016) 'Children with profound and multiple learning difficulties: Laughter, capability and relating to others', *Disability & Society*, 31(9): 1175–89.

Butler, C. (2018) 'Developing the capacity to recognise the capabilities of pupils with PMLD, to promote learning opportunities and to reduce isolation', report to the Harpur Trust, University of Bedfordshire. Available at: https://uobrep.openrepository.com/handle/10547/622853 (accessed 21 January 2021).

Carpenter, B. (2007) 'Changing children– changing schools? Concerns for the future of teacher training in special education', *PMLD–Link*, 19(2): 2–4.

Carpenter, B., Egerton, J., Brooks, T., Cockbill, B., Fotheringham, J. and Rawson, H. (2011) 'The complex learning difficulties and disabilities research project: Developing meaningful pathways to personalised learning', project report, Specialist Schools and Academies Trust, London. Available at: http://complexneeds.org.uk/modules/Module-3.2-Engaging-in-learning—key-approaches/All/downloads/m10p010d/the_complex_learning_difficulties.pdf (accessed 27 September 2020).

Colley, A. (2018) 'To what extent have learners with severe, profound and multiple learning difficulties been excluded from the policy and practice?', *International Journal of Inclusive Education*, 24(7): 721–38.

CCEA (Council for the Curriculum, Examinations, and Assessment) (2012) 'Quest for learning'. Available at: https://ccea.org.uk/downloads/docs/ccea-asset/Curriculum/Quest%20for%20learning%2C%20Guidance%20%26amp%3B%20Assessment%20Materials%20Profound%20%26amp%3B%20Multiple%20Learning%20Difficulties.pdf (accessed 18 September 2020).

Dee, L. (2002) *Enhancing Quality of Life: A Literature Review*, Cambridge: Skill and University of Cambridge.

DfE (Department for Education) (2017) 'Performance – P Scale – attainment targets for pupils with special educational needs'. Available at: https://assets.publishing.service.gov.uk/government/uploads/system/uploads/attachment_data/file/903590/Performance_-_P_Scale_-_attainment_targets_for_pupils_with_special_educational_needs_June_2017.pdf f (accessed 18 September 2020).

Donnelly, V. (2005) 'Inclusion: Celebrating diversity?' Paper presented at Inclusive and Supportive Education Congress, International Special Education Conference, Glasgow, Scotland. Available at http://www.isec2005.org.uk/isec/abstracts/papers_d/donnelly_v.shtml (accessed 18 July 2018).

Francis, H. (2011) 'Effects of "The Listening Program" on children with profound and multiple learning difficulties', *International Journal of Therapy and Rehabilitation*, 18(11): 611–21.

Gittins, D. and Rose, N. (2008) 'An audit of adults with profound and multiple learning disabilities within a West Midlands Community Health Trust: Implications for service development', *British Journal of Learning Disabilities*, 36(1): 38–47.

Goldbart, J., Chadwick, D. and Buell, S. (2014) 'Speech and language therapists' approaches to communication intervention with children and adults with profound and multiple learning disability', *International Journal of Language & Communication Disorders*, 49(6): 687–701.

Gray, G. and Chasey, C. (2006) 'SMILE: A new service development for people with profound and multiple learning disabilities', *PMLD Link*, 18(3): 27–31.

Green C.W. and Reid, D.H. (1999) 'Reducing indices of unhappiness among individuals with profound multiple disabilities during therapeutic exercise routines', *Journal of Applied Behavior Analysis*, 32: 137–48.

Griffiths, C. and Smith, M. (2016) 'Attuning: A communication process between people with severe and profound intellectual disability and their interaction partners', *Journal of Applied Research in Intellectual Disabilities*, 29(2): 124–38.

Hill, V., Croydon, A., Greathead, S., Kenny, L., Yates, R. and Pellicano, E. (2016) 'Research methods for children with multiple needs', *Educational and Child Psychology*, 33(3): 26–43.

Hostyn, I. and Maes, B. (2009) 'Interaction between persons with profound intellectual and multiple disabilities and their partners: A literature review', *Journal of Intellectual & Developmental Disability*, 34: 296–312.

Hughes R., Redley, M. and Ring H. (2011) 'Friendship and adults with profound intellectual and multiple disabilities and English disability policy'. *Journal of Policy and Practice in Intellectual Disabilities*, 8: 197–206.

Imray, P. and Hinchcliffe, V. (2012) 'Not fit for purpose: A call for separate and distinct pedagogies as part of a national framework for those with severe and profound learning difficulties', *Support for Learning*, 27(4): 150–7.

Jones, F., Pring, T. and Grove, N. (2002) 'Developing communication in adults with profound and multiple learning difficulties using objects of reference', *International Journal of Language & Communication Disorders*, 37(2): 173–84.

Jones, P. and Riley, M.W. (2017) '"Trying, failing, succeeding, and trying again and again": Perspectives of teachers of pupils with severe profound multiple learning difficulties', *European Journal of Teacher Education*, 40(2): 271–85.

Lacey, P. (1998) 'Meeting complex needs through multidisciplinary teamwork', in P. Lacey and C. Ouvry (eds), *People with Profound and Multiple Learning Difficulties: A Collaborative Approach to Meeting Complex Needs*, London: David Fulton, pp. ix–xvii.

Lacey, P. (2009) 'Developing the thinking of learners with PMLD', *PMLD Link*, 63: 15–19.

Lewis, A. and Norwich, B. (2000) 'Is there a distinctive special educational needs pedagogy?' In NASEN, *Special Teaching for Special Educational Needs*, Tamworth: NASEN.

Lyons, G. and Arthur-Kelly, M. (2014) 'UNESCO inclusion policy and the education of school students with profound intellectual and multiple disabilities: Where to now?' *Creative Education*, 5: 445–56.

Male, D. and Rayner, M. (2009) 'Who goes to SLD schools in England? A follow-up study', *Educational & Child Psychology*, 26(4): 19–30.

Martin A. (2006) 'Assessment using the P Scales: Best fit – fit for the purpose?' *British Journal of Special Education*, 33(2): 68–75.

McDermott, H. and Atkinson, C. (2016) 'Routes for Learning: Professionals' implementation of the approach in supporting children with profound and multiple learning difficulties', *The SLD Experience*, 75(1): 10–17.

McNicholas, J. (2000) 'The assessment of pupils with profound and multiple learning difficulties', *British Journal of Special Education*, 27(3): 150–3.

Mencap (1999) *Reading for All*. London: Mencap.

Munde, V. and Vlaskamp, C. (2015) 'Initiation of activities and alertness in individuals with profound intellectual and multiple disabilities', *Journal of Intellectual Disability Research*, 59(3): 284–92.

Nijs, S., Vlaskamp, C. and Maes, B. (2016) 'Children with PIMD in interaction with peers with PIMD or siblings', *Journal of Intellectual Disability Research*, 60(1): 28–42.

Pinney, A. (2017) 'Understanding the needs of disabled children with complex needs or life-limiting conditions: What can we learn from national data?' London: Council for Disabled Children. Available at: https://councilfordisabledchildren.org.uk/sites/default/files/field/attachemnt/Data%20Report.pdf (accessed 18 September 2020).

Poppes, P., van der Putten, A.J.J., Brug, A. and Vlaskamp, C. (2016a) 'Staff attributions of the causes of challenging behaviour in children and adults with profound intellectual and multiple disabilities', *Research in Developmental Disabilities*, 48: 95–102.

Poppes, P., van der Putten, A.J.J., Post, W.J. and Vlaskamp, C. (2016b) 'Risk factors associated with challenging behaviour in people with profound intellectual and multiple disabilities', *Journal of Intellectual Disability Research*, 60(6): 537–52.

Poppes, P., van der Putten, A.J.J. and Vlaskamp, C. (2010) 'Frequency and severity of challenging behaviour in people with profound intellectual and multiple disabilities', *Research in Developmental Disabilities*, 31(6): 1269–75.

Porter, J., Ouvry, C., Morgan, M. and Downs, C. (2001) 'Interpreting the communication of people with profound and multiple learning difficulties', *British Journal of Learning Disabilities*, 2 (1): 12–16.

Qualifications and Curriculum Group (2006) *Routes for Learning*. Cardiff: Welsh Department of Education.

Rayner, K., Bradley, S., Johnson, G., Mrozik, J.H., Appiah, A. and Nagra, M.K. (2016) 'Teaching intensive interaction to paid carers: Using the "communities of practice" model to inform training', *British Journal of Learning Disabilities*, 44(1): 63–70.

Rayner, M. (2010) 'The curriculum for children with severe and profound learning difficulties at Stephen Hawking School', *Support for Learning*, 26(1).

Rayner, M. and Male, D.B. (2013) 'Specialist support services received by pupils in special (SLD) schools in England: Level of support received and head teachers' perceptions of usefulness', *The SLD Experience*, 58: 14–20.

Rees, K. (2017) 'Models of disability and the categorisation of children with severe and profound learning difficulties: Informing educational approaches based on an understanding of individual needs', *Educational & Child Psychology*, 34(4): 30–9.

Rochford, D. (2016) *The Rochford Review: Final Report, Review of Assessment for Pupils Working Below the Standard of National Curriculum Tests*, London: The Stationery Office.

Salt, T. (2010) *Salt Review: Independent Review of Teacher Supply for Pupils with Severe, Profound and Multiple Learning Difficulties (SLD and PMLD)*, London: Department for Children, Schools and Families.

Samuel, J. and Pritchard, M. (2001) 'The ignored minority: Meeting the needs of people with profound learning disability', *Tizard Learning Disability Review*, 6: 34–44.

Simmons, B. and Bayliss, P. (2007) 'The role of special schools for children with profound and multiple learning difficulties: Is segregation always best?', *British Journal of Special Education*, 34(1): 19–24.

Simmons, B. and Watson, D. (2015) 'From individualism to co-construction and back again: Rethinking research methodology for children with profound and multiple learning disabilities', *Child Care in Practice*, 21(1): 50–66.

Smith, E., Critten, V. and Vardill, R. (2020) 'Assessing progress in children with severe/profound intellectual disabilities: What are the issues?', *Disability & Society*, doi:10.1 080/09687599.2020.1719042

Standards and Testing Agency (2018) 'Piloting the 7 aspects of engagement for summative assessment: qualitative evaluation'. Available at: https://assets.publishing.service.gov.uk/government/uploads/system/uploads/attachment_data/file/757524/Seven_Aspects_evaluation_report.pdf (accessed 18 September 2020).

Stewart, C. and Walker-Gleaves, C. (2020) 'A narrative exploration of how curricula for children with profound and multiple learning difficulties shape and are shaped by the practices of their teachers', *British Journal of Special Education*. doi:10.1111/1467-8578.12313

Uzgiris, I. and Hunt, J.McV. (1975) *Assessment in Infancy: Ordinal Scales of Psychological Development*, Chicago: University of Illinois Press.

Vorhaus, J. (2017) 'Sharing in a common life: people with profound and multiple learning difficulties', *Res Publica*, 23(1): 61–79.

Ware, J. (1996) *Creating a Responsive Environment for People with Profound and Multiple Learning Difficulties*, London: Fulton.

Ware, J. (2005) 'Profound and multiple learning difficulties', in B. Norwich and A. Lewis (eds), *Special Teaching for Special Children? Pedagogies for Inclusion*, Maidenhead: Open University Press, pp. 67–80.

Ware, J. and Healy, I. (1994) 'Conceptualising progress in children with profound and multiple learning difficulties', in J. Ware (ed.), *Educating Children with Profound and Multiple Learning Difficulties*, London: David Fulton, pp. 1–14.

Welsh Assembly Government (2006) 'Routes for Learning – Assessment materials for learners with profound learning difficulties and additional disabilities', Cardiff: Crown Copyright.

Welsh Assembly Government (2019) 'Routes for Learning Routemap'. Available at: https://hwb.gov.wales/api/storage/2bbe3615-64d0-48c6-8002-a65239fb6ee9/routes-for-learning-routemap.pdf (accessed 18 September 2020).

Part **3**

Creative engagement in the curriculum

A deliberate intention to facilitate creative engagement is a powerful way to bring the curriculum to life. In Part 3, Chapter 5 takes the example of the teaching of English in the secondary curriculum in England and, in discussing how to bring this aspect of the school curriculum to life, the author considers moving away from what he sees as the rather formulaic and GCSE-dominated approaches that have taken hold in recent years and turning back to being a curriculum area focused on celebrating the best that the discipline of English has to offer. Chapter 6 continues the theme of engagement in literacy learning and adopts the view that, even within the tight prescription of the National Curriculum framework, there can be room for a degree of flexibility to enable cultural responsiveness and sensitive engagement with students' own views, aimed at addressing literacy difficulties at secondary level. The research discussed in this chapter illustrates how the use of culturally responsive pedagogy, together with an emancipatory approach in one supplementary school, contributed to overcoming issues of disaffection and lack of interest in reading and writing experienced by a group of culturally diverse students aged 11–14. In Chapter 7, the authors focus specifically on the power of student voice in bringing the curriculum to life, and describe a 5-year study in progress on the formation and development of 'dialogic groups' at a secondary school in the east of England. Their discussion suggests the potential of dialogic group work for enhancing student engagement across the English National Curriculum.

Next in Part 3, Chapter 8 outlines a case study of effective personalized provision made for one rather disaffected young man that used the concept of his hobby, pigeon racing, to re-kindle his engagement with literacy learning and achievement. Then, Chapter 9 again takes the theme of student engagement and challenges the oft-cited notion that contemporary teaching practices are better and more innovative than their historical counterparts. With specific relation to physical education (PE), the authors show how the historical legacy of both Rudolf Laban (dance) and Kurt Hahn (outdoor learning and adventure education) (OAA) has contemporary vibrancy, and suggest a way in which the subject would benefit from embracing rather than obscuring the 'tool-box' for practice each provides. Chapter 10 focuses specifically on the physical education curriculum to argue for a broad and balanced curriculum offer, where all children and young people are challenged, engaged, included and inspired to achieve their full potential in PE.

5 Planning and designing a creative secondary English curriculum

James Shea

Major questions addressed in this chapter are:

- How can teachers reduce the constraints of current assessment practices on the English curriculum in secondary schools?
- What might replace such practices and at the same time be seen to maintain standards?
- There appears to be some evidence that the current curriculum in secondary English is falling in popularity. How can English teachers cultivate curiosity and re-engage interest in the discipline?

Abstract

This chapter focuses on moving the teaching of English in the secondary curriculum in England away from what is seen as the rather formulaic and GCSE-dominated approaches that have taken hold in recent years and turning back to being a curriculum area focused on celebrating the best that the discipline of English has to offer. It takes the view that pupils need to become knowledgeable in English in all respects, skilful in English, curious in English, able to use English as a lens through which to view the world, and at the same time exemplary at articulating their knowledge and ability in English through formal examinations. The English National Curriculum sets out broad and ambitious aims. Yet those aims may be constrained as a result of the dominance of the GCSE curriculum and the importance of GCSE results to the institutions that deliver the curriculum. The chapter explores how English teachers have an opportunity to redesign their curriculum in English creatively to achieve this ambitious set of aims using the space provided by the new Office for Standards in Education (Ofsted) Framework of Inspection 2019.

Introduction

The teaching of English in secondary classrooms across the breadth of England has changed considerably in recent years. Standish and Sehgal-Cuthbert (2017) effectively capture the early years of how English as a subject emerged, but the current chapter is more concerned with capturing the recent restrictions of curriculum innovation in the teaching of secondary English and suggesting, further, a path forward which uses creativity as a means by which to achieve this.

This chapter begins by discussing the national context within which English is taught in schools in England and some of the resulting restrictions on the curriculum, and moves on to consider challenges in the teaching of English and the way in which the curriculum in English can be revitalized. It concludes by pointing to teachers' potential agency in creating a curriculum that will enthuse and engage their pupils, and support the development of informed, critical thinking.

The current national context for secondary English teaching

Following the introduction of school league tables as part of a marketization strategy (Ball, 2013) and the resultant competition between them, the outcome of the English curriculum in school is now measured predominantly by the collective end grades of school cohorts sitting General Certificate of Secondary Education (GCSE) examinations in English Language and English Literature, usually taken at the age of 16. Being beholden to produce consistently high examination results affects how English is taught, as described by James and McCormick (2009), whose study of 40 schools found teachers increasingly teaching to the test. Further, the examination system itself has changed over the last two decades, moving away from the pre-2017 GCSEs in English Language and Literature which consisted of a mixture of speaking and listening, examination and of drafted coursework (whether in timed or untimed conditions). Instead, since 2017, knowledge of the English curriculum is demonstrated solely by handwritten answers to timed examination papers. The literature examination is all 'closed book' (the pupils are not allowed to have recourse to copies of poems, plays or novels) and heavily weighted towards recall of the text. The language paper predominantly looks to ensure pupils can extract precise knowledge from unseen non-fiction texts and set this out in analytical essays. The creative arts side of English fares badly. Creative writing is reduced to a small section of a single paper while speaking and listening are not included in the final grade. This is not a curriculum or an examination model which has been advocated by the English teachers of England, parents or indeed any other educational organization. When surveyed by the Department for Education on the removal of

Speaking and Listening from the GCSE (Ofqual, 2013), over 92 per cent of respondents rejected this proposal. It was implemented by the Department for Education regardless.

Restrictions on the English curriculum

The teaching of English and the curriculum for English have subsequently been influenced by these changes and the imperative to find ways to enable pupils to achieve good examination grades. Influenced by some of the work from cognitive scientists, such as Sweller, some teachers have looked to reduce the extraneous load and thus, they hope, the cognitive load, but not the intrinsic load (Sweller, 2010) inherent within the challenges of writing during English lessons by, for example, introducing structured supports such as writing strips which specify tightly the content required within essays. The intrinsic load is the inherent difficulty of the task, whereas the cognitive load is how much working memory in terms of resources is being used. The extraneous load is the extra challenge which can make it harder to achieve the task without making the actual difficulty of the innate challenge harder (e.g., unclear instructions can create extraneous load while the inherent task remains the same whether the instructions are clear or unclear). Initiatives to reduce cognitive load can be contentious, e.g., writing frames designed for weaker writers such as Point, Evidence Explain (PEE) and the many derivatives from that original model which have permeated teaching (Gibbons, 2019). While such support is helpful to the pupil, at the same time it can actually reduce the intrinsic load and there are issues with trying to reduce extraneous load without reducing the intrinsic load – for example, pre-teaching all potentially unknown words before reading a chapter (Shea, 2020a; 2020b). The post-2017s GCES have proved to be problematic for schools in England. Many secondary schools have expanded their GCSE years from two years to between three and five years long in response. This latter point has alarmed the Office of Standards in Education (Ofsted) so much that they changed their inspection framework in 2019 to make schools justify extending the GCCE years beyond two years in length, citing a requirement that a curriculum needs to be broad and balanced (Ofsted, 2019).

In many cases, what is present here is a need for the English curriculum not to be tightly constrained by examinations and there is now a precedent. The coronavirus crisis of 2020 led to examinations being converted into teacher assessments (Ofqual, 2020). At once, the resulting clamour was that some pupils who had been *preparing* for the examinations were upset, as set out by the National Education Union: 'It is a huge upset for them. They picked their subjects years ago and have been working really hard' (*The Portsmouth News*, 2020). Learning how to pass the examinations has become far more important than learning a broad-based curriculum and reflects an international concern in countries ranging from Sweden (Larsson and Scheller, 2020) to the USA (Fjortoft, Gettig and Vedone, 2018).

Concerns about lack of attention to aesthetic meaning and reader response

For the subject of English there are more concerns as this increased teaching to the test runs in contradiction to the fundamental notions of English literacy theory. Since the work of Rosenblatt (1938), a text is seen as incomplete without its audience. The meaning of a text is made up of two aspects: the text itself and the reader. The reader also infers two types of meaning from the text: *efferent* meaning and *aesthetic* meaning. Some texts are wholly meant for efferent consumption: the instruction manual for a device or a recipe book. Some books seek to provoke a more profound aesthetic response in the reader, such as Emily Brontë's *Wuthering Heights* or George Orwell's *1984*. Yet the books exist in their own right without the author or the author's intentions as captured by Barthes' seminal essay, 'The death of the author' (1977). Readers are free to *read* the text as they wish. The aesthetic response they have is wholly theirs to have and joins with the text to create a singular and unique meaning of the text. This notion of *reader response* is key to all teaching of English. The writer and the reader co-exist and yet are wholly separated through the text. This causes tensions for the discipline of English when it comes to formulating knowledge organizers (Hirsch, 2006) and ensuring that outcomes for GCSEs are predictable and reliable – despite the well-documented issues with assessing English literature examination scripts with a high level of reliability (Ofqual, 2014). What seems to be pushed to the foreground are the efferent components of the text: plots, language devices, profound or popularized quotations, historical contexts and authorial intention. What is sometimes held back is the right to have an aesthetic response. The teaching of poetry for GCSE pupils in England can sometimes be almost rote in its lavish transcribing of notes from the teacher to the pupil (Dymoke, 2012). The ability of the pupil to have time and space to have an aesthetic reaction to the poem is removed in the urgent pursuit of analytical writing skills which carefully and considerately rehash quasi-similar statements and devices together in the form of a mock response to an old or made-up examination question. For example, the effort that the poet Simon Armitage put into creating the poem *Remains* from his collection of poems, *The Not Dead* (2008) can sometimes be lost amidst a need for pupils to demonstrate 'fine-grained' responses to the GCSE criteria (AQA, 2015a). The opportunity for originality in being able to form a wholly unique aesthetic response to the poem is made ever more difficult by the need to produce evidence of an efferent reading of the text and this causes problems. If a pupil has no aesthetic meaning of the text, then they have not created a unique reading of the text and in a sense, they have not read it – they have consumed it for the purpose of demonstrating their writing skills for the GCSE examination. This is not to say that demonstrating a good level of English through the GCSE examination is not important – on the contrary, it is possible to design a creative curriculum, using creative pedagogies which *also* lead to good outcomes in the GCSE examinations or any other aspect of life where the knowledge and skills of English will be used. It is this latter part that is important to emphasize. To be able to

consume a text and have a wholly unique aesthetic reaction to it, is a fundamental life skill founded on central tenets: to be able to infer, to imagine, to
relate, to empathize, sympathize, to have notions of self and others and to be
able to express these through speaking and writing in a range of forms. This
forms the way forward then, in designing a creative curriculum for English.

Challenges in the teaching of English

The first step in creating an English curriculum must be in grasping some of the
difficulties of English for the English teacher. Teachers cannot order pupils to
'develop a love of literature' (DfE, 2013), or insist they react to a text with a
prescribed emotion. They cannot teach the epistemically curious questions (Litman, 2008) that their pupils need to ask to drive their self-regulated learning
forward. Yet they are in a position to create the conditions for these things to
happen and that is what this chapter is about: setting out an approach to the
teaching of English where a teacher considers the aesthetic as well as the efferent nature of texts and writing (Rosenblatt, 1938). To begin, let us look at a
classic author that all children in England study, regardless of which type of
secondary school they are in: William Shakespeare.

Vignette: Epistemic challenges in teaching Shakespeare

Shakespeare is typical of the challenge faced by an English teacher. Shakespeare's plays contain efferent content (the general plot and characters), the
comprehension of which poses challenges to achieve as much as the aesthetic responses (e.g. to react profoundly to a character or a line in the play)
we wish, as English teachers, for the pupils to have. Indeed, in many cases,
English teachers themselves may have had only negative aesthetic experiences of Shakespeare before beginning to plan to teach one of his plays. It
is all too easy for the planning to be wholly focused on teaching the context,
the plot, the characters and what have been established as the key scenes
and lines from those who have read or seen the play before. What sometimes does not feature in the planning is the aesthetic experience itself.
Take, for example, the fact that many lines, soliloquies and scenes remain
difficult to follow, even with a professional actor reading them out. This difficulty of comprehending the play can be seen as a negative experience by a
novice English teacher. Such teachers might offer modern translations or, as
set out at the start of this chapter, pre-teach key vocabulary to try to reduce
the perceived extraneous load (Sweller, 2010) of the scene. Yet, this difficulty of understanding the play is a key *appealing* feature of a Shakespeare
text. The ambiguity of the language, the many intertextual references, the
layers of hidden meaning all contribute to the *experience* of revisiting the text
to enjoy it again and again and revealing more meaning. Rosenblatt's (1938)
notion of reader response – this central idea, that each time we read a text

it is different – really applies to the experience of reading and understanding Shakespeare. In holding up the text as something that changes and offers something new with each reading, the pupils learn to welcome the challenge of this shape-shifting text. They see that their unique and individual responses can co-contribute to a unique class of pupils' exploration of the text. Their unique class experience of the text will be different to that of an adjoining class in the next room reading the same text. This is where the examination system needs to be more focused – it needs to reward the deep and insightful exploration of the text rather than the exposition of familiar efferent interpretations. In addition, this experience where we celebrate the difficult means we are beginning to develop their epistemic curiosity. Litman (2008) divides epistemic curiosity into two aspects: a desire to know more through curiosity and a desire to know more because we have a deficit – the so-called, *fear of missing out* (FOMO) effect. This does not just apply to inter-pretation of texts, but also the decoding of unknown words. By developing a system to decode unknown words – looking at the type of word class which it is, the sentence within which it sits, the Greek or Roman roots or even if it seems to be a borrowed word, thus, pupils begin to develop epistemic curi-osity with words, their origins and how they are used. They begin to curate their own developing vocabulary from their self-regulated reading. Instead of shying away from a new word or always having to look it up, they are able to enjoy the extraneous and intrinsic load of meeting a new word and decoding it. The tension between being able to pass an examination (be able to write about a text) and being able to do well in English (being an autonomous reader and communicator) can be felt in the space between the need for pupils to understand a text in order to pass a timed closed text examination in English and the need for pupils to explore and express an understanding of a text because that is what it means to learn English.

Issues in revitalizing the English curriculum

Taking Litman's (2008) ideas, then, we can begin to consider how the curriculum for English needs to be revitalized. There is a great deal of emphasis in the English curriculum on knowledge as part of a Department for Education's push (Gibb, 2017a; 2017b) to bring the ideas of Hirsch (1987; 1996, 2006) into the curriculum. The idea that there are certain pieces of knowledge which are prioritized over oth-ers has influenced the design of the English curriculum (Gove, 2012). Even further, this knowledge must be remembered over time (Ofsted, 2019) and thus we see the drivers of curriculum and pedagogical design pointing directly to an examination system which checks that the important knowledge has been retained. This may be all very well for subjects like mathematics or science, but, for English, the reality is that for both the discipline of English and for the examinations of English, pupils are expected to have personal interpretations of texts, unique ideas for their cre-ative writing and highly idiosyncratic reactions to the comparisons of multiple texts. As much as efferent knowledge features in knowledge organizers for English, that trio of words: personal, unique and idiosyncratic, requires planning beyond that of teaching pre-selected knowledge.

Poetry in the English curriculum

One area where this can be considered is in poetry. The GCSE examinations for English require pupils to be able to respond to seen and unseen poetry, to be able to compare poems and to be able to express their ideas in those 'fine-grained' essay compositions. The journey to this begins at the start of the secondary experience at the age of 11. Here pupils begin to be introduced to poetry which contains adult themes – war poetry, for example. The current GCSE specification uses Simon Armitage's poem *Remains*: 'one of my mates goes by and tosses his guts back into his body' (Armitage, 2008). The graphic nature of the language is provocative by nature and quite typical of war poetry. It is not enough to simply teach the pupil the efferent information in the poem – that these images are typical of a war scenario. Instead, a considerate and carefully supervised exploration of the poem is undertaken as a class. Different opinions from the class will be used to create a reading. Further than this, however, the English teacher must teach each pupil to be a sensitive and thoughtful reader who, when they face unseen poetry on their own, responds with insight and personal perspicuity. To create such a reader for a wide range of literature takes the repeated exposure to literature and experiences of exploring literature through a range of lenses, over a number of years.

Development of critical, informed thinking through the English curriculum

It is not the repeated teaching of the efferent meaning in texts and the remembrance of them, but the experience of reacting to literature in a group (and alone) and being able to draw upon the knowledge of those experiences to help shape further experiences that encourages critical thinking. Through exploring texts with pupils, English teachers can hone the ability to view themes and uniquely interpret the text within their pupils. This is not something that is easy to do. For example, the Black Lives Matter movement which gained prominence in 2020 has brought a fresh perspective to many texts. Whether it is the curriculum itself which they study or the voice of others within the texts themselves, just like feminism, neo-Marxism and other lenses such as eco-criticism, so the Black Lives Matter view enables the reader to look at a text through a new lens. Texts which have been taught for decades in the UK, such as Steinbeck's *Of Mice and Men* (1937), are revisited with all sorts of implications, including the use of racial epithets and how they should be read within the class – even though Steinbeck himself was virulently anti-racist and used such language to draw attention to racism within his time and English teachers had always explored these ideas. The very fact that the Black Lives Matter movement happened has changed the teaching and the meaning of such texts.

The diversity of the curriculum is thus something that is going to be revisited more as the 2020s unfold. In a creative and exciting curriculum, the multitudinous identities of contemporary civilization should be considered when selecting texts for study. Gender, sexuality, race and affluence are all areas which would inspire modern pupils should they feature in texts chosen for inclusion on the curriculum. The English curriculum is currently very much led by those who pay homage to the notion of a canon of classics as set out by F.R. Leavis (1948) and championed further by those who feel, like Hirsch, that there are timeless texts which everyone should study. Yet, many of those classics reflect the societies which produced them. Societies where lower-class characters do not even warrant a name despite being what today one would term a 'critical worker' (DfE, 2020). It is important that where English teachers have control of the curriculum – for example Key Stage 3 – that they are bold in their choices of seminal texts for study. Even when limited by the thin list of choices provided by an examination board, they should be courageous and select more interesting and epistemically intriguing texts from the list wherever possible. English teachers should select texts which explore contemporary themes and identities so that pupils can form their own meaning of the text through a personal reaction where, according to transactional theory (Rosenblatt, 1938), the meaning is different to every reader. The notion of 'live reading' (sometimes called pedagogic literary narration) where the teacher reads aloud along with a class is a vital and instrumental part of the English teacher's classroom. As the class read the text, so each pupil is making their own meaning. When they share those meanings collaboratively, so they begin to influence another's interpretation. Discussion ensues in which moments of epiphany emerge for the class and often for the teacher. Those discussions enable the pupil to explore their own identity within their life and society and to begin to make critical sense of the world within which they live. Unless pupils are exposed to compelling classical *and* contemporary texts which ferment epistemic curiosity, then the curriculum will struggle to stay vibrant and relevant. Already, we see that the GCSE curriculum of 2015 onwards has led to fewer pupils going on to A level English with drops of 22 per cent for English Language and 8 per cent for English Literature from 2018 to 2019 (DfE, 2019). The effects of not teaching inference of language by removing the extraneous load through pre-teaching vocabulary and the lack of diversity in the choices of texts can be directly seen here in this lack of take-up of English at post 16. If we are to excite and inspire a new generation of pupils to want to study English in a post-16 world, then our choices of text and approaches to teaching must be those that inspire them to want to read and study more.

The writing curriculum

One clear aspect of English that has experienced rapid change over recent years is the notion of writing. From the overuse of PEE writing frames (Gibbons, 2019) to the notion of writing strips (where each section of the essay has been tightly controlled by content descriptors), there has been a large push towards enabling pupils to create 'fine-grained' essays in which all the efferent aspects of the criteria for each of the assessment objectives are clearly met. There is a trade-off here between the need for pupils to perform well in examinations and the need to enable pupils to be able to write well for their future home and work lives. Those two objectives do not always work in tandem with each other. Yet, if the notion from Litman (2008) is embraced, that English teachers want to foster the epistemic curiosity within pupils to explore and use writing as a tool, then the area of writing must be revisited with the notion of creativity in mind.

The first aspect must be that which features everywhere in English – the notion of exploring texts through writing. When one explores a text through writing, one does not actually know what the content is going to be until one has finished it. It is an aesthetic event in its own right and which delivers a moment of epiphany to the writer as well as the reader upon its conclusion. Yet, the teaching of essay writing in English secondary schools seems to be all too often beset with the challenges of reproducing the efferent knowledge necessary to meet the GCSE criteria. Points must be slavishly rooted to predetermined ideas and themes found in the text. Evidence can often be drawn from the agreed list of 'good quotations' endlessly mined and regurgitated through internet-based resources. The 'right' poems must be selected for comparison. There is sometimes no epiphany for the writer or reader of the essay within the secondary school as the reader is the examiner rather than the examiner *and* the writer. What is important is that the 'correct' type of essay is created, containing the 'correct' types of points and with reliable quotations in support.

Teaching writing is founded on both the process approach and the genre approach (Maybin, 2005). Both approaches are examined in the GCSE English language paper through the ability of the pupil to create pieces of writing within the traditions of both. However, the fact that the majority of the GCSE Literature and Language examination questions ask the pupils to produce essay writing has rather reduced the focus on those two approaches to writing. Now, the most common approach to writing is a sub-division of the genre approach – the analytical essay. Some pupils are inherently exposed to extensive structured approaches to analytical writing to the point where 'analytical paragraphs' are part of the English teaching. There is no 'unknown writing' in these analytical paragraphs, no moments of epiphany for the writer and the reader. Instead, tightly controlled writing created against strict writing frames are rehearsed ready for the regurgitation process which happens in examinations. We should not blame English teachers who teach children to do this, however. The careful control of the percentage who pass or fail each year by the Office for Qualifications (Ofqual) ensures that similar numbers of pupils (around 30 per cent) must fail to attain the notional pass mark of a grade 4 each year – *regardless of the standard of their writing*. Pupils are not writing to a standard, but rather are writing in opposition to their peers. They must better meet the rigid criteria than others who sit the examinations in the same year as them. It could be that a pupil's writing in one year might be equal to that of a grade 4 while in another year the same writing could attain a grade 5.

Personal agency of teachers of English

While there is not much English teachers can do about Ofqual or about the limits of what is best termed a norm-referenced system (despite Ofqual's protestations to the contrary), where some pupils must fail to attain a 'passing' grade regardless of their standard, there are things English teachers can do to help enhance the curriculum around writing. It remains that in Assessment Objective 1 of the GCSE Specifications of the English Literature GCSEs for England, pupils are required to 'Maintain a critical style and develop an informed personal response' (AQA, 2015b) and in Assessment Objective 5 of the English Language GCSEs for England, pupils are required to 'Communicate clearly, effectively and imaginatively, selecting and adapting tone, style and register for different forms, purposes and audiences' (ibid.). These assessment objectives can be used as a strong starting point for making the curriculum for writing in English creative again. They draw upon the process approach to English which seeks to enable pupils to act in the guise of 'writer'. Rather than writing solely for the examiner, pupils write for themselves and for an audience. They seek to explore their options and create a unique and autonomous critical style to both their literary essays and their creative writing. Rather than produce identikit pieces of writing, their writing should be distinctive and informed by personal lenses which they bring to their work. Just as those in higher education bring lenses to texts and creative writing, so their younger counterparts in secondary school should be beginning that journey. Looking at texts through the common literary lenses of feminism, class, diversity and even lenses from other subject areas, such as ecology and psychology, can also be reflected within creative writing. Teachers can harness these 'big' ideas and use them as lenses so pupils can begin to develop their ability to explore universal and contemporary themes through their creative writing. Encouraging pupils to embrace vocabulary and phrasing which are typical of such lenses enables them to work with complex abstract nouns and the knowledge, which sits behind the nouns, needed to confidently and correctly write, using such vocabulary. Designing a curriculum which empowers pupils to research, to read, to gather and process new knowledge returns us to that key idea of epistemic curiosity. While we cannot tell a pupil to be curious, we can give them the infrastructure through which to foster curiosity and how to ensure that this new knowledge is represented through their analytical work and their creative writing.

Conclusion

In some ways, the English curriculum always had the mechanics within it to be innovative, creative and inspiring. Rosenblatt's Principles of Instruction

(Shea, 2020a) set out how the unique contribution of each pupil conspires and inspires new meaning and interpretation to be made each time a text is read or written in the English classroom. The focus within such teaching is on strong autonomous writing of the sort that meets the Assessment Objectives set by the examination boards very well. It is possible to have good examination outcomes and a creative English curriculum which together inspire a new generation to go on and study English further. However, it will take bold English teachers who see that autonomy is a good thing for pupils: teachers who see that writing to a high standard is something which relies on bringing together a wide range of knowledge – some learned in schools and some learned through self-regulated epistemic curiosity; teachers who select contemporary and challenging texts from the curriculums of Key Stages 3 and 4, and, lastly, teachers who appreciate that passing the examination is just one part of the English curriculum and that a rich and evocative classroom brings a vast range of knowledge to the table from which pupils dine together and share their experiences.

References

AQA (2015a) 'GCSE English Literature Assessment Resources'. Available at https://www.aqa.org.uk/subjects/english/gcse/english-literature-8702/assessment-resources?f.Sub-category%7CF=Sample+papers+and+mark+schemes (accessed 23 April 2020).

AQA (2015b) 'GCSE English Specifications'. Available at https://www.aqa.org.uk/subjects/english/gcse (accessed 23 April 2020).

Armitage, S. (2008) *The Not Dead*. Claremont, CA: Pomona Press.

Ball, S. (2013) 'Education, justice and democracy: The struggle over ignorance and opportunity'. Available at: http://classonline.org.uk/docs/2013_Policy_Paper_-_Education,_justice_and_democracy_(Stephen_Ball).pdf (accessed 23 April 2020).

Barthes, R. (1977) 'The death of the author', in R. Barthes, *Image, Music, Text*, London: Fontana, pp. 142–8.

DfE (Department for Education) (2013) 'National Curriculum in England'. Available at: https://www.gov.uk/government/publications/national-curriculum-in-england-english-programmes-of-study/national-curriculum-in-england-english-programmes-of-study (accessed 23 April 2020).

DfE (Department for Education) (2019) 'A Levels in 2019'. Available at: https://assets.publishing.service.gov.uk/government/uploads/system/uploads/attachment_data/file/825429/A-Level-infographic_current___3_.pdf (accessed 3 June 2020).

DfE (Department for Education) (2020) 'Critical Workers who can access schools or educational settings', available at: https://www.gov.uk/government/publications/coronavirus-covid-19-maintaining-educational-provision/guidance-for-schools-colleges-and-local-authorities-on-maintaining-educational-provision (accessed 3 June 2020).

Dymoke, S. (2012) 'Opportunities or constraints? Where is the space for culturally responsive poetry teaching within high-stakes testing regimes at 16+ in Aotearoa New Zealand and England?', *English Teaching: Practice and Critique*, 11(4): 19–35.

Fjortoft, N., Gettig, J. and Verdone, M. (2018) 'Teaching innovation and creativity, or teaching to the test', *American Journal of Pharmaceutical Education*, 82(10).

Gibb, N. (2017a) 'The evidence in favour of teacher led instruction'. Available at: https://www.gov.uk/government/speeches/nick-gibb-the-evidence-in-favour-of-teacher-led-instruction (accessed 2 June 2020).

Gibb, N. (2017b) 'The importance of knowledge-based education'. Available at: https://www.gov.uk/government/speeches/nick-gibb-the-importance-of-knowledge-based-education (accessed 2 June 2020).

Gibbons., S. (2019) 'Death by PEEL? The teaching of writing in the English classroom', *English in Education*, 53(1).

Gove, M. (2012) Letter from Secretary of State for Education to Tim Oates of the Expert Review Panel. Available at: http://data.parliament.uk/DepositedPapers/Files/DEP2012-0902/LetterfromSoStoTimOates.pdf (accessed 2 June 2020).

Hirsch, E.D. (1987) *Cultural Literacy: What Every American Needs to Know*, Boston, MA: Houghton Mifflin.

Hirsch, E.D. (1996) *The Schools We Need and Why We Don't Have Them*, New York: Doubleday.

Hirsch, E.D. (2006) *The Knowledge Deficit: Closing the Shocking Education Gap*, Boston, MA: Houghton Mifflin.

James, M. and McCormick, R. (2009) 'Teachers learning how to learn', *Teaching and Teacher Education*, 25(7): 973–982.

Larsson, M. and Scheller, O. (2020) 'Adaptation and resistance: Washback effects of the national test on upper secondary Swedish teaching', *Curriculum Journal*. Available online at https://onlinelibrary.wiley.com/doi/full/10.1002/curj.31 (accessed 23 April 2020).

Leavis, F. (1948) *The Great Tradition*, London: Chatto and Windus.

Litman, J. A. (2008) 'Interest and deprivation factors of epistemic curiosity', *Personality and Individual Differences*, 44(7): 1585–95.

Maybin, J. (2005) 'Teaching writing: Process or genre?', in S. Brindley (ed.), *Teaching English*, London: Routledge.

Ofqual (2013) 'Analysis of responses to the consultation on the proposal to remove speaking and listening assessment from the GCSE English and GCSE English Language Grade'. Available at: https://dera.ioe.ac.uk/17586/7/2013-08-29-analysis-of-responses-to-the-consultation-removal-of-speaking-and-listening.pdf (accessed 23 April 2020).

Ofqual (2014) 'A review of literature on marking reliability research'. Available at: https://assets.publishing.service.gov.uk/government/uploads/system/uploads/attachment_data/file/605659/2014-02-14-quality-of-marking-review-of-literature-on-item-level-marking-research.pdf (accessed 23 April 2020).

Ofqual (2020) 'How GCSES, AS and A levels will be awarded in summer 2020'. Available at: https://www.gov.uk/government/news/how-gcses-as-a-levels-will-be-awarded-in-summer-2020 (accessed 23 April 2020).

Ofsted (2019) 'Education Inspection Framework'. Available at: https://www.gov.uk/government/publications/education-inspection-framework (accessed 23 April 2020).

Rosenblatt, L. (1938) *Literature as Exploration*, London: Heinemann.

Shea, J. (2020a) 'Rosenblatt's Principles of Instruction', *The Peer Reviewed Education Blog*, available at: https://peerrevieweducationblog.com/2020/06/01/rosenblatts-principles-of-instruction/ (accessed 23 April 2020).

Shea, J. (2020b) 'Fast reading and fast readers', *The Peer Reviewed Education Blog*, available at: https://peerrevieweducationblog.com/2019/10/30/fast-reading-and-fast-readers/ (accessed 25 January 2021).

Standish, A. and Sehgal-Cuthbert, A. (2017) *Why Should Schools Teach?: Disciplines, Subjects and the Pursuit of Truth*, London: IOE Press.

Steinbeck, J. (1937) *Of Mice and Men*, New York: Covici-Friede.

Sweller, J. (2010) 'Element interactivity and intrinsic, extraneous, and germane cognitive load', *Educational Psychology Review*, 22: 123–38.

The Portsmouth News (2020) 'Coronavirus: Portsmouth A-level student speaks out about disappointment over exam cancellations'. Available at: https://www.portsmouth.co.uk/health/coronavirus/coronavirus-portsmouth-level-student-speaks-out-about-disappointment-over-exam-cancellations-2516527 (accessed 23 April 2020).

6 Using culturally responsive pedagogy to improve literacy learning within a supplementary school

Margaret Olugbaro, Janice Wearmouth and Uvanney Maylor

Major questions addressed in this chapter are:

- What degree of flexibility is there to enable cultural responsiveness and sensitive engagement with students' own views within the tight prescription of the National Curriculum?
- What is the potential of a supplementary school to re-engage students who are disengaged from their literacy learning?
- Can a culturally responsive approach address literacy difficulties effectively in a supplementary school?
- How can parents/carers and teachers work collaboratively to address students' specific literacy needs in the context of a supplementary school?

Abstract

The research discussed here is taken from a PhD study undertaken between 2012 and 2014 by one of the authors of the current chapter. It illustrates how the use of culturally responsive pedagogy together with an emancipatory approach of the sort advocated by Paulo Freire in one supplementary school contributed to overcoming issues of disaffection and lack of interest in reading and writing experienced by a group of culturally diverse students aged 11–14. The significance of such pedagogy is that it takes account of the individuality and cultural backgrounds of students, and what, therefore, students bring with them into the learning context, of which teachers should be aware. The students were referred to the researcher by their parents who were concerned about their levels of progress in their mainstream schools. A supplementary school was established in a community centre for the purpose of addressing the literacy difficulties that were identified. Sessions were based on the National Curriculum in England but pedagogy was adapted to meet students' expressed interests and literacy learning needs as well as their diverse cultural backgrounds. Students were involved in every aspect of the sessions from planning to evaluation as befits an emancipatory approach. The outcomes were improved levels of attainment and re-engagement with literacy learning. The approach and its results cannot be generalized from such a small sample of participants. Nevertheless, there is the implication that even within the tight prescription of the National Curriculum, there is room for a degree of flexibility to enable cultural responsiveness and sensitive engagement with students' own views to improve their literacy learning.

Introduction

The current chapter details a step-by-step description and discussion of how culturally responsive pedagogy and an emancipatory approach were used to address identified literacy needs among a group of Key Stage 3 (ages 11–14) students within the context of a supplementary school. It begins by stating the requirements of literacy at Key Stage 3 and the type of literacy difficulties evident at Key Stage 3. Then it provides an overview of Freire's (2009) emancipatory approach alongside culturally responsive teaching. This is followed by a description of the way in which the researcher was able to address the literacy difficulties identified among the students through the establishment of a supplementary school in a community centre, aimed at raising the attainment levels of participants by actively engaging them and enabling them to take agency of their learning. It gives details of students' progress over a year and concludes with a recommendation for supplementary schools to work collaboratively with mainstream schools.

Literacy at Key Stage 3

Requirements of literacy at Key Stage 3

The National Curriculum has been in force in England since 1988. By law, state-maintained schools must adhere to the prescriptions of the National Curriculum, and this includes English at Key Stage 3. The English curriculum requires that particular topics are included in the learning programme. The focus and the purpose of literacy learning at Key Stage 3 as outlined in the National Curriculum (DfE, 2013, pp. 4–5) are, first, communication 'to communicate their [students'] ideas and emotions to others'. Second, to support students to 'develop culturally, emotionally, intellectually, socially and spiritually'. Third, it is to support the acquisition of knowledge through reading, 'which also enables pupils both to acquire knowledge and to build on what they already know'. Above all, the purpose is seen as enabling young people to participate 'fully' as members of society who can communicate with others, have acquired cultural, motivational, social and spiritual attributes and are knowledgeable.

The prescriptive nature of this National Curriculum has been heavily critiqued by many educators as too narrow and restrictive, as reported by, for example, Shepherd in an article in *The Guardian* newspaper of 13 April, 2009. However, as Wragg and Wragg (1997) note, even with prescription it is not possible for central government to prescribe every detail of a school's curriculum. Teachers may still have the opportunity to make decisions which may have a profound effect over the quality of students' learning. As Wearmouth, Soler and Reid (2003) comment, schools' and teachers' autonomy over curricular decision-making is a particularly important issue where students experience difficulties in learning, such as in the acquisition of literacy, and/or have lost interest in it. The National Curriculum, while prescriptive, is at the same time 'broad' (DfE, 2013). It is crucial, therefore, that teachers are fully conversant with details of the requirements of the National Curriculum and the room for manoeuvre they have within it to respond appropriately to individual students' learning needs. Moreover, the 'broadness' of the National Curriculum offers scope to adopt a culturally responsive and emancipatory approach in English teaching and learning as discussed below.

Research (Finch, 2008, p. 61) suggests that the more students are familiar with practices in pedagogy and are allowed to 'think differently, the greater the feeling of inclusion and the higher the probability of success'. The key is helping students relate lesson content to their own backgrounds. It is therefore the teacher's role to create a classroom culture where all students, regardless of their 'cultural and linguistic background are welcomed, supported and provided with the best opportunity to learn'. All this is compatible with a culturally responsive and emancipatory approach that in the end aims to support learners to develop awareness of the working of society as well as free themselves from the oppression of others and experience more equitable educational outcomes (Bennett *et al.*, 2018, pp. 244–5).

Literacy difficulties at Key Stage 3

According to the National Curriculum (DfE, 2013), literacy difficulties experienced by Key Stage 3 students include reading (comprehension, presentation of answers, deducing, and inferring and text reference) and writing (sentence structure, spelling and grammar). Students' low performance in literacy at Key Stage 3 as observed in a survey carried out by Clark (2012, pp. 9–13) on behalf of the National Literacy Trust, revealed that more than 50 per cent of Key Stage 3 students (11–14 years) do not enjoy reading or writing. The survey findings suggest that a lot more needs to be done to support children who are struggling with reading and writing. Brooks (2013, p. 8) contends that when children experience literacy difficulties through primary into secondary schools, they 'are likely to have difficulty in coping with the steadily increasing demands of the curriculum in Key Stage 3 and beyond'. A major concern should therefore be to find ways of helping children who struggle with reading and writing. Every child is unique, and the areas of difficulties often differ. However, the danger of leaving intervention too late is that students can become disengaged, demotivated and might begin to experience what Seligman (1974) and Peterson (2010) identified as 'learned helplessness'. Most mainstream schools in England employ teaching assistants (TAs) to support students' learning, but Blatchford *et al.* (2014) found that many TAs are not trained in the specialist areas in which they support students. Consequently, the needs of students experiencing difficulties in literacy, including a lack of engagement, can go unrecognized and unaddressed.

Using an emancipatory approach to address lack of engagement

Freire's (2009) emancipatory approach advocates encouraging students to develop a sense of autonomy over their learning. In the research study described here, adopting an emancipatory approach was decided upon from the beginning. The students (see participants) were introduced to an approach which gives room for self-expression and active participation in their own learning.

Freire describes pedagogy in a classroom where an emancipatory approach has been adopted as one implemented through dialogue between the students and the teacher as well as the teacher and the students. In this case the teacher teaches and learns while students learn and teach too. In the classroom setting, both the teacher and students are responsible for the achievement of teaching and learning goals. This is seen as an emancipatory form of pedagogy which promotes freedom in learning.

Culturally responsive pedagogy

Research (Gay, 2010; Pai, Adler and Shaidow, 2001, cited in O'Neal, 2006) suggest that culture is at the heart of all we do in the name of education. Culture determines how we think, believe and behave, which also affects how we teach and learn and is therefore an obvious corollary to a socio-cultural view of learning. Culture therefore is central to learning and it plays a role not only in communicating and receiving information, but also in shaping the thinking process of groups and individuals (Gay, 2002; 2010).

Culture underpins culturally responsive pedagogy which is a method of teaching that acknowledges, responds to and celebrates fundamental cultures and offers full, equitable access to education for students from all cultures. Gay

(2010) observed that culturally responsive teaching makes use of the cultural knowledge, prior experiences and performance styles of diverse students to make learning more appropriate and effective for them. In other words, it teaches to and through the strengths of culturally diverse students. Culturally responsive teachers design student-centred pedagogy which as Sullo (2009) and Tileston (2010) commented, must be aimed at motivating students to be active participants in their learning. They must also be aware of the challenges that may occur when implementing culturally responsive pedagogy (Ladson-Billings, 1994). One way of tackling such challenges is to motivate learning by looking for themes that are reflected in students' own lives, thus bringing topics to life.

In their outline of specific activities for culturally responsive pedagogy, Finch (2008) and Gay (2010) advised that teachers should acknowledge students' differences as well as their commonalities. For instance, students' attitudes to certain tasks or duties can be determined by their cultural beliefs and recognition of these differences makes it easier for the teacher to address the individual needs. Through building on students' cultural, socio-economic and linguistic backgrounds, culturally responsive teaching can lessen the cultural dissonance students face when engaging with curricula that is 'mismatched' with and/or outside of their own cultural background (Hilaski, 2016), and in this way their academic achievement can be enhanced (DeCapua, 2016). Culturally responsive teaching is also central to enabling culturally diverse learners to develop and/or extend their literacy skills (DeCapua 2016; Harmon, 2012; Moje and Hinchman, 2004; Piazza et al., 2015).

The concept of supplementary schools

Pedagogy in a supplementary school has the potential to take an emancipatory, culturally responsive approach. Supplementary schools offer out-of-hours (weekday evenings/weekends) educational opportunities for children and young people whose parents would like them to receive additional support for education in addition to that offered by the mainstream schools they attend. This type of provision is often available to minority ethnic communities and is typically run by volunteers who are either parents or teachers of similar ethnic background (Maylor et al., 2013; Reay and Mirza, 1997). Supplementary schools offer educational support (language, core curriculum, faith and culture) and other out-of-school activities. Teaching is in small groups, pairs and one-to-one. In terms of class sizes, supplementary schools are at an advantage because class sizes are smaller than in mainstream schools.

Purpose of supplementary schools

Research (Creese et al., 2006; Maylor et al., 2013; Mirza, 2009) has suggested that supplementary schools can offer a range of learning opportunities which include National Curriculum subjects, such as English, Mathematics, and Science. They can also provide an avenue for self-expression and enable students to engage with their learning in order to ensure progress (Freiberg and Waxman, 1996, cited in Gordon *et al.*, 2005). In this way supplementary schools aim to increase minority ethnic children's knowledge, improve their skills and promote their educational achievement in mainstream schools. Bastiani (2000, p. 30) noticed that the attendance of some Black children at supplementary schools is essential to 'getting special encouragement and attention and building competence and confidence' which are missing from mainstream schools. Moreover, Gordon *et al.* (2005), Strand (2007) and Maylor *et al.* (2013) suggested that the advantages of group, peer and individual work are more visible in a supplementary school owing to the smaller student numbers, which gives room for teachers to attend to specific students' needs by breaking down topics and explaining points better, checking their work and tracking progress on a given topic.

Judging by the purpose for the establishment of supplementary schools, one of which is to create an avenue for children from different cultures to access forms of tuition aimed at addressing their specific learning needs, culturally responsive pedagogy can be seen as a relevant form of intervention that can be adopted by such schools, especially as both have high expectations for students' success (Bennett *et al.*, 2018; Maylor *et al.*, 2013) as exemplified in the research project discussed next.

The research project

Participants

This research project involved five male participants in Key Stage 3 who were experiencing difficulties in literacy that needed to be addressed. These students were referred to the researcher by their parents because they were disengaged from learning. Parents shared their son's school results which revealed that their attainment levels in literacy were low. These students were from low-income families, hence the researcher's decision to offer her services free of charge. Four participants were Black British African and, also shared the same cultural heritage (Nigerian) as the researcher, while the other one was White British. The common ground was low attainment in literacy. Table 6.1 details the participants' demographic details.

Location of the research project

As a PhD student, the researcher was aware of the literature relevant to supplementary schools, and therefore decided to establish a small supplementary school in which she could address the participants' literacy needs in her local area, an urban area in the East of England. Supplementary school sessions were held on Saturdays in a community centre (which offered an ethnically inclusive learning community space to local residents) as recommended by research (Jeynes, 2011; Maylor *et al.*, 2013; Warmington, 2014).

Table 6.1   Summary of participants by age, year group, ethnicity and parent/guardian

Student	Age	Year group	Ethnic group	Parent/carer
*Fafa Deba	12	8	British African	*Mrs Deba
*Moises Ewarina	12	8	British African	*Mrs Ewarina
*Riley Turner	12	8	White British	*Mrs Turner
*John Areola	13	9	British African	*Mrs James
*Shawn James	13	9	British African	*Mrs James

*Pseudonyms.

The community centre was the cheapest option (for the researcher who paid to use the venue) and the most accessible to the participants who lived nearby. Local authority health and safety expectations required that the community centre manager be present during the sessions.

Data collection

For this research project, data were collected initially from two sources:

- informal discussion with each participant's parent/carer;
- needs analyses of the participants to establish the difficulties they experienced in literacy acquisition and their feelings towards literacy learning and school in general.

The data collection took place over one academic year (2013/2014) and complied with the British Educational Research Association (2011) ethical guidelines.

Discussion with parents/carer

Prior to commencing the study, the researcher had informal discussions with the parents/carers to ascertain their concerns and the type of educational support they sought for their children. The first parent, 'Mrs Deba' approached the researcher after a church service, requesting additional English tuition sessions for her son. She introduced her friend, 'Mrs Ewarina', whose son had similar issues. 'Mrs Turner' spoke to the researcher on the phone at first and then in person shortly before the first session where she explained her son's (Riley) problems with literacy. The fourth parent, 'Mrs James' was the mother of Shawn and the guardian of John. She told the researcher that both of her 'boys' were working below their abilities in literacy and therefore needed 'additional help' to help them improve.

The parents and carer explained the issues as they saw them.

- Mrs Deba spoke about Fafa's 'poor spellings' and her desire to see him improve in his English.
- Mrs Ewarina, the mother of Moises, wanted extra tuition for her son who was struggling with reading and writing.

- Mrs Turner wanted Riley to have tuition sessions with 'someone else' so that he could take his work 'more seriously' and improve his reading and especially his writing. His handwriting was a reason for his low level in writing. She had tried to help, but she felt that as his mother, he found it difficult to see her as a teacher.
- Mrs James spoke for John, her ward, and Shawn, her son. John's mother was her older sister and had relocated to Africa after living in the UK for 16 years. Previously John had been a very good student of English, but his performance level had 'dropped' and Mrs James became worried that 'he might fall below national standard'. She explained that Shawn needed 'encouragement' because he would 'rather not do anything'. Tuition sessions would be of benefit to him because; it would give him 'a sense of purpose' and encourage him to study and work hard.

The issues that arose from their comments in relation to the support for their children's learning that these parents/carers were hoping for were:

- having an external person (not a family member) who was an English teacher, who could work with them in a formal way in a venue that was not home would give the parents/carers confidence that their children were being taught by someone who was well informed about the school curriculum and the Key Stage 3 requirements;
- the importance they attributed to their children doing well at school. They all wanted their children to do extra work to improve their grades. This clearly reflects the findings of Mirza (2009) and Onwughalu (2011) on parental involvement as a key to children's academic success.

Assessment of students' literacy needs

The researcher identified the students' literacy needs in several ways:

- initial assessment of literacy levels using National Curriculum-recommended tests with rubrics;
- standardized reading tests (Neale Analysis; Neale, 2011) to check reading age and ability;
- discussion sessions aimed at getting to know the students more and to find out their literacy learning experiences as well as their specific areas of literacy difficulty.

Table 6.2 presents the assessment of the students' literacy needs.

Summary of initial discussion with students

Fafa reported that he had lost interest in literacy because the reading and writing themes became 'boring and irrelevant'. Moises said that he was disengaged

Table 6.2 Summary of reading and writing outcomes[1]

Student	Age	Initial reading age (years and months)	National Curriculum reading level at the beginning	Difficulties in reading	National Curriculum writing level on school report	National Curriculum writing level at the beginning	Difficulties in writing
Fafa	11+	10.2	4a	Comprehension and accuracy problems	3a	3a	Spellings, punctuation and choice of words for writing
Moises	12	11.4	4a	Comprehension	4c	4c	Spellings and vocabulary
Riley	12	10.8	3a	Comprehension and pronunciation	3a	3a	Spellings, punctuation and choice of words for writing
John	13	11.9	4a	Comprehension and presentation of answers	4a	4a	Spellings and vocabulary
Shawn	13	11.9	4a	Comprehension	4c	4b	Spellings, punctuation and choice of words for writing

[1] Level 3 is working below expectation at KS 2. Level 4 is the expected level at the end of KS 2 and a starting point for KS 3.

from learning especially because he did not see any improvement in his literacy. He added that he needed 'help' in reading, writing and spellings to re-engage with his learning. Riley stated that he loved to read but his handwriting was 'horrible' and he needed a 'little' encouragement to get better. John reported that he lost interest in literacy due to his 'consistent low levels' (in mainstream school) and that he was sure that 'specific tuition' aimed at addressing his difficulties would help him improve and stay 'on top'. Shawn commented that he was struggling with reading and writing especially comprehension where he often got 'confused' and 'stuck'.

The issues that emerged from the discussion were:

- lack of interest in reading and writing due to lack of engagement;
- disengagement from learning which was attributed to consistent lack of progress in literacy;
- acknowledgement of areas of difficulty and the need for intervention aimed at addressing these areas.

Research approach

The researcher adopted a student-centred approach to addressing the literacy difficulties identified which were framed around an emancipatory (Freire, 2009) and culturally responsive approach (Gay, 2010; Ladson-Billings, 1994). The emancipatory approach advocated by Freire (2009) suggested that one way of ensuring student involvement is by giving them some degree of control over what they learn and how they are taught. There are several ways of doing this but one of the ways explored in this research was the use of students' suggestions and feedback to inform lesson planning. Freire advised that the student is not expected to just aim at reproducing the words that exist already but that they should be creative. He describes the act of being solely dependent on what was taught without attempting to change or make personal findings as to how it affects our lives as 'oppression'. A socio-cultural pedagogy (Vygotsky, 1978, p. 87) is compatible with an emancipatory approach in supporting children's active agency in their learning and assisting them in becoming self-regulated learners.

Two specific sessions illustrate what culturally responsive pedagogy could look like and show the student-centred approach that the researcher adopted. In one of the sessions with the Year 8 group, a critical incident (Tripp, 2011) led her to appreciate just how important this pedagogy was in addressing students' writing difficulties.

Session 1

The objective of Session 1 was to practise a different genre of writing (letters) as required at Key Stage 3 using a standardized assessment question and to create an avenue to address any difficulties they might be experiencing with writing letters. In that task, three students were to present themselves as a dog's owner and then write a letter of apology to another dog's owner whose dog was being harassed by their dog. They were asked to apologize for their dog's behaviour, assuring the dog owner that it would never happen again and discuss measures that had been taken to ensure this. The students struggled with the task and could barely write more than two to three sentences after about 15 minutes. When asked why that was so, two Black British African boys said that they did not know what else to write since they did not have dogs. Sharing ethnicity with these boys, the researcher was similarly culturally unfamiliar with owning pets. She had often seen dogs roaming around and was aware that some did not seem to have owners. She had, however, given the task with the hope that the students would be able to carry it out since they had read the story of a troublesome dog previously in the reading task for the same assessment. However, in the writing task the three students were asked to assume the role of the pet owner in the story which they found difficult. The challenge for the students was the fact that two of them did not have pets and the third student only had a pet hamster which he could not compare with having a dog as a pet.

The researcher reflected personally to determine a way forward (Archer, 2003; Sayer, 2011). Her reflections exemplify how culturally responsive teaching can help teachers to clarify understandings of their 'self' as a teacher (Martin and Spencer, 2020) and how culturally responsive teaching can adapt according to the teaching context (Bennett *et al.*, 2018). Accordingly, the researcher decided to bring the theme of the writing task to life by making it applicable to the students by telling them to imagine that it was not a dog but their sibling or relative who was in that situation. They were advised to give the dog a name and write as if it was about a person. This encouraged them to come up with ideas and write more paragraphs without deviating from the aim of the task.

This experience enabled the researcher to apply the principles of culturally responsive teaching to address the students' writing difficulty. Students were motivated to carry out the task and to see themselves within the context of the question, even though they did not have dogs and one had a pet hamster that he stated was different from having a dog. One way of tackling issues relating to cultural diversity in the classroom is to motivate learning within the context of culture by looking for themes that are reflected in students' own lives, thus bringing topics to life and allowing a degree of flexibility in order to motivate students. Although Riley was White British and owning a dog in White British culture is common, not having a dog as a pet put him at the same level as the two Black African students who did not have any pets. Thus, in line with Freire's emancipatory approach (Freire, 2009), he had to reimagine himself within the context of the task to complete it.

Session 2

The objective of Session 2 was to use a recommended play, Shakespeare's *Romeo and Juliet*, to explore how relationships in a European (Italian) context can be contextualized and made more meaningful to young people who come from a different culture and therefore have a different perspective of how love should be demonstrated. The rationale for the session was to use talk between peers to deepen understanding of the play on the interpersonal then the intrapersonal plane. The speaking tasks were based on a play (book) they had studied (Dole *et al.*, 1991; Glynn *et al.*, 2006; Stead, 2006), which had been suggested by students and which they read at school in order to maintain their interest and engagement, as well as put them in a position to work more confidently in their mainstream school (Stead, 2006; Wearmouth, 2009). The session was also intended to encourage students to translate their reading into writing as a way of encouraging them to develop their use of grammar, vocabulary and spelling (Glynn *et al.*, 2006; McCormack and Pasquerelli, 2009; Smith, 1994), as well as gain interest and support from families as the more knowledgeable other (Gordon *et al.*, 2005; Onwughalu, 2011; Reay and Mirza, 1997; Vygotsky, 1978).

Students were to carry out a creative writing task using a picture prompt. A picture of the scene where Romeo was standing outside Juliet's window (far below) with the nurse talking to her was displayed for students to discuss. They talked about the significance of the picture on the rest of the play as well as what it tells us about the character of Juliet's nurse. Students made points about the nurse serving as an alibi to the relationship between Romeo and Juliet despite her awareness of the long-standing family feud between the Capulets and Montagues which posed a hindrance to the love between Romeo and Juliet. The picture showed the nurse encouraging Juliet to go to Romeo and telling her that she would be on guard so that no one could see them together in the garden.

The task afforded an opportunity for culturally responsive teaching as two students in the Year 9 group were of African origin and they tried to compare the love situation in the play to what happens in some modern-day African contexts. Nowadays, despite several attempts to stop child marriages, some African cultures still approve of love relationships and early marriage between young people because it is seen as a preservation of culture, just as it was at the time Romeo and Juliet was written in 1594, when early marriage was not uncommon in Europe. However, in Nigeria, in the researcher's experience, most parents would rather have their children complete their education before falling in love or contemplating marriage. The students observed that if Romeo and Juliet were Africans, they would not have died a tragic death borne out of undying love for each other and that the nurse, instead of being an alibi would probably (as a result of her allegiance to the dictates of culture and tradition) have been a spy or a 'tell-tale'.

The supplementary school session provided time to break down the topic, while the creative writing task was done at home and brought into the following session. This is a key strength of supplementary schools where the teacher is able to dissect topics as a way of making them clearer to students before they carry out the assigned task (Maylor *et al.*, 2013; Strand 2007). In such situations, longer time can be spent on topics which at the end give students a better understanding.

Progress in Literacy learning

Reading

Fafa started at level 4a and progressed steadily to level 5b (two levels up) equivalent to a year's progress while Moises progressed from 4a to 5a (three levels up) similar to a year and a half levels of progress by the end of the study. Their improved levels of progress can be attributed to increased levels of motivation to read. Also, Riley made good progress throughout the study. He developed a genuine interest in his reading as indicated in his increased attainment level from 3a to 4b (a year's progress). Additionally, John and Shawn both progressed from level 4a to 5a (3 levels up and a year's progress). All the boys developed an interest for reading, especially with the approach recommended by the National Curriculum (DfE, 2010) which encourages students to read widely for pleasure and enjoyment, which in the case of this study included books such as *Terror Kid* by Benjamin Zephaniah, *Boys Don't Knit* by T.S. Easton and *SMART* by Kin Slater.

Writing

In writing, Fafa progressed by two sub-levels from 4b to 5c and Moises from 4a to 5b which indicates, in National Curriculum terms, three sub-levels of progress and one and a half years of what might be expected. Riley, on the other hand started at level 3a, approximately one and a half years behind what was expected of him. His progress to level to 4b represents a year's progress in his writing. One year's progress in writing was made by John, from 4a to 5b and by Shawn who moved from 4b to 5c.

Discussion of the findings

The study findings indicate that culturally responsive pedagogy and an emancipatory approach can contribute to students' learning. In Key Stage 3 it is possible to see how a culturally responsive and emancipatory approach that aims to support learners to develop can be achieved within the Key Stage 3 framework. As can be seen from this research, there is a need to find culturally diverse ways of addressing literacy difficulties at Key Stage 3 since it can help to develop more confident and engaged potential Key Stage 4 students from Black and White groups. The supplementary school interventions aimed at addressing specific literacy needs in a culturally responsive way can be valuable in raising student literacy attainment levels in mainstream schools as exemplified by participant comments. For example, Fafa said that he 'benefitted especially in spellings' which has 'improved' his 'writing at school'. All participants reported increased levels of engagement and motivation to work at school and on their own. The supplementary school sessions encouraged the participants to continue to build on what they had learnt through consistent practice. The parents also confirmed their children's re-engagement and increased levels of attainment which was reflected in their 'better grades in their schoolwork'.

Conclusion

The findings from this research led the researcher to conclude that a supplementary school using culturally responsive pedagogy and an emancipatory approach can serve as an avenue for addressing difficulties and re-engaging otherwise disengaged students. One strong point for supplementary schools is the small number of students who attend (Maylor *et al.*, 2013; Strand, 2007), which makes it possible for the teacher to address specific needs. There were five participants in this study which implies that a small number of students in a group can create room for learning through positive engagement with each other. The teacher (though guided by a prescriptive curriculum) can adopt creative and innovative approaches to address literacy difficulties. One such is a culturally responsive form of pedagogy which considers students' cultural backgrounds, experiences and beliefs and incorporates these into teaching and learning to bring out the best in students as well as encouraging them to be active learners. This is because when students realize that the topic of a lesson is of no interest or relevance to them, they switch off or become disengaged. Thus, re-engaging such students can serve as a way of encouraging them to take agency of their learning. In addition, the emancipatory approach gives students the opportunity to get involved and therefore play a significant role in deciding how they learn, which can be a great source of motivation. This study therefore lays bare the effect of student-centred teaching outside a mainstream school setting aimed at addressing literacy difficulties and disengagement with learning.

Despite these possibilities, the approach and its results cannot be generalized from such a small sample. Nevertheless, there is an implication that even within the tight prescription of the National Curriculum there is room for a degree of flexibility to enable cultural responsiveness and sensitive engagement with students' own views to improve their literacy learning. Moreover, this study highlights implications for collaborative working between supplementary and mainstream schools as a way of supporting students to develop higher levels of literacy learning. One way of achieving this is for students to identify their areas of difficulty, have these addressed in smaller groups within the context of a supplementary school and apply what has been learnt within the context of their mainstream schools. Teachers in mainstream schools should be able to identify learners who are getting additional help outside of school due to their increased attainment levels. Sadly, there seems to be little interaction with parents whose children attend supplementary schools and supplementary schools have no access to gain information on students' performance outside of what they glean from parents (Maylor *et al.*, 2013).

References

Archer, L. (2003) *Race, Masculinity and Schooling*, Maidenhead: McGraw-Hill Education.

Bastiani, J. (2000) *Supplementary Schooling in the Lambeth Education Action Zone*, London: Institute for Public Policy Research.

Bennett, S., Gunn, A., Gayle-Evans, G., Barrera IV, E. and Leung, C. (2018) 'Culturally responsive literacy practices in an early childhood community', *Early Childhood Education Journal*, 46: 241–8.

Blatchford, P., Russell, A., Basett, P., Brown, P. and Martin, C. (2014) 'The role and effects of teaching assistants in English primary schools (Years 4–6) 2000–2003: Results from Class Size and Pupil-Adult Ratios (CSPAR) KS 2 Project', Nottingham: DfES.

British Educational Research Association (2011) 'BERA ethical guidelines for educational research 2011'. Available at http:/www.bera.ac.uk/publications.

Brooks, B. (2013) *What Works for Children and Young People with Literacy Difficulties? The Effectiveness of Intervention Schemes*, London: DfES.

Clark, I. (2012) 'Formative assessment: Assessment is for self-regulated learning', *Educational Psychology Review*, 24(2): 205–49.

Creese, A., Bhatt, A., Bhojani, N. and Martin, P. (2006) 'Multicultural, heritage and learner identities in complementary schools', *Language and Education*, 20(1): 23–43.

DeCapua, A. (2016) 'Reaching students with limited or interrupted formal education through culturally responsive teaching', *Language and Linguistics Compass*, 10(5): 225–37.

DfE (Department for Education) (2010) *The National Curriculum*, London: DfE.

DfE (Department for Education) (2013) *The National Curriculum*, London: DfE.

Dole, J.A., Duffy, G.G., Roehler, L.R. and Pearson, P.D. (1991) 'Moving from the old to the new: Research on reading comprehension instruction', *Review of Educational Research*, 61(2): 239–64.

Finch, J.T. (2008) 'Perceptions of preservice and in-service teachers working toward culturally responsive teaching: A study of multicultural education graduate course at an urban society', thesis, University of Louisville: Kentucky, pp. 59–65.

Freire, P. (2009) 'Chapter 2 from Pedagogy of the Oppressed', in P. Freire and M.B. Ramos (eds), *Race/Ethnicity: Multidisciplinary Global Contexts*, 2: 163–74.

Gay, G. (2002) 'Culturally responsive teaching in special education for ethnically diverse students: Setting the stage', *International Journal of Qualitative Studies in Education*, 15(6): 613–29.

Gay, G. (2010) *Culturally Responsive Teaching: Theory, Research, and Practice*, New York: Teachers College Press.

Glynn, T., Wearmouth, J. and Berryman, M. (2006) *Supporting Students with Literacy Difficulties: A Responsive Approach*, Maidenhead: Open University Press.

Gordon, E.W., Bridglall, B.L. and Meroe, A.S. (eds) (2005) *Supplementary Education: The Hidden Curriculum of High Academic Achievement*, Lanham, MD: Rowman and Littlefield Publishers Inc.

Harmon, D. (2012) 'Culturally responsive teaching though a historical lens: Will history repeat itself?' *Interdisciplinary Journal of Teaching and Learning*, 2(1): 12–22.

Hilaski, D. (2016) 'A collaborative inquiry: Working together to make our Reading Recovery lessons culturally responsive', unpublished doctoral dissertation, Georgia State University, Atlanta, GA.

Jeynes, W.H. (2011) *Parental Involvement and Academic Success*, London: Taylor and Francis.

Ladson-Billings, G. (1994) *The Dream Keepers*, San Francisco, CA: Jossey-Bass.

Martin, A.D. and Spencer, T. (2020) 'Children's literature, culturally responsive teaching, and teacher identity: an action research inquiry in teacher education', *Action in Teacher Education*, 42(4): 387–404.

Maylor, U., Rose, A., Minty, S., Ross, A., Issa, T. and Kuyok, A.K. (2013) 'Exploring the impact of supplementary schools on Black and minority ethnic pupils' mainstream attainment', *British Educational Research Journal*, 39(1): 107–25.

McCormack, R.L. and Pasquarelli, S.L. (2009) *Teaching Reading: Strategies and Resources for Grades K-6*, New York: Guilford Press.

Mirza, H. (2009) *Race, Gender and Educational Desire*, Abingdon: Routledge.

Moje, E.B., and Hinchman, K. (2004) 'Culturally responsive practices for youth literacy learning', in J. Dole and T. Jetton (eds), *Adolescent Literacy Research and Practice*, New York: Guilford Press, pp. 331–50.

Neale, M.D. (2011) *Neale Analysis of Reading Ability (NARA)*, London: ACER Press.

O'Neal, G.S. (2006) 'Using multicultural resources in groups', *GROUPWORK-LONDON*, 16(1): 48.

Onwughalu, O.J. (2011) 'Parents' involvement in education: The experience of an African immigrant community in Chicago', New York: iUniverse.

Peterson, C. (2010) 'Learned helplessness', in *The Corsini Encyclopedia of Psychology*, Chichester: Wiley, pp. 1–2.

Piazza, S., Rao, S. and Protacio, M. (2015) 'Converging recommendations for culturally responsive literacy practices: Students with learning disabilities, English language learners, and socio-culturally diverse learners', *International Journal of Multicultural Education*, 17(3): 1–20.

Reay, D. and Mirza, H.S. (1997) 'Uncovering genealogies of the margins: Black supplementary schools', *British Journal of Sociology of Education*, 18(4): 477–99.

Sayer, A. (2011) *Why Things Matter to People: Social Science, Values and Ethical Life*, Cambridge: Cambridge University Press.

Seligman, M.E. (1974) *Depression and Learned Helplessness*, Chichester: John Wiley & Sons.

Shepherd, J. (2009) 'Prescriptive national curriculum restricts teachers', *Guardian*, 13 April, 2009.

Smith, B. (1994) *Through Reading to Writing: Classroom Strategies for Supporting Literacy*, London: Routledge Falmer.

Stead, T. (2006) *Reality Checks: Teaching Reading Comprehension with Nonfiction*, Toronto, Canada: Pembroke Publishers Ltd.

Strand, S. (2007) 'Surveying the views of pupils attending supplementary schools in England', *Educational Research*, 49(1): 1–19.

Sullo, B. (2009) *The Motivated Student: Unlocking the Enthusiasm for Learning*, Washington, DC: ASCD.

Tileston, W.D. (2010) *What Every Teacher Should Know About Student Motivation*, London: Sage.

Tripp, D. (2011) *Critical Incidents in Teaching: Developing Professional Judgement*, London: Routledge.

Vygotsky, L.S. (1978) *Mind in Society*, Cambridge, MA: Harvard University Press.

Warmington, M. (2014) *Black British Intellectuals and Education: Multiculturalism's Hidden History*, London: SAGE.

Wearmouth, J. (2009) *A Beginning Teacher's Guide to Special Educational Needs*, Buckingham: Open University Press.

Wearmouth, J., Soler, J. and Reid, G. (2003) *Meeting Difficulties in Literacy Development: Research, Policy and Practice*, Hove: Psychology Press.

Wragg, E.C. and Wragg, T. (1997) *Assessment and Learning: Primary and Secondary*, Hove: Psychology Press.

7 Oracy, dialogic learning and education for democracy

Developing an authentic 'student voice' in an Eastern Region secondary school

Mike Berrill and Neil Hopkins

Major questions addressed in this chapter are:

- Is there a way of facilitating an authentic student voice in a large secondary school?
- If so, how can student voice be developed and extended across the whole school curriculum?

Abstract

The focus of this chapter is an ongoing 5-year study on the formation and development of 'dialogic groups' at a secondary school in a town in Eastern England. The project, entitled 'Oracy, dialogic learning and education for democracy', was initiated by a desire to improve the articulation of student voice at the school. The text is written largely from the perspective of the recently retired Executive Principal at the school, hence employs the first person. Discussion in the chapter suggests the potential of dialogic group work for enhancing student engagement in the English National Curriculum.

Introduction

This chapter focuses on the first three years of a 5-year programme of work that has involved the authors engaging with students at a secondary school in a large town in the Eastern Region in England. As is discussed below, the project that we have called 'Oracy, dialogic learning and education for democracy', sprang from a desire to improve the articulation of the student voice at the school. The changes implemented at the beginning of the project proved to be positive and encouraged us to explore with staff and students the whole organizational approach to structured conversation at the school, how this might extended to enrich the school curriculum and support students to acquire the values, skills and dispositions to become active and assertive citizens in the classroom and the world beyond. The theoretical framework is taken from the work of Dewey ([1916] 2007), Alexander (2008) and, especially, Mercer (2019), each of whom is concerned with talk and discussion in educational settings, and the implications these can have for learning and democratic society.

The text is written largely from the perspective of the recently retired Executive Principal at the school and hence employs the first person. It begins with an outline of the school's approach to improving the student voice process, turns to the theoretical frameworks on which the on-going developments rest, and concludes with an outline of the exciting and innovative ways in which the school proposes to take the project forward in the coming years.

Context

The school is arguably one of the most socially and ethnically diverse in the Eastern Region. Following the reorganization of the town where the school is located from a three- to a two-tier structure in 2015 (lower, middle and upper to primary and secondary) the school is now an oversubscribed, 1,200 strong, 70 per cent minority ethnic comprehensive school that serves the inner-urban area. Following mass secondary academization, it is the only remaining local authority (LA) maintained 11–18 secondary school in the area.

Executive Principal's recollections

I was the Principal of the school from 1997 until my retirement in 2010 but was retained part-time and given the largely honorary title of Executive Principal with responsibility for heading up a three-school Foundation Trust, strategic planning and external liaison. During my 13 years as head teacher, I was adamant that the school should have a strong student voice, not only so students' views could inform school leadership and governance, but to equip students with the skills and dispositions for civic and democratic engagement in later life. My efforts were redoubled in 2012, when it became increasingly apparent that the radical changes in curriculum and assessment that began in 2010 were progressively marginalizing activities not directly related to academic achievement. As imperatives associated with meeting high stakes, externally set exam targets came to take centre stage, student voice activities had gone into abeyance. As a result, I decided to bring together a group of students to consider how we might re-energize the student voice and to begin by considering why they had not always been successful in the past.

Engaging with student voice

Prior to beginning this new initiative, I carried out my own review of the past. There were very few stand-out memories from the previous 15 years and even fewer instances of positive impact. I had to go back to the complete reorganization of the school in 2000 for anything particularly noteworthy. Each year following my appointment in 1997, I had asked an enthusiastic middle manager to organize elections for 'Tutor Group Reps' to form 'Year Councils', which then contributed to the 'School Council'. They were always led by young, committed staff, but I recollected that by Christmas each year the enthusiasm and energy that marked the early stages of the student voice process were dwindling, and, by Easter, in anticipation of the examination season, it seemed that staff were always glad to allow the whole exercise to fade into the background for another year. However, the following September the whole process would restart with renewed vigour and determination, often with fresh staff in charge. And so it went on for the 13 years of my headship. The question was how to ensure that any new initiative could be sustained and impactful.

I began my student meetings in 2012 by asking why School Councils had never really worked in the past and was surprised by the consensus view that emerged. In the students' opinion, they had failed because the wrong students tended to be elected. Those securing the most votes were invariably the 'popular students', the 'good-looking ones', the ones who 'everyone wanted to be', and, as they went on to argue compellingly, the last thing these students wanted to do after school was to sit in a room discussing how to address smoking in the toilets. In the memorable words of one student at the time, they wanted to be 'hangin with their homies'. In short, in their view, the voting exercises in the past had been more of a beauty pageant than a genuine exercise in democracy, and as a result they had mostly selected the students perceived to be 'cool'.

The Student Forum

The solution, jointly agreed with the students, was a group called the 'Student Forum', which began from the simple premise articulated by one student who said that the 'students you want in the room are the students who want to be in the room'. Accordingly, a group was formed through an application and interview process, not to sift out 'unworthy candidates' but to test the resolve of students who wanted to join. Our thinking on this came from a student who argued that anyone who could be bothered to fill in an application form, get a signature from a parent and form tutor, and attend for an interview, was probably serious about joining and would be committed to long-term membership.

In the event, over the seven years I chaired the Forum, no one who applied and went through the interview process was ever turned down. The ethnic and intellectual diversity of the group was nurtured by Year Heads 'encouraging' a range of candidates who might be interested to apply. Though not everyone responded to this encouragement, enough always did to achieve a good spread of age, achievement, gender and ethnicity, and the Forum always came to reflect the broad make-up of the school.

The first group in 2012 numbered just 12 students, spread across years 9–12. All meetings took place fortnightly after school and lasted about one and a half hours. There were agendas and Minutes to provide a sense of seriousness, formality and continuity. Conversely the facilitation of the meetings was always light-hearted and there was always a good deal of laughter. This 'tight-loose' mixture of the formal and informal, preceded by generous refreshments, proved to be an ideal format.

Apart from the traditional formalities like Minutes, Matters Arising and Any Other Business (AOB), the general format of meetings was that an agenda issue would be tabled and a question for discussion formulated. The group would then split into 'diverse triads' which were groups of three students of mixed age, gender and ethnicity. Initially these groups were set and remained the same for each meeting, but over time this changed and the students competed with each other at each meeting to see who could construct the most diverse group from those attending. The triads would consider the issue before them for 3-4 minutes and a spokesperson from each group would report back to the full group in turn.

During the first 2 years, the meetings, while engaging and enjoyable, were slightly reserved as the group explored the boundaries of what issues it was possible to talk about, what kinds of things it was permissible to say and what potential outcomes might be achievable, but by the third year things began to change significantly. By this time the group had risen to 25 in number, several students had been members from the beginning and a distinctive 'culture' began to emerge, marked by some important features:

- The students were more relaxed and talked more freely as they realized that very few issues were 'out of bounds' (basically the only rules were no swearing, discussing individual staff or students, and no side conversations).
- They became more open and friendly with each other, 'bonded' as a group across age, gender and ethnicity and were frequently seen talking with each other around school.
- The older students began to actively nurture the younger ones and encourage them to raise issues; they were increasingly chosen to do triad feedbacks to the main group.
- The younger students began to 'model' themselves on the older ones and often mirrored gestures, vocabulary and verbal mannerisms.
- Over time the student topics became more serious (e.g. teaching quality, LGBTQ and transgender issues, exam stress, anxiety and mental health).

- The students became more fluent, articulate and expressive with each other, and were able to spontaneously construct longer sentences and express more complex and nuanced ideas.
- Whereas at the beginning they could be quite dismissive of each other, they began to listen more actively – probing and summarizing – and generally acting in a more respectful way.
- They clearly enjoyed the sessions as absenteeism was low (usually dental appointments or sports fixtures) and meetings sometimes lost a sense of time and had to be halted at 4.15.
- They needed less and less facilitation.

The last point is probably the most significant. After they had discussed an issue in their diverse triads, and taken turns to share their thoughts, initially I needed to introduce a new stimulus question to maintain the flow of dialogue. But as the group matured, they began to take issues off on their own with respectful sentence stems like, 'Can I pick up on your point and say… ?' or, 'Can I ask you what you mean by … ?' As the chair and facilitator, I often became an observer and summarizer and, as the group entered a 'flow state', it became more creative both at problem framing and problem solving. At no stage did my work with the students involve teaching them about how human groups work more effectively. With just simple protocols and ground rules built on courtesy and respect, skill levels grew organically.

At this point I, as Executive Principal, met the second author of this chapter at a book group exploring key chapters from John Dewey's book, *Democracy and Education* (Dewey, [1916] 2007). This began a period of critical reflection on these developments and cemented our subsequent working relationship. Dewey argued that democracy is much more than voting. He argued that at its heart it is a form of 'associated living' (ibid., p. 68). These words seemed to describe precisely what we were achieving in the Student Forum and led us to explore other key features of what was being achieved:

- A major strength of the Student Forum – in the context of compulsory schooling — was that the group was entirely voluntary and everyone who attended did so freely, which speaks to the importance of building aspects of voluntarism into the curriculum.
- It thrived on the long-term continuity that came from students being together and developing strong relationships over several years; many joined in Year 9 and stayed until Year 13.
- Over time it nurtured confident, articulate, morally aware young adults with a strong sense of civic engagement and personal agency.

In short, I felt that in 40+ years in education, it was the closest to a spirit of open democracy that I had experienced in the context of compulsory education. This was made all the more remarkable given that the purpose of state education at secondary level was being increasingly restricted to 'teaching-to-the-test' and the passing of exams.

Development of the Student Forum

By the third year, however, there was a growing sense of unease within the group about the actual 'voting' element. In the students' view the 'democratic' spirit of the Student Forum was missing. Given their critique of former processes as resembling 'beauty pageants', the group itself came up with a solution. When the students were not confident that their views were an expression of the wider student body, they went out and asked other students using a process they called 'vox-pop'. Each of the 25 members nominated five other students from their year groups who were of mixed gender and ethnicity, and representative of the broader student body. Forum members then either discussed the issue with them or presented them with a questionnaire that the students devised themselves.

A good example was their analysis of what made for 'good' and 'bad' homework. They completed a detailed exercise themselves and used the results to create a questionnaire, which they administered and analyzed. They were delighted when the results from the 118 responses (over 10 per cent of the school population at that point) closely resembled their own. These were then presented to both the Senior Leadership Team (SLT) and the governors.

Another development that provided the group with an enhanced sense of personal agency and engagement was when they suggested that the Head Girl and Head Boy – both members of the Student Forum – should be invited to attend a 20-minute section of Senior Leadership Team (SLT) meetings once per fortnight. From the beginning, the minutes of Student Forum meetings had been copied to governors and SLT members, but there was always a feeling in the group that this was a paper exercise as they rarely received feedback. In the Student Forum's view, this new protocol would 'close the loop'. The proposal was accepted and became standard practice as did student attendance at governors' meetings to share a summary of Student Forum business between their meetings.

This was far from a tension-free process. On occasions the group could become quite indignant if they thought their views were being 'brushed off' or not taken seriously. On more than one occasion a sub-group of more senior students formed a deputation and requested a meeting with the head teacher to press the Forum's case on an issue. Sometimes this worked and sometimes it did not. But over time they came to accept that their voice was advisory and one of many stakeholder voices at the school. As they went on to argue, however, their direct involvement in governance, management and school development 'felt real', their voice was articulated and their impact was apparent. This sense of agency and impact led to the Student Forum winning the 'Speaker's School Action Award' for their work on mental health and the fact that a 'School Wellbeing Coordinator' was appointed as a result. Their award was presented to them by John Bercow in the Houses of Parliament in March 2018.

By this time, though there was considerable confidence within the school that membership of the Student Forum was beneficial for students and not a distraction from their examination work. In 2018, this was demonstrated unequivocally when an analysis was undertaken into the examination performance of students who had joined and remained on the Student Forum for two years or more. Both staff and students were delighted to discover that far from being a distraction, their examination results showed enhanced performance when compared to their target grades, especially at Key Stage 4. This confirmed a notion that had been developing at the school for some time: the idea of 'achievement through social engagement'. It was in this way that the work of the Student Forum began to underpin the idea we should extend the benefits of dialogic group work and problem solving to the wider school. As a consequence, the SLT decided to embark on the development of a whole-school oracy and dialogic learning programme.

There was a recognition by the senior leadership in the school, however, that given the necessary focus on 'exam performance', any new initiative of this kind might be perceived as marginal to the dominant focus of most teachers and most departments at the time. It was therefore accepted that this would involve a long process of awareness raising and professional skill development; one that might take between 5 and 8 years to build and embed. The question then became, could we create a curriculum that would grow organically over time and develop oracy and dialogic learning as a consciously nurtured combination of knowledge, skills, values and dispositions? From this point onwards, it was the work of Dewey, Alexander and Mercer and the continuing dialogue between the two authors of this chapter that informed the work at the school.

Theoretical framework underpinning the school's Oracy Programme

Dialogic learning

The school set out to base its approach on a clear understanding that:

> Democratic pedagogy rejects the traditional domination-subordination relationship between teacher and taught, makes knowledge reflexive rather than disciplinary, the child an active agent in his or her learning, and the classroom a workshop or laboratory. In all these respects the classroom seeks to enact the ideals of the wider democratic society. Negotiation thus stands in conscious antithesis to both transmission and induction,
>
> (Alexander, 2008, p. 80)

Also, as Hopkins (2019, p. 38) comments:

> Beliefs and values do play an important part in both the teacher's and students' notions of what constitutes effective teaching and learning. Dialogical learning epitomises the idea that we come to acquire knowledge and understanding through our interaction with others.

Indeed, 'in order to have a large number of values in common, all members of the group must have an equable opportunity to receive and to take from others' (Dewey, [1916] 2007, p. 66). The exchange of different viewpoints that comes with dialogical forms of pedagogy enables students to peer into a problem and look at it from the various sides before establishing a fact or coming to a conclusion. The solution is more stable because it has been built by many hands, is the product not of a hierarchy where the information is fed to students in an 'input-output' manner but where they have had some ownership of the process and the endeavour that has gone into it.

Alexander (2008, pp. 112–13) outlines a number of what he sees as principles of dialogic teaching:

- *collective*: teachers and children address learning tasks together, whether as a group or as a class;
- *reciprocal*: teachers and children listen to each other, share ideas and consider alternative viewpoints;
- *supportive*: children articulate their ideas freely, without fear of embarrassment over 'wrong' answers; and they help each other to reach common understandings;
- *cumulative*: teachers and children build on their own and each other's ideas and chain them into coherent lines of thinking and enquiry;
- *purposeful*: teachers plan and steer classroom talk with specific educational goals in view.

What this summary of dialogic teaching and learning contains is an emphasis on the common and collective without sacrificing the individual student's attitudes and ideas. Students, in collaboration with each other and the teacher, are able to explore, through supported speech, the issues, experiments or problems they are working on in an atmosphere of 'two heads are better than one'. The learning is inherently social. By adopting such a process, in Alexander's words:

> We see young children discussing with increasing sophistication and sensitivity the dynamics and mechanisms of interaction: the use of eye contact, listening, taking turns, handling the dominant individual and supporting the reticent one, engaging with what others say rather than merely voicing their own opinions.
>
> (2008, p. 115)

What we have here, in effect, is a pedagogical model for what democratic education (in the Deweyan mode) ought to look like. The students described in the passage above are developing the skills and attitudes one associates with active citizenship in a democratic society. It is through such exchanges that a sense of commonality can prevail.

Mercer's theories of dialogic learning

Mercer approaches the issue of dialogic teaching and learning from a perspective that uses linguistics and psychology alongside recent research into

cognition, memory and the impact on knowledge. Mercer (2019, p. 56) catego-
rizes classroom talk and thinking into the following three groupings:

- *Disputational talk* which is characterized by disagreement and individualized decision-making.
- *Cumulative talk* in which speakers build positively but uncritically on what
  others have said.
- *Exploratory talk* which occurs when partners engage critically but con-
  structively with each other's ideas.

We can identify elements of each of Mercer's categories for talk and thinking in
the passage below:

> If the living, experiencing being is an intimate participant in the activities of
> the world to which it belongs, then knowledge is a mode of participation,
> valuable in the degree in which it is effective. It cannot be the idle view of an
> unconcerned spectator.
>
> (Dewey, [1916] 2007, p. 247)

Mercer, however, is not an advocate of group or paired learning simply for the
sake of it. Where he has concerns is in learning situations where there is a pronounced difference in the abilities or levels of confidence between students.
Mercer (2019, p. 47) concludes from his research that children appear to learn
more effectively when working with a partner of similar ability rather than a
more capable one whose insistence on their own strategies for solving problems may stifle rather than help the less able or confident.

Mercer makes clear the importance of teacher-led input, especially with
young children or at the initial stages of dialogic learning where: 'there are
no good reasons for assuming that children already possess a good understanding and awareness of how best to go about "learning together in the
classroom"' (Mercer, 2019, p. 63). Collaboration does not absolve the teacher
of authority and responsibility (a criticism levelled at some progressive
educators) – they 'can arrange conditions that are conducive to community
activity' (Dewey, [1938] 1950, p. 64). The teacher, due to their level of maturity
in relation to the children, has a particular role within any collective endeavour to guide and maintain the educational aspect of any experience in the
classroom. Dewey neatly defined the teacher's function in this context as
'los[ing] the position of external boss or dictator but tak[ing] on that of
leader of group activities' (ibid., p. 66).

Another important concept associated with Mercer's theories on dialogic
learning is the 'intermental development zone' (IDZ). Mercer (2019, p.121)
calls the IDZ a 'dynamic frame of reference' that changes and amends as discussion goes forward, enabling both teacher and learner to 'think through'
the endeavour they are participating in. As with the discussion above on how
the teacher retains a special role and responsibility in relation to dialogic

discussion generally, Mercer sees a critical role for the teacher with regards to the creation and maintenance of the IDZ:

> The IDZ is a mutual achievement ... *but the teacher must take a special responsibility for its creation and maintenance.* [Its] ... effectiveness is likely to depend on how well a teacher can create and maintain connections between the curriculum-based goals of activity and a learner's existing knowledge, capabilities and motivations.
>
> (Mercer, 2019, p. 121; emphasis added)

Unlike the caricature of progressive education that Dewey is often accused of advocating, where the teacher absolves themself of any responsibility in the learning process, Dewey is clear on the need for the teacher to embrace these professional duties. It could be said that this is the difference, in an educational context, between democracy and anarchy:

> The educator's part in the enterprise of education is to furnish the environment which stimulates responses and directs the learner's course ... the teacher should be occupied not with subject matter in itself but in its interaction with the pupils' present needs and capacities.
>
> (Dewey, [1916] 2007, pp. 137, 139)

School Oracy Programme

From our work with the Student Forum we knew that effective dialogic group work was important for developing the skills, values and dispositions associated with personal agency, civic engagement and collaborative problem solving. Though these are seen as unimportant in relation to the intense individualism of GCSE and A levels examinations, they are nevertheless essential for a flourishing economy and a vibrant democracy. Despite the significant time pressures that the school was under, the SLT recognized that these should become an integral part of the curriculum.

The theoretical consideration above and our wish to extend the work of the Student Forum to the whole school, quickly took us to the concept of 'oracy' and to the work of the 'Voice 21' organization. This was set up by Peter Hyman and grew from his pioneering work on oracy as the Head of the newly formed 'School 21' in London.

From the beginning the work of Voice 21 was built on the Cambridge Oracy Skills Framework created by Neil Mercer and his team at Hughes College, Cambridge. What began with a sense of inspiration from the work of Dewey and Alexander brought us to Mercer's concept of 'exploratory talk' and his detailed practical framework of skills. (https://www.educ.cam.ac.uk/research/projects/oracytoolkit/oracyskillsframework/).

A simple definition of oracy suggests that it is merely the ability to express oneself fluently and grammatically in speech but Mercer's framework clearly incorporates the multi-level social, emotional and cognitive skills that underpin dialogic group learning. His team had mapped out four practical dimensions of oracy:

- *Physical* – relating to the voice, its fluency, pace, tonal variation, clarity and projection; and body language including gesture, posture, facial expression and eye contact;
- *Linguistic* – relating to the appropriate use of vocabulary, register, grammar and structure; and the use of rhetorical techniques, such as metaphor, humour, irony and mimicry;
- *Cognitive* – relating to the conveying of meaning and intention, building on the views of others, seeking information and clarification through questioning and summarizing; the focus on task, time management and giving reasons to support views; critically examining ideas and views expressed and taking account of the level of understanding of others;
- *Social and Emotional* – relating to guiding or managing interactions; turn-taking, active listening and responding appropriately; self-assurance, liveliness and flair.

From the school's work with Voice 21, Mercer's framework and the authors' own experience, five simple guidelines were formulated:

- Unstructured and poorly planned talk in the classroom is often worse than no talk at all and potentially a waste of valuable time.
- Effective classroom talk, and the dialogic learning that grows from it, do not happen naturally or by accident; its basic elements have to be taught, discussion has to be well facilitated and classrooms must have the right ground rules.
- Achieving all of this takes time, and the development of high-level planning and facilitation skills.
- Oracy and dialogic learning cannot simply be tacked on to a lesson (the 'oracy bit'); they need to infuse a teacher's whole approach to lesson planning, teaching and learning.
- Although the various elements of oracy can be taught and practised separately, like sports skills, they only become fully embedded as an active skill set through extended practice in real discursive activities.

Vignette: Oracy-based curriculum development

With the above guidelines in mind, the staff and students began to develop their own skill levels by introducing a dedicated oracy lesson into Years 7 and 8 in September 2018. This involved using a range of discursive group games and activities to introduce the basic vocabulary of oracy with terms like:

- 'active listening' – showing through voice cues, gesture, posture, facial expression and eye contact, and by probing and clarifying that you are both listening and seeking to understand;

- 'turn taking' and 'courtesy' – the importance of equity, 'sharing the air', rule following and avoiding aggression in effective group work;
- useful 'sentence stems' for clarifying, probing, challenging and summarizing (e.g. 'sentence openings' that build on previous speakers like, 'Picking up Halima's point, I'd like to add…' or to probe like, 'Can you tell me a bit more about…?').

In Year 7, the curriculum is built around a real-time activity with the charity 'First Give' (https://firstgive.co.uk/) that involves developing student advocacy and social action. Basically, over a term they explore the local charity landscape, form into groups, each choose a charity, contact them and arrange a visit. Ultimately, with guidance and training, each group creates a 'pitch' which they present to parents and an outside panel to win a sum of money for their chosen charity. This involves oracy milestones like making a telephone call to the charity, organizing a meeting, researching a presentation and ultimately presenting to an external panel.

In Year 8 the curriculum is built around the Pixl 'Up for Debate' programme (https://upfordebate.co.uk/), which provides detailed training on effective forms of argument and presentation. It engages the students in researching and planning a debating position against other teams in the school and ultimately locally and regionally. Further up the school there are special focus weeks which provide opportunities to reinforce these skills by considering and debating issues relating to the 17 Sustainable Development Goals of the United Nations' 'Agenda 2030' (https://www.un.org/sustainabledevelopment/development-agenda/).

As we write, the school is moving into the third year of its oracy and dialogic learning strategy which involves an upward roll-out from this strong and developing Year 7 and 8 base. All departments are now required to indicate in their development plans how they will access and use the growing database of ideas and resources, including suspended timetable days, to introduce oracy groupwork activities into their particular subject areas across Years 9–13, not as a 'bolt on' but as an integral part of their teaching and learning. An innovation this year is to encourage greater parental involvement by sending out 'nudge texts' suggesting topics for discussion at home. No doubt this will all change and develop over the coming years as we gain experience and feedback from our research but a strong and resolute start has been made.

Evaluation of developments in oracy

The Executive Principal, one of the authors, and Professor Mercer collaborated to create a research tool designed to help map – and feed back into – the longer-term growth and development of oracy and dialogic group work across the school. This is based upon the 'Oracy Skills Framework' and involved turning each of the skill elements into a competence statement with an assessment grid alongside to score skill levels on a five-point scale. It yields both individual and cohort scores (tutor group, year group and school) so that we can make formative judgements about how skill levels are changing over time. Following a year of trials in 2018/9, this was introduced to Year 11 teachers in 2019/20 and, following the disruption of the Covid 19 pandemic, will hopefully be repeated in the 2020/21 academic year.

Conclusion

Significant progress has already been made with the oracy programme at the school. Using materials from Voice 21 and additional stimulus materials from 'Just Give', Pixl's 'Up for Debate' and the UN's Agenda 2030, we are slowly developing an exciting and innovative oracy curriculum framework. The research tool, devised with support from Professor Mercer, has provided staff and students with a comprehensive vocabulary around oracy and overview of its key competences. It has also enabled both staff and students to identify specific aspects of practice that are already sound and areas for improvement so that students can steadily become more aware, articulate, expressive and confident as emerging adults and citizens. As this is a project that is in 'midstream', we are still in the process of finding new results and refining our approach both on the basis of what the staff and students are telling us and our own observations. We hope that other schools, colleges and educational providers may be able to adapt and develop the framework around oracy presented in this chapter to enhance their own practice regarding speech, dialogic learning, curriculum development and citizenship education.

References

Alexander, R. (2008) *Essays on Pedagogy*, Abingdon: Routledge.

Dewey, J. ([1938] 1950) *Experience and Education*, New York: Macmillan.

Dewey, J. ([1916] 2007) *Democracy and Education*, Teddington: Echo Library.

Hopkins, N. (2019) *Democratic Socialism and Education: New Perspectives in Policy and Practice*, Dordrecht: Springer.

Mercer, N. (2019) *Language and the Joint Creation of Knowledge: The Selected Works of Neil Mercer*, Abingdon: Routledge.

8 A creative approach to supporting literacy acquisition for a young man with difficulties

Philippa Smith, Janice Wearmouth and Karen Lindley

The major question addressed in this chapter is:

- What kind of creative approach might enthuse and reinvigorate a student who is disaffected and frustrated by his own lack of progress in literacy learning?

Abstract

This chapter describes a case study of the design, implementation and evaluation of personalized provision made for one young man. Concerns had been raised about him by both teaching staff and parents, the most serious of which were writing and illegibility when reading back, retention of information as a result of slow pace, the young man's disaffection from classroom activities, and his seeming inability to engage with staff about his difficulties in literacy acquisition. None of the attempts to help him, including provision of a laptop for use in class, had been successful. In order to support the young man, it was determined by the special educational needs co-ordinator (SENCo) that, in order to move forward productively and effectively, the initial task was to help the student 'find his voice'. Once she had found a way to do this through the use of a projective interview technique, 'Talking Stones', he was able to verbalize his specific needs and interests and, in doing so, enabled the SENCo's team to help him find a creative and effective solution to overcome his barriers to literacy learning and achievement in other curriculum areas also.

Introduction

Under Section 19(d) of Part 3 of the 2014 Children and Families Act in England, young people with special educational needs and/or disabilities are entitled to access to education that enables them to 'achieve the best possible' educational and other outcomes. The school or college that a young person attends should put support in place to make sure this is happening. Not all learners are happy to be singled out for special attention, however. Sometimes this issue can be addressed by thinking creatively, finding a way to communicate with a young person and gain his/her confidence, and paying special attention to a young person's strengths and interests as well as the barriers to learning that s/he faces.

In all four countries of the UK the right of learners to self-advocacy during the process of assessing and drawing up plans to address individual difficulties in learning is enshrined in law, as, for example, in the Children and Families Act, 2014, in England. Engaging with learners' views may not always be easy, however. In many schools professionals may have met learners with whom communication is difficult. For a number of reasons, it is particularly important to understand how learners who are disaffected from school and disengaged with school learning feel about the learning environment and themselves as learners. Failure to address the issue of non-engagement with their education of significant numbers of disaffected learners costs society dearly, both in terms of reduced economic contribution in adult life and, for some, of criminal activity and prison. Following this line of thinking requires a conceptualization of the learner as active agent in his/her own learning, and of both learning and behaviour as dynamic between learner and context if students are to become active participants in schools' communities of learners (Glyn, Wearmouth and Berryman, 2006). Everyone both creates his/her own world and is created by it and by others around. If this is the case, schools need to take account of how learners make sense of their own circumstances and what impression is conveyed of others' constructions of them (Wearmouth, 2019). The questions to be asked in the current study were, first, how might the SENCo and her team engage with the young man sufficiently to understand his perception of himself and the difficulties he experienced in his literacy learning? And, second, how could this knowledge enable an approach that might enthuse him sufficiently to be prepared to try again to overcome the barriers he faced and make some progress?

Background to the study

The research study discussed in this chapter was carried out in the special educational needs and disability (SEND) department of a secondary school in the Midlands in England. The young man at the centre of the study, 'Jack', was a pre-adolescent Year 8 student from a large supportive family. He had a diagnosis of dyslexia and dyspraxia and encountered extreme difficulties with scribing and retention of information. He was an intelligent, interesting and extremely polite and compliant boy. Through discussion and agreement between the boy's mother and the special educational needs co-ordinator (SENCo), a range of strategies were put into place in the attempt to assist the young man to overcome his literacy difficulties. These included specialist writing tools and paper; coloured overlays; the assistance of a teaching assistant (TA); considered seating plans; breaks in schedules; extra time; provided written and visual guidance support and help with tasks refining fine motor skills. 'Jack' would attempt the strategies but did not seem to benefit from any of them and withdrew further from engagement. Unfortunately, this resulted in staff becoming agitated with his lack of focus and issuing behaviour points which proved to be quite counterproductive. Although 'Jack' was tolerating school, he nevertheless became disenchanted with it and associated school with negativity. It was clear that 'Jack' was not only finding it difficult to acquire and use the fundamental literacy skills he needed to make progress across the curriculum, but also that he had no real interest in any of the topics and usual strategies often used to encourage learners of his age. Where some children may react to barriers to their learning by being purposefully disruptive, 'Jack' withdrew and entered his own 'world', apparently daydreaming of things that interested him. The major difficulty associated with this was that he was unable, or chose not, to open himself to staff and so became quite an enigma. Parents attempted to offer solutions to assist his engagement, however, he seemed to take umbrage at being the object of focus and the sharing of his personal life. The SENCo and her team were determined not to give up on him, however, but to try to help him find his voice. Once this had been established, the team might be able to find some sort of incentive for him to motivate his learning. They really felt that a possible route forward for 'Jack' was the use of technology to support him with his writing, so it was imperative to find a way to enable him to open up to staff about why he was opposed to using the laptop.

Theoretical framework

The study discussed in this chapter is conceptualized within a social constructivist view of mind (Vygotsky, 1978), an approach that is pertinent to claims that pedagogies for school literacy learning should be responsive to the strengths and needs of its students and the frames of reference they bring to their school learning. The distinctiveness of this view, sometimes called 'cultural-historical psychology', is that there is an intimate connection between the learning environment and the distinguishing qualities of human psychological processes. From this perspective everything in the learning environment in schools is seen as fundamental to learning: materials, interactions between teacher and students, interactions student to student, student interactions with the learning task, the way success and failure is mediated, and so on. The underpinning of pedagogy with a socio-cultural perspective on the learning process, therefore, has a particular rationale. It enables acknowledgement of the learner's social situatedness in literacy learning in school (Kozulin, 2003), while at the same time focusing attention on the social practices that character-ize the settings in which young people's literacy learning in schools is acquired. The theory also forces a focus on the agency of the teacher as a mediator of learning who needs to adopt a responsive approach to young people's learning by recognizing and responding to the frameworks for learning brought into the school by students (Glynn *et al.*, 2006; Wearmouth, 2017), and also have a high degree of relevant specialist and pedagogical knowledge to support students' appropriation of skills and the construction of knowledge relevant to current learning activities.

Vygotsky (1978, p. 57) proposed that there are two planes where the learning process takes place: the interpersonal, that is the 'between the people' plane, and the intrapersonal, 'within the individual' plane, as s/he thinks about and reflects on new concepts and learning and appropriates psychological tools, skills and knowledge. From this perspective, personal identity as a learner in the classroom is associated with:

- the kinds of activities that students experience and in which they engage or are prevented from engaging in;
- the process of scaffolding of new learning by more expert others such as teachers and peers;
- the messages that students hear or see about themselves and their achieve-ments, or failures to achieve.

Social and cognitive development are seen as mutually facilitative and insepa-rable (Glynn *et al.*, 2006) and depend on the presence of mediators during interactions between the individual and the environment. In schools, teach-ers-as-mediators can guide and model the use of symbolic cultural tools, as, for example, language and literacy. In schools, learners' understanding increases as they participate in learning conversations on the interpersonal plane, as is illustrated in the discussion of the case study below. There is an assumption also that learning occurs through communication within relation-ships between students and staff, but in the case of this particular young man, he had yet to develop a rapport with any staff member. It became clear that a technique was required to help him verbalize his needs, ideally with one trusted member of staff.

Research focus

The aim of this study was to help the young man overcome his lack of ability and lack of interest in literacy which was proving to be a huge stumbling block in his attainment in all subjects. The hoped-for outcome was for him to develop his reading and writing to a stage where he would be able to record information in lessons in order to revisit and reflect at a later date. It was also important for him to keep a similar pace in his learning as his peers so that he could achieve positive educational outcomes.

Research design and methods

The research was designed to develop a rapport and understanding between the SENCo and 'Jack' in order to help identify the difficulties he was experiencing at school and discover why he was not engaging with any strategies offered to support him. It was already identified that his main obstacle was his difficulties in literacy acquisition and that these were creating barriers in all areas of his study. Further observation and investigation were required to identify reasons why he was not engaging in strategies offered.

The study was carried out in the manner of participant action research through a series of stages:

- investigation of the difficulties experienced and the nature of the young man's barriers to learning;
- design of appropriate solutions and strategies to engage the young man in learning;
- implementation of the strategies;
- evaluation of the project.

The interviews carried out by the SENCo with the young man were recorded and transcribed, after she had gained the requisite permissions.

Ethical considerations

Permission was sought for classroom observations and interviews with the young man from his family and from the young man himself. Consent was sought from the teacher and the head teacher for the in-class observations, and for all interviews. The young man was informed of his right to withdraw from the interview at any stage. A pseudonym has been used to refer to the young man in order to maintain anonymity.

Investigation of the young man's difficulties

The young man's difficulties were explored through a series of interviews, using a method entitled 'Talking Stones', a pedagogic tool that addresses the challenge of engaging with a student's perspective meaningfully (Wearmouth, 2004). This is a powerful projective technique originally derived from techniques related to Personal Construct Psychology. In serving as a sensitive device to support student self-advocacy, it views learners as active agents in their own learning. During an individual interview, 'Jack' was given a pile of stones of varying shapes, sizes, colours and textures and encouraged to explore his thoughts and feelings about literacy learning in school and himself in relation to it by projection onto these stones. He selected one from the pile to represent himself in school and discussed his choice. He then selected more stones to represent reading and writing at school and at home, described why the stones had been chosen, and then placed them on a large, rectangular, light-coloured cloth whose edges set a boundary to the positioning of the stones and their distance from each other. 'Jack' then interpreted the stones, their attributes and their positions in relation to each other as representing his own constructed meanings. This technique was used with 'Jack' during three 30-minute sessions with the SENCo. The sessions were arranged through discussion with him in order to engage him from the outset. He was asked to select three different lessons from which to be withdrawn and he selected English, mathematics and PE.

A thematic analysis of all data was undertaken by the researchers who had carried out the fieldwork. Participants' words are quoted verbatim below.

Findings from interviews

'Jack' was initially quite guarded and a little bemused about the stones, however, after it was explained to him, he was willing to give it a go. During the first session 'Jack' sorted through approximately ten different stones. The SENCo asked him which one would best describe him as a person. He chose a small nondescript stone. He explained his choice as:

I don't know … small and normal … I guess …

It was no surprise to the SENCo as she was not initially expecting much of a disclosure. She proceeded to ask him to choose a stone he would like to be. He selected another rather nondescript, slightly larger stone with the explanation:

Maybe I'd like to be a bit taller but still normal …

When questioned what 'normal' was, he indicated that it was when one 'didn't stand out and was left alone'. The SENCo proceeded to ask 'Jack' to choose three more stones: a stone that represented school; a stone that represented reading; and a stone that represented writing. He very quickly and without consideration chose three random stones and when asked to elaborate said:

Dunno …

At this stage he became disengaged and started fiddling with his pencil and avoiding eye contact so the SENCo offered to close the session. He responded by saying that he did not want to go back to English. The SENCo attempted to glean his reasons, however, he just shrugged and looked out of the window. They sat quietly for a further 15 minutes until it was time to go.

During the second session 'Jack' appeared more relaxed with the SENCo and even chatted a bit prior to looking at the stones. She posed the question: 'What type of stone are you at home?' 'Jack' rummaged through and selected a colourful large round stone. His reasoning was:

I like being at home because I play with my toys and do what I want ...

This opened the discussion to toys. It transpired that 'Jack' still showed an interest in toys usually favoured by younger children, mostly animal related. At this stage the SENCo approached the topic of animals which sparked a little more interest in 'Jack' than she had witnessed prior to this. She asked questions about his pets, but he soon turned the questions around and was seemingly interested in discussing the pets of the SENCo. Sensing a potential opening to developing the relationship positively, she proceeded to tell 'Jack' about her cats, dog and chickens. 'Jack' responded by chatting about chickens and explained the process of hypnotizing chickens, which resulted in both SENCo and 'Jack' having a little chuckle together. At this stage, the SENCo asked 'Jack' once again to select three stones representing school, reading and writing. He more thoughtfully selected the least attractive stones. He stated that they were not his favourite ones and neither was school. When prompted, his response was:

I like my friends and break time but I don't see the point of school. I don't like reading and I can't write ...

The SENCo asked 'Jack' if he had tried any of the help offered to him to help him write and he shrugged. She asked:

What about the laptop? Can you type?

He replied:

Yeah, a bit ...

Her response was:

Is it easier to type than write?

His answer:

Yes.

She responded by saying:

So wouldn't it be easier to type in class?

His reply was:

> Nope. I'm not doing that. I've told everyone and no one is listening ...

The SENCo proceeded to ask him:

> Have you told anyone why? You keep on saying you won't use the laptop but never why.

'Jack' replied:

> It's nobody's business.

It was clear that 'Jack' was using avoidance to stop the conversation. He became physically withdrawn by crossing his legs away from the SENCo and folding his arms. He appeared to think he was in trouble or was going to get into trouble. The SENCo assured him that this was not the case. 'Jack' relaxed and volunteered that he would feel 'like an idiot and people will laugh'.

At this stage the SENCo picked up the stone 'Jack' had originally selected as himself. She asked:

> If you had a laptop in class, would this still be the 'you' stone?

He said:

> No. It would be different and stand out and everyone would see it.

She asked him to select the stone he would be if he had the laptop and he chose a large quite rough stone. He placed it on the opposite side of the desk with distaste.

At this stage he disengaged and asked to go back to lessons. The SENCo closed by asking if he wanted to return for his session the following week. He agreed to this.

Although ending on a disgruntled note, the session had proved to be successful in identifying what was already suspected by the team. Jack knew his difficulties but his fear of standing out in a crowd far outweighed his desire to find solutions to ease them. On a negative note, however, there was still no progress in encouraging the young man to use the tools that would assist him.

The third and final session where 'Talking Stones' were used was very short but appeared to be the most beneficial of the three. 'Jack' arrived, thrilled that he was missing PE. The SENCo and he had a laugh together as he had almost forgotten the session and had changed into his kit and was dreading dodgeball. Being removed was a pleasant surprise. He said with a grin:

> Even coming here is better than dodgeball.

The SENCo asked 'Jack' to select a stone that he wished he could own and take with him. He spent a while looking and chose a smooth organic white stone. The SENCo asked him:

> If you could magically change it to anything in the world that you desired what it would be?

After a great deal of thought, he replied:

> A racing pigeon.

It was at this stage that his demeanour and interest changed dramatically. 'Jack' proceeded to chat with great vigour about racing pigeons and turned out to be most knowledgeable. Naturally, as the subject was unusual for a boy of his age, the SENCo asked many questions about the interest and the conversation opened up and exposed her to an excited and engaged young man. The SENCo asked 'Jack' if she could in any way include this love of pigeons into his learning – would it make him more engaged – to which he replied:

> Yes, of course…it's interesting and I like it.

They discussed pigeons for approximately 30 minutes after which he agreed to meet regularly to work on methods to help him conquer his worries regarding the laptop use in class if she incorporated this topic. It was almost posed as a challenge to her – a major breakthrough for both the young man and the team.

Much more could be quoted from the transcript to exemplify 'Jack's' use of the stones, but space precludes further description. However, in it, 'Jack' demonstrates how he was using the attributes of size, shape and aesthetics to describe himself and activities at school. Although the stones helped the SENCo identify his keen interest and hobby, the method largely developed and opened up the communication channels between SENCo and student. The content of his disclosures was telling and informative, however, the feeling of ownership and safety they offered him was far more beneficial to the study.

The interview transcript provides powerful evidence of 'Jack's' lack of interest in school and highlights that he wished to remain anonymous. He had constructed a view of himself as someone who blended in and wanted to remain there. He knew that if he 'flew under the radar' he would not draw any attention to his inadequacies in lessons and the trouble he faced when reading or writing. He had a sense of failure at school and felt that he was wasting his time and energies there. Coupled with his literacy issues, it indicated that school was a very sad place for him to be.

Design of intervention strategy

The SENCo recognized the need for a creative approach to re-engage 'Jack'. Being a creative art teacher she recognized and understood the importance of alternative approaches to literacy and numeracy and wanted to create a fun and exciting incentive tool to encourage 'Jack' to use technology in class to help him access and respond to text. Initially she prepared the technology for 'Jack' to get him accustomed to using it and spent a session working through the software with him. He was equipped with earphones to listen to the text if required, and could both type and use voice recognition software to ease his issues with writing. The SENCo liaised with staff and conducted a series of observations to identify the best position for 'Jack' in each classroom and asked him to choose a friend he would be comfortable sitting next to. By pre-preparing the setting and equipment with 'Jack's' input, she was removing any self-imposed barriers that he would often use as excuses. The relationship between the two of them had blossomed and her transparent approach to her plans were imperative in his participation.

Once 'Jack' was satisfied with the arrangements, the SENCo 'revealed' the incentive. She had designed a 'pigeon racing' game. The game was presented to 'Jack' as a shell of an idea in order for the two of them to design it together.

Concept of the game

The game was to be a progressive 'race' whereby each contestant would have a racing pigeon which started at the pigeon coop. Each contestant would have to complete a series of challenges to 'fly' a step closer to a cloud (See Figure 8.1).

There would be a number of clouds to reach, however, as the clouds rose in height, so the steps became more frequent and more challenging. Each step would carry a small prize if met, such as a Kinder egg or a doughnut or something from the 'prize box'. Each cloud would contain a larger prize such as a lunchtime queue jump pass for him and a friend, or time to play games on the computers at break. The final cloud contained the ultimate prize, which was for him to visit the local county Injured and Lost Racing Pigeon Rescue and become a sponsor of his own rescued pigeon. Although the prizes were a great incentive, the SENCo added an additional element of competition by joining as the second contestant. Keeping in mind it was a race, the young man would set the SENCo a weekly challenge and, if she met her objectives, she would also claim a prize. The SENCo recalled: 'I did drop his mum some hints about things that I find challenging, such as maths problems and keeping to an exercise regime!'

The tasks

The tasks were to be issued each week and the pace at which they were tackled was up to 'Jack'. Should he choose to complete a full 'cloud flight' pre-deadline (if it was an open-ended task), then that was his prerogative. Each time he completed a step, he would have to report to the Assistant SENCo who would liaise with the SENCo. He was being monitored throughout by participating teaching staff as well as teaching assistants (TAs) who were instructed to gen-

Figure 8.1 Racing pigeon game

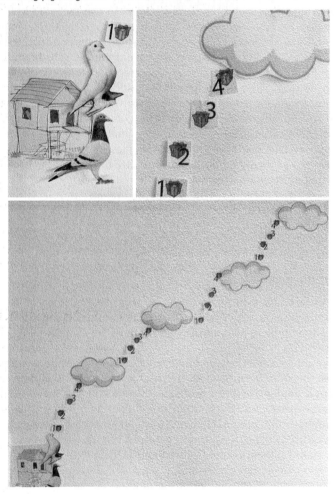

tly encourage and praise any progress he was making. Examples of the tasks were laid out as below:

- Take the laptop to English lessons for a week. He did not have to use it, but rather keep it on the desk and show that he was able to remember to collect it and return it. If he wanted to reduce the time step to two lessons – he could use the laptop to complete his tasks.
- Use the laptop in English lessons for a week.
- Continue to use it in English and take it to History lessons for a week.
- Continue to use it in English and use it in History.
- Sit a test in English using the laptop and not a scribe.

The tasks would grow alongside his progress and, if he had any setbacks, he would not be reprimanded nor would his pigeon fly backwards. It was important that his confidence was nurtured and that a careful use of mindfulness was considered throughout the process.

Implementing the strategy: playing the game

The first week, 'Jack' was a little nonplussed by the idea until he entered the SENCo's office. She had dedicated an entire wall to the game. The first session was spent in selecting the pigeons they both preferred, copying, cutting and positioning them and discussing how he felt about the first task (see Figure 8.1). 'Jack' knew that was expected of him. He acknowledged that he did not want to participate but would as he wanted to play for the rewards.

'Jack' did participate and spent the following three weeks doing really well. He reached the first cloud with what appeared to be quite a lot of ease. He realized that other students did not take much notice of his laptop and soon understood that many children across the school used different aids to assist them in learning. It wasn't, however, a miraculous success. The second round of steps heading towards the second cloud was much more challenging for Jack. He began to lose interest in the game and old habits began to emerge such as 'forgetting' to collect the laptop or refusing to use it in class. Interestingly, many of these discrepancies took place when the SENCo (also a member of the senior team) was unavailable for a session. The assistant SENCo would sit in, however, 'Jack' did not develop a rapport with her and was quite vocal about his dislike of her and a TA who was assisting. It became very apparent that he would require another mentor/support system to help maintain his focus when the SENCo was absent or required on the other campus. His tutor, who was also his maths teacher, agreed to take on the role and him meeting with 'Jack' regularly did appear to make a difference and he got back on track. His History teacher was also very good at encouraging his progress and he soon started to earn his prizes. 'Jack' soon started to develop his confidence and clearly wanted to work towards the coveted final prize.

Unfortunately, the game was not completed due to time circumstances and a bout of absence due to illness. The young man eventually moved schools for family and personal reasons and did not complete his school year at the school. He did, however, make steps to conquer his own fears and beat a barrier he had created for himself as a result of his additional learning needs.

Evaluation of strategy

From an emotional, social and mental health perspective, this method was largely successful for 'Jack'. He realized that there was more than one way of learning and that applying one's interests and strengths to learning can make a great difference. Most interestingly the data from 'Jack's' progress charts also showed a great deal of positive difference. His assignments were more legible and more easily assessed. His pace was better and his attention in class had improved. He performed better in tests using the voice recognition software and he himself recognized the benefits of using technology and how it could assist his difficulties. His attainment rose within a term primarily in English and History and also showed improvement in mathematics.

From a social constructivist view of mind (Vygotsky, 1978), it is clear that the approach was responsive to Jack's needs and strengths. The SENCo deliberately set out to listen to him and build on his expressed strengths and interests in order to develop a responsive approach to the difficulties he experienced in his literacy learning. The way she integrated his interest in pigeon racing into activities that were designed to stimulate his willingness to engage in new literacy learning, the positive rapport that developed between them and his consequent developing sense of self-efficacy – 'I can do' – serve to illustrate the fundamental importance of the SENCo's awareness of her agency in mediating his learning. She understood the significance of taking account of the frames of reference he brought with him to school; in this she acknowledged the power of a technique, 'Talking Stones', that helped him verbalize his needs so that she could scaffold his participation in learning conversations on the interpersonal plane. This was, importantly, something that, until this point, Jack had been unwilling to do. Subsequently he could begin to reflect and use appropriate literacy tools and skills that were new to him.

From a CPD perspective, this intervention was applied successfully in staff training as a case study with the hope of encouraging teachers to view their students as individuals and a means to demonstrate how a creative approach to the curriculum could positively influence learners with alternative methods of learning and understanding.

Conclusion

The creative approach to this young man's difficulties did prove to assist him in a small but effective manner. The method used was in this case successful, however, it must also be noted that there are also a number of pragmatic aspects that need to be taken into account if it is to be embedded into the curriculum. For example:

- it can only be carried out on an individual basis;
- it is time-consuming;
- it requires an understanding of counselling theory and practice.
  In terms of practice it is important to recognize that:
- true listening is an art;
- children will make decisions about people they can talk to and trust, and those they cannot;

- we know from the counselling literature that good listeners offer time, support, non-directive questions, acknowledgement of feelings, reflecting back, and such non-verbal behaviour as eye contact, sitting next to (rather than opposite, behind a desk), and a basically trusting atmosphere which communicates that it is all right to speak honestly.

These are not easy situations to create in school but with a dedicated team of professionals who advocate this type of learning it is achievable.

References

Glynn, T., Wearmouth, J. and Berryman, M. (2006) *Supporting Students With Literacy Difficulties: A Responsive Approach*, Maidenhead: Open University Press.

Kozulin, A. (2003) 'Psychological tools and mediated learning', in A. Kozulin, B. Gindis, V.S. Ageyev and S.M. Miller (eds), *Vygotsky's Educational Theory in Cultural Context*, Cambridge: Cambridge University Press, pp. 15–38.

Vygotsky, L.S. (1978) *Mind in Society: The Development of Higher Psychological Processes*, Cambridge, MA: Harvard University Press.

Wearmouth, J. (2004) '"Talking Stones", an interview technique for disaffected young people', *Journal of Pastoral Care in Education*, 22(2): 7–13.

Wearmouth, J. (2017) 'Employing culturally responsive pedagogy to foster literacy learning in schools', *Cogent Education*, 4(1), DOI: 10.1080/2331186X.2017.1295824.

Wearmouth, J. (2019) *Special Educational Needs and Disability: The Basics*, 3rd ed., London: Routledge.

The future of physical education is in the mix

Establishing the DJ as a metaphor for innovative curriculum design

Saul Keyworth and Danny Golding

Major questions addressed in this chapter are:

- How can metaphors be productively used to bring the curriculum to life in teaching?
- To what extent are educational innovations innovative?
- How far can historical traditions/thinkers inform and benefit contemporary educational practices?

Abstract

This chapter seeks to challenge the oft-cited notion that contemporary teaching practices are better and more innovative than their historical counterparts. With specific relation to physical education (PE), the chapter seeks to show how the historical legacy of both Rudolf Laban (dance) and John Dewey (OAA) has contemporary vibrancy and that the subject would benefit from embracing rather than obscuring the 'toolbox' for practice each provides. Drawing upon the notion of teacher as DJ, this chapter acknowledges the power of employing metaphors in education. In so doing, it advocates that teachers need to take responsibility for innovative curriculum design that honours past, present and future.

Introduction

Monday 10.00 a.m.: Careers appointment …

Gardener, scaffolder, sculptor, dancer, adventurer, stand-up comedian, counsellor and lighthouse operative.[1] Any thoughts? ...

I actually quite fancy being a physical education teacher by day and a DJ (Disc Jockey) by night.

Although this fictional exchange between careers advisor and student may seem a little far-fetched, the scenario is anything but trivial. Above all else, it reaffirms schools as sites of hope, exploration and transformation wherein teachers nurture 'agendas of possibility' (McLaren, 2009, p. 80). The agendas to which McLaren refers are the various threads woven to compose the educational experience, namely, pedagogies employed, theoretical insights drawn upon, activities selected, and so on. By school-leaving age, it is hoped these agendas have resonated to afford each student the competence and confidence to entertain a plethora of 'possible futures'. Sadly, research attests this does not always materialize as schools in general (Youdell, 2011) and physical education (PE) in particular (Kirk, 2010), are often-times 'troubling' spaces that reproduce rather than ameliorate social inequalities, despite policy to the contrary. By way of example, the National Curriculum for Physical Education, at its inception, noted the child came before subject with factors such as gender, race, ethnicity, sexuality, class and ability needing careful thought and action (see DES/WO, 1991a; 1991b; Penney, 2002). How has the subject been faring here? Chiming with research more recent and past, Evans (2012, p. 5) lamented, 'progress was piecemeal and painfully slow' and that physical education 'wasn't always too clever at dealing with issues of elitism, racism, sexism, disability, etc.'. In light of this, calls for change and reform have been voluminous, emanating from both the academic (e.g. Casey and Larsson, 2018) and populist (Kessel, 2016) press. Collectively these remind us that the 'world and its students have changed a great deal, yet many physical education programmes have not' (Randall and Robinson, 2016, p. 7).

This chapter begins with an overview of physical education's historical legacy and contested present and goes on to challenge the view that contemporary teaching practices are better and more innovative than their historical counterparts. It seeks to show how the legacy of both Rudolf Laban (dance) and John Dewey (OAA) has contemporary vibrancy and how the subject would benefit from embracing rather than obscuring the 'toolbox' for practice each provides.

Historical legacy: obscured practices

Engaging lenses both historical and futuristic, Kirk's (2010) *Physical Education Futures* asks, 'What futures might be possible for PE?' Despite much success, he reminds us that sometimes students leave our programmes devoid of the confidence and/or competence to embrace physically active lifestyles. Reaching somewhat of a 'historical' crossroads, Kirk (2010) presents three potential directions for the subject's traversing, the most likely in the short to mid-term being more of the same with equally differing results. The strength of 'occupational socialisation' (Lawson, 1986) and teachers' over-whelming 'love affair with sport' (Ferry and McCaughtry, 2013) are key reasons why 'sport-as-techniques' has reigned and continues to reign dominant in recent times. Kirk (1992) and Fletcher (1984) note that sport, along with a scientized outlook, began to dominate PE in the 1970s to bolster credibility and security. Issues such as gender, sexuality, race and 'class' can be overlooked and/or dismissed here (Evans and Davies, 2008; 2014) alongside the voices of those protesting to be other than 'games-persons' (Myerson, 2005). In short, there is often a disjunction between the subject's core aspirations of equitable lifelong healthy lifestyles and their materialization. Kirk (2010) bleakly warns of the danger of 'extinction' if the subject continues to remain distant to, at odds with and off the pace with societal change(s). Kirk, alongside Sykes (2011), offers radical reform as the most positive direction for engaging and equitable travel. Acknowledging teachers as lynchpins of change, Kirk calls for reform that embraces an awareness of physical culture's ongoing transformations, a desire to entertain 'new visions and voices' (Bain, 1990), both within/beyond the sporting stage, as well as becoming historically conversant with physical education's contested roots. He suggests Outdoor and Adventurous Activities (OAA) and dance are two, albeit sometimes marginal practices in PE, having considerable purchase in effecting the reforms envisioned. As specialists in these areas, this warrants our due 'care and attention' (Kirk 2010, p. xi), as does embracing the insights of experiential education visionaries such as John Dewey (1859–1952) and Rudlof Laban (1879–1958). Thinking deeply and moving freely with Dewey and Laban answers Evans' call for embracing 'alternative vocabularies, voices and ways of thinking about delivering education and PE' (2014, p. 555). Casting our gaze on their oeuvre, we seek to 'look beneath the surface appearances of progress and innovation' (Evans and Davies, 2008, p. 205) to mine the contemporary vibrancy of their insights for rich and meaningful experiences in OAA and dance.

'Oldies but goodies'

Much like Bradley (2009) describes in her personal and pedagogic relationship to Laban, we continue to live their ideas and find nourishment in the pathways, branches and new journeys their various rearticulations in practice afford. Neither is set in stone and can be creatively re-mixed for future use. Both Dewey and Laban provide a toolbox enabling movement beyond practices which are merely introductory in nature. Regrettably, with dance and OAA being marginalized in much contemporary practice, the toolbox derived from Dewey and Laban's oeuvre remains closed to many practitioners, as it was to us for many years. To counter this 'disappearance' (Kirk, 2010, p. 67) or as Hodgson and Preston-Dunlop (1995) would term it, 'forgetting and/or confusion', we re-examine and reappraise the power and potential of their work for contemporary practice. We believe it is both a shame and to the subject's detriment that both are paid 'lip service' with the mere mention of their names often eliciting 'blank stares' (Newlove and Dalby, 2004, p. 11). It is clear physical education needs to acknowledge equitable reform with valuable and timely lessons being gleaned from its rich heritage. To coin the phraseology of Killingbeck (2016, p. 101), Dewey and Laban, like vinyl records, are 'oldies but goodies' and deserve their place on the contemporary (turn)table. As Leibnitz sagely postulated, the present is saturated with the past yet pregnant with the future. Some change is undeniably happening, albeit piecemeal and often in slow motion.

The slow speed of change

Up and down the country the daily drama of physical educators berating pupils to hurry along with their changing, while donning something suitable for what ensues is commonplace. As we have been detailing, calls have been getting louder and louder for teachers to heed their own call. To what degree and how are they changing? Despite forty plus years of pro-feminist, post-structural, critical race, queer and most recently new materialist scholarship/activism, there appears to be more continuity rather than change in both outlook and practice. In an attempt to 'shake and stir' (Evans *et al.*, 1996) teachers out of this impasse, we have turned to artful practices that as Greene (2008) denotes, have the ability to open worlds of possibility that create rather than merely mirror possible worlds. Here we agree with Boler, who suggested, 'if education is a commitment to growth and change, then that change will require facing up to our investments and experiencing the discomforts of new thinking<-->*moving*' (2004, p. 199; emphasis added). To 'break with the taken for granted' (Greene, 2001, p. 5) or as Dewey (1988) coined it, movement from fixed habits to more flexible/fluid modes of being, we employ New York-based crochet artist Nathan Vincent's (2013) 'Locker Room' and Victoria Marks 'Outside In' (1994) performed by Candoco Dance Company. We have used both in our teaching as points of critical departure to begin the important process of encouraging PE teacher trainees/teachers to look at society/education as if they could be otherwise (Greene, 2001, p. vii).

Vignette: Rendering the 'familiar strange'

Nathan Vincent's (2013) 'Locker Room' is a wonderful conduit to render the 'familiar strange' (e.g. Foucault, 1985; Jeanes and De Cock, 2005) as he uses 'fiber in unexpected and unorthodox ways' (Stark, 2017). His work often evokes masculine imagery through the oft-held feminine practice/craft of crochet. In doing so, he seeks to explore 'gender permissions' and the challenges of straying from what Butler (1990) terms 'intelligible (read stereotypical/prescribed) gender displays/norms'. 'Locker Room' is a large-scale installation that encourages viewers to question their potential dis/locations with gendered norms and their embodiment and emplacement. For many, the PE changing room can be an uncomfortable, exposing and alienating space which serves to negate the joys and pleasures of moving, both within and outside PE. This can often be overlooked by and alien to PE teachers who largely experience PE practices and spaces in positive ways. Enacting 'pedagogies of discomfort' (Wolgemuth and Donohue, 2006) has the potential to create an affective engagement with feelings of inadequacy, vulnerability and the constant need to measure up to prescribed (s)expectations alongside other limiting and intersecting vectors of power. The aim here is to dislodge comfort by hopefully eliciting a heightened empathetic and caring response to those deemed Other. As one author notes through personal recollection, the changing room and PE experience thereafter were a 'strip-tease' and varied tale of embodied 'pride and prejudice' as narrowly prescribed notions of masculinity were both achieved and unmet.

Critical reflections

In this chapter, we argue that teachers, like DJs, are more productive when they have honed their capabilities to 'notice' and 'respond' to learners and variations in the educational mix – what we term 'notice-abilities' and 'response-abilities'. The *teacher as DJ* that we are envisioning needs to be *'wide-awake'* (Greene, 1995; 2001) to socio-cultural milieu, pedagogically astute, attuned to students' life-worlds as well as being a *'connoisseur'* (Eisner, 2003; 2004) of their craft. Put simply, connoisseurship denotes 'the art of appreciation' (Eisner, 2003, p. 153) and this is enhanced by the quality and diversity of one's frames of reference (Eisner, 2004; Killingbeck and Whitehead, 2015). It is useful to consider an optician's eye-glasses here and the trialling of lenses to determine one's prescription. Rather than lenses of various strength that can add clarity or haze, think of each lens as theoretical filters which provide a panoramic angle of repose illuminating a heightened perception to both what is/is not going on in our classes. Eisner posits the quality of curricular and teaching, alongside the 'intellectual significance of the ideas to which students are exposed' (2003, p. 154) can inspire, bore and/or alienate. Failing to hone our craft here will see attention wane and ultimately our dancers/learners disengaging and vacating the dance floor.

Vignette: Everyone can be a dancer

Victoria Marks' (1994) 'Outside In' performed by integrated dance company Candoco brings into critical relief Laban's notion that everyone can be a dancer. Ward-Hutchinson (2009, p. 52) posits this piece 'challenges the viewer to see dance and dancers in a different way to create an imaginative world where anything is possible'. With many PE teacher trainees/teachers professing to be neither dancers or comfortable with creativity, 'Outside In' can renegotiate a critical reflection towards poss(abilities) and unrealized potentialities for self and other. Engaging with 'Outside In' can create a sense of 'wide-awakeness' (Greene, 1995; 2001) to how bodies and selves (as in Nathan Vincent's 'Locker Room'), are socio-culturally materialized, rendered with value and made intelligible. The particular scene selected (think DJ sample) is a short duet between Kuldip Singh-Barmi and David Toole (the latter being a self-trained dancer with no legs). As the duet ends, Singh-Barmi moves towards a mirror, briefly pausing to catch his reflection. This can provoke the asking of numerous questions ranging from the superficial (measuring up to (s)expectation) to the more deep-seated and provocative (why and how are such norms constructed, policed and ultimately undone?). Singh-Barmi proceeds to lean forward with his head and torso slowly submerging deep into the mirror. This brings to mind the need for teachers to become critically reflective practitioners possessing the abilities to both 'notice' and 'respond' to the various educational dramas weaving and unfolding before them. In concert with Eisner (2004) and Killingbeck and Whitehead (2015), we note a teacher's capacity to notice and competence in response are enriched and/or hampered by the quality of tools they employ.

Engaging metaphors

Metaphors are a powerful cognitive-linguistic vehicle for enhancing learning that can be used to develop understanding and guide action. Providing gravitas to this claim, Bruner (1996) suggests that the use of metaphor is the pinnacle of higher-order thinking. This may explain why they are widely used in education (Low, 2008). Indeed, Craig (2018) argues that using metaphors is particularly pertinent to teacher education where they can be used to capture the lived experience of teaching 'to bring coherence to their knowing, doing and being' (p. 300). The skilful use of metaphors can help bridge meaning and experience (Pope and Gilbert, 1983).

Using metaphors as an established and advanced learning tool, we argue that physical educators should be empowered to draw upon the richness of obscured practices and pedagogies in crafting a 'bricolage' that views curriculum design and teaching as a creative process. We offer the metaphor of the disc jockey (DJ) to situate the PE teacher as a 'connoisseur' (Eisner, 2003; 2004), who can facilitate edutaining experiences both theoretically astute and vibrant in sight, sound and feeling. Through a thorough and detailed appreciation of past rhythms the DJ can mix new and contemporary sounds to engage the senses that resonate with future generations of learners.

Possible futures: remixed

Careers Office: 10.05 a.m.:

> So, you wish to be a PE teacher by day, DJ by night? That's great but have you ever considered combining the two? Thinking of the PE teacher as a DJ? It seems to me both desire the same goal of enthusing and captivating an audience. The DJ uses records and sounds while the teacher draws on various resources to instil and illuminate educational insights. Both need to plan, to consider what materials they use and the order in which they use them. I've dabbled a bit in both and know that when 'structure' isn't given due thought, the atmosphere can turn sour and the audience departs.

The diverse range of jobs proffered by the careers advisor have each been used 'metaphorically' to illuminate the profession of education and conduct of teachers. So, too, the student's nightly desire towards enthusing and enthralling clubbers on the dancefloor. As many view teaching as an artful endeavour (e.g. Robinson, 2014; 2020), it is not surprising parallels have been drawn between the teacher and DJ (Adams, 2013; McGregor and Mills, 2006), musician (Breault, 2006; Humphreys and Hyland, 2002), emcee (Rose, 2018) and artist (Eisner, 2003; 2004; Greene, 1995; 2001). The late (and great) Sir Ken Robinson has left behind a wonderful legacy reminding educators, both poignantly and always with good humour, that the real skill in education is finding imaginative, creative, engaging, learner-centred and memorable ways to communicate the depth of one's knowledge. As this book notes, the curriculum needs to be brought to life and lived beyond the school gates/years. In short, it should leave an abiding and inspiring imprint.

In tune with physical culture: hip hopping to justice

We believe the artful practice of the DJ has fruitful resonance to both physical education teaching and vast numbers of contemporary students. The soundtrack to the past 40 years could arguably be termed 'The Hip Hop Years' (Ogg and Upshal, 1999) with its attendant music, fashion, film and art 'becoming the dominant language of youth culture worldwide' (Rose, 2018, p. 1). Dance historian Sally Banes noted, 'hip hop was originally born of kids evolving their own social networks from crews to karate clubs, making their own dances, poetry and music, in an attempt to make a harsh, cruel and often incomprehensible city a liveable environment' (George, 1985, p. xvii). Hip hop's various elements, DJing, emceeing, graffiti art and b-boy/b-girling have each been appropriated to garner 'peace, love and unity whilst having fun' – hip hop's mantra as coined by Afrika Bambaataa. Most recently it could be reasoned hip hop has gone TikTok with the sights and sounds of this lexicon seemingly knowing no bounds. We wonder how much this passion has been harnessed in schools in general and physical education in particular.

Hip hop clearly holds potential in contributing to the socially just and transformative practices many call for in physical education (e.g. Lynch and Curtner-Smith, 2019). In tune with Sir Ken Robinson's belief that 'creative delivery' is key, Lynch and Curtner-Smith (ibid., p. 370) suggest there 'is no best way to teach social justice' and that 'teachers should find their own groove and slant for transformative practice'. Although the metaphor of the teacher as DJ has found a natural home in music education (McGregor and Mills, 2006), we believe this can usefully 'six-step' its way over to physical education where, as illuminated above, engaging and inclusive practices are the playlist of the day. Regrettably, there is evidence to suggest music education is often out of tune with the musical preferences of students (e.g. McGregor and Mills, 2006) while physical education (e.g., Kirk, 2010) has been critiqued for being 'off the pace' with many falling through its spaces.

The creative pedagogic usage of music (and its attendant lyrics) has been cited as being productive to furthering social justice agendas (Levy and Byrd, 2011; Zagerman, 2018). Although all musical genres can serve this task, hip hop has been shown to be particularly salient, not least due to its historical roots/ genesis (Hill, 2009; Rose, 2018). Of particular significance here is its purveyance of what Boogie Down Productions termed 'edutainment'. Villanueva (2020, p. 2) outlines this 'refers to the consciousness-raising capacity of hip hop delivered through a fusion of education and entertainment'. Critical hip hop pedagogies (e.g. Hill, 2009; Rose, 2018) regularly build on Freirean foundations and seek to raise consciousness via dialogic and student-centred teaching approaches. Taking impetus from student life-worlds, this enables cultural relevance and promotes engagement as education unfolds *with* rather than *on* students. In Rose's (2018) examination of one professor's critical hip hop pedagogy, the teacher likened their role to that of an emcee (MC), with the MC referring to moving the crowd, both physically and emotionally as well as the more conventional Master of Ceremony and Content. To recall the thoughts of Robinson, it is not enough to have a strong command of your subject area(s). This needs to be married to a creative, engaging, relevant and memorable delivery. Within the English educational context, mastering content and ceremony can be seen as the nuts and bolts of Teachers' Standards (DfE, 2012). Taking to the 'decks', we aspire to be masters of both content and ceremony in OAA and dance (and PE more broadly) and argue an attunement to the educational oeuvres of John Dewey and Rudolf Laban is harmonious to our intent.

Facilitating dance: employing Laban's toolbox

Laban's impact on physical education, although 'waxing and waning' (Vertinsky, 2015, p. 540) since his arrival in England in the 1930s, has been immense. Although we are specifically discussing dance here, his introduction of 'expressive forms of movement' (Vertinsky, 2009, p. 2031) has equal purchase in gymnastics alongside other creative and aesthetic elements of a broad and balanced physical education provision. Despite initially gaining popularity with female physical educators (see Fletcher, 1984), his ideas have (and continue) to hold salience to all in the profession. Sansom (2007, p. 231) notes Laban 'brought a form of literacy to dance', that served the dual purpose of elevating its status as well as opening access to all. Working within physical education it is not uncommon to hear trainees, teachers and/or pupils protest to being neither dancers nor creatively literate. Laban's movement analysis, which clearly articulates movement into its action (what), spatial (where), dynamic (how) and relationship (whom, etc.) features provides an inclusive entryway. As Laban (1988, pp. 11–12) professed, it was not 'artistic perfection or the creation and performance of sensational dances which is aimed at, but the beneficial effect of the creative activity of dancing upon the personality of the pupil'. Although many may not consider themselves dancers, this should not detract from the frequency and quality of dance offerings provided to students. To enable this to come to productive fruition, we agree that all in PE should 'learn the elements of Laban's toolkit' (Thomson, 2014, p. 14; see also Killingbeck, 2016; Smith-Autard, 2002). In practice, teachers can employ this language to compose clear and articulate 'movement tasks' affording students structure and purpose in their explorations. This is in stark contrast to the sadly all too common situation whereby students are sent away for long periods of time (e.g. 25 minutes) in which to create a sequence for performance. Laban's elements allow a more facilitated approach where constructed motifs show innovation and developments are varied and maintain interest. Composing work through short, structured tasks enables focused performance and appreciative episodes which ultimately serve to enhance the quality of work generated.

To return to the notion of teacher as DJ, McGregor and Mills (2006) postulate, equitable music education requires teachers to weave together complex threads of culture, music and pedagogy. With respect to dance education, this is afforded by Smith-Autard's (2002) Midway Model, which, since its inception in 1976, has become the 'accepted model for dance teaching' (Killingbeck, 2016, p. 100). The Midway Model exemplifies the 'meddler in the middle' approach to dance which Pickard *et al.* (2016, p. 63) explain has grown from the 'guide-on-the-side' and initial 'sage-on-the-stage'. Using a resource-based approach and drawing upon Laban's elements as a vocabulary, students' confidence and competence in composition, performance and appreciation are furnished as well as their overarching artistic, aesthetic and cultural understanding. Much as the DJ selects captivating songs/sounds, the dance teacher 'selects' from a range of resources that can (but not exhaustively include), poems, text and clips from professional works. To engage as many students as possible, selections need to be rich in breadth and balance and incorporate a range of cultural and stylistic influences. To captivate the resistant and often novice dancer, hip hop fused dance may be productive as it can potentially 'comfort' the afflicted. Once more at ease, rhizomatic roots and shoots delving into the richness of dance can be explored.

In his poignant TED talk (2015), Jonzi D of Lyrikal Fearta, questioned why hip hop was often peripheral in schools. Drawing on his own trajectory of dancing from the street corner to the stage, he queried why hip hop seemed to lack theatrical value in some quarters, and levelled 'is hip hop not quite high art enough?' Once considered peripheral to music and dance education, turntablism and urban/street dance have recently found their way onto GCSE examination syllabi as well as gracing esteemed performing venues such as the Royal Albert Hall and Sadler's Wells. In 2004, Jonzi D, in collaboration with Sadler's Wells, founded 'Breakin Convention'. Now entering its 15th year, this is an annual international festival of hip hop theatre. One of the initial acts, Boy Blue Entertainment, have grown to grace the opening ceremony of London's Olympics (2012) as well as having their (2013) production, 'Emancipation from Expressionism' form part of the current GCSE syllabi. The knowledgeable dance teacher can find many hooks in this piece with which to build their lessons/unit of work. One potential avenue could be towards exploring Laban's (1988) warning of becoming 'lop' or 'one-sided'. If one reads gender through Laban's movement analysis, in particular the dynamic register, one can see that moving directly with virtuosity and power holds a particular gender intelligibility. As for most things made, these can be unmade and made over in more fulsome ways.

As for the DJ, teachers need to select their educational samples with care and beat-match them in edutaining ways. Beat matching is the art of getting two records perfectly in sync with each other. We are broadening beat-matching to denote how theory and practice (praxis) can be married in clear, articulate and engaging ways. Here theory can critically illuminate the resources employed (such as 'Locker Room', 'Outside In' and 'Emancipation from Expressionism'), while the resources selected can breathe life into and animate theory. A deep understanding of Smith-Autard's (2002) Midway Model, Laban's movement analysis and the skillset of a DJ has much to offer the physical education teacher in composing and performing insightful dance lessons/units that students appreciate, remember and hopefully find 'moving' for the life-course.

Outdoor education and OAA

Outdoor learning has a rich and eclectic heritage evident in its prominent position in both formal and extended school curricula (Leather, 2018). In a broad pedagogical mix it might feature as a distinctive subject area exemplified by Outdoor and Adventurous Activities (OAA) in physical education (PE) or could be significantly more discreet as in informal outdoor play. There are of course many blends and possibilities for using the outdoors as a powerful learning medium. Further, these are manifested in many guises notably: outdoor education, adventure learning, the pedagogy of place, environmental learning, field studies, expeditions and residential education. This presents the teacher as DJ with a palate of genres to explore when creating engaging learning opportunities. The benefits of outdoor learning are both credible and substantial. Among contemporary findings are: improved mental health, increased well-being, enhanced socio-ecological health, self-acceptance, personal growth, autonomy and connectedness with nature (Carpenter and Harper, 2016).

Historically it is suggested that outdoor education has experienced six interlinked waves of development (Allison, 2016). These have advanced through:

exploration, personal and social development, environmental education, curriculum connections, sustainability and climate change, and intercultural education. The teacher as DJ might see these as evolving and connected musical movements enabling curiosity, collaboration and innovation. Many of these developments have not been translated into the PE curriculum, leading some to question OAA's ability to champion outdoor learning (Humberstone, 1993). Despite Ennis and Chen's (1993) recognition that PE value orientations can inculcate some of these contemporary themes, currently PE teachers may be ill prepared to embrace pedagogies and competencies needed to facilitate learning experience beyond narrowly conceived notions of physical education. Further, prescribed and restricted curriculum content may compound existing values incongruity (Chen *et al.*, 2017). High-quality outdoor education necessitates advanced skills sets that include practical knowledge drawn from social, psychological, ecological, spiritual and ecological domains. Just as the DJ needs to be fully conversant with polyphonic tones, so the outdoor facilitator needs to be deeply familiar with a diverse range of appropriate pedagogies.

Outdoor learning flourished in the period prior to the Education Reform Act (HMSO, 1988) which is demonstrated in the prolific growth of outdoor centres and specialist education advisors. From a teacher as DJ perspective, this could be seen as a 'golden period' of creativity and innovation; the 'scene' was thriving and flourishing. However, subsequently the position of outdoor education has been more contested and challenging. After considerable debate, OAA was devised as the preferred platform for outdoor learning in the formal curriculum. Initially OAA aspired to capture adventurous activities in tandem with outdoor living and travelling (Leather, 2018). However, despite the claim of being broad and balanced, it has been argued that this development creates ideological tensions between an approach to learning which, on one hand, are esoteric, progressive and learner-centred; juxtaposed with a subject at least partially driven by skill development, compartmentalization and outcome measurement (Humberstone, 1993). Within PE there has been a strong advocacy for embracing aspects of outdoor education (Stidder, 2007) but even Ofsted's (2004) report into best practice in OAA recognizes that these are highly credible, but relatively rarely optimized in PE. Further, levels of specialist expertise are identified as often low and compounded by barriers relating to risk aversion, resourcing, training and curriculum prioritizing. John Dewey (1931) recognizes such polemic dilemmas as 'educational confusion' that detracts from developing authentic and holistic learning. This is representative of a 'DJ battle' with competing styles both trying to attract a partisan and sometimes fractured audience. However, such conflicts can become harmonious and mutually supportive when stakeholders are prepared to listen.

At the heart of any DJ set is rhythm; it is Dewey and his contemporaries that provide these beats in outdoor education. Such sophisticated and widely acknowledged pedagogical philosophies have been celebrated extensively by communities of practice that exist outside mainstream physical education. Sadly these powerful voices are muted and do not always resonate in OAA or in PE in general (Thorburn and MacAllister, 2013). Drawing on a soundscape of experiential learning, Dewey (1938) identifies growth, connectivity and meaning making fostered through direct experience. Further, the transformative potential of real experience informs the work of pioneering educator Kurt Hahn whose legacy provided the template for the Outward Bound movement and the Duke of Edinburgh's award. The emphasis on learning as a progressive process also features as a central part of Kolb's learning cycle (1984), widely adopted in many outdoor programmes (Allison and Wurdinger, 2005). The DJ might think of these as core sources that are built into multiple samples in homage to the roots of the music. Dewey's (1938) notion of sequential learning and experience-based theory testing, simplified via Kolb to 'plan-do-review-apply', provides a valuable template for any aspirant DJ and more significantly a valuable tool for a dynamic PE teacher. Sadly, Thorburn (2018) observes that Dewey's work is underutilized in establishing contemporary arguments that substantiate PE's unique contribution to education. This is probably also true of the substantial body of knowledge that flourishes in outdoor education, but is rarely heard in PE and what we describe as obscured practice.

Conclusion: rewind and remix

This chapter has sought to challenge the oft-cited notion that contemporary teaching practices are better and more innovative than their historical counterparts. Our aim was to highlight the educative power of metaphor alongside the contemporary vibrancy of John Dewey and Rudolf Laban's oeuvre to physical education. We hope our suggestion that the subject would benefit from embracing rather than obscuring the 'toolbox' each provides has been tuneful. That is for the reader to decide.

Careers Office: 10.10 a.m.:

So what made you decide to be a PE teacher?

A love of moving and being in fresh air. My family are keen 'outdoorsy' types and this has rubbed off as I've a real passion for mountain biking, climbing and sailing. I'm also a huge music lover, all genres, hence the desire to be a DJ too. I say all genres, I've a particular soft spot for hip hop at the moment and am taking breakdance (b-boying) lessons as I think that's really cool. I'm going to look into parkour as well, you know, free running. I just love the coming together of music and being physically active that these cultures seem to embrace. Physical education here doesn't really buy into that. Don't get me wrong, I enjoy games but I feel they could be doing more, you know reaching out to a wider audience. I love watching old clips of how alternative physical cultures started and have transformed through the years. I find that really interesting. I want to be an informed and eclectic teacher, DJ also. I don't just want to play one record at a time, I want to mix and match and find a groove that more people feel they can tune into ...

We leave teachers with three reflective questions:

1 Do you employ the use of metaphors in your teaching? If so, which have served to be most productive and why?
2 In your own experience, to what extent would you say that educational innovations are innovative?
3 How do you feel historical traditions/thinkers can inform and benefit contemporary educational practices?

Note

1 Our esteemed colleague, Sophy Bassett-Dubsky, skilfully employs the lighthouse to illuminate effective educational practices.

References

Adams, J. (2013) 'Teachers as DJ's: making music in unlikely spaces', in T.M. Kress and R. Lake (eds) *We Saved the Best for You: Letters of Hope, Imagination and Wisdom for 21st Century Educators*, Rotterdam: Sense Publishers, pp. 69–74.
Allison, P. (2016) 'Six waves of outdoor education and still in a state of confusion: Dominant thinking and category mistakes', *Kwartalnik Pedagogiczny*, 240(2): 176–84.
Allison, P.A. and Wurdinger, S.D. (2005) 'Understanding the power, promise and peril of the experiential learning process', *Teacher Education and Practice*, 18(4): 386–99.
Bain, L. (1990) 'Visions and voices', *Quest*, 42(1): 2–12.
Boler, M. (2004) 'Teaching for hope: the ethics of shattering world views', in D. Liston and J. Garrison (eds) *Teaching, Learning and Loving*, New York: Routledge Falmer, pp. 117–31.
Bradley, K. (2009) *Rudolf Laban*, London: Routledge.
Breault, R.A. (2006) 'Finding the Blue Note: A metaphor for the practice of teaching', *Journal of Educational Thought*, 40(2): 159–76.
Bruner, J. (1996) *The Culture of Education*, Cambridge. MA: Harvard University Press.
Butler, J. (1990) *Gender Trouble: Feminism and the Subversion of Identity*, New York: Routledge.
Carpenter, C. and Harper, N.J. (2016) 'Health and wellbeing benefits of activities in the outdoors', in B. Humberstone, H. Prince and K.A. Henderson (eds), *International Handbook of Outdoor Studies*, London: Routledge, pp. 59–68.
Casey, A. and Larsson, H. (2018) 'It's groundhog day: Foucault's governmentality and crisis discourses in physical education', *Quest*, 70(4): 438–55.
Chen, A., Zhang, T., Wells, S.L., Schweighardt, R. and Ennis, C.D. (2017) 'Impact of teacher value orientations on student learning in physical education', *Journal of Teaching in Physical Education*, 36(2): 152–61.
Craig, C. (2018) 'Metaphors of knowing, doing and being: capturing experience in teaching and teacher education', *Teaching and Teacher Education*, 69: 300–11.

DfE (Department for Education) (2012) *Teacher's Standards: Guidance for School Leaders, School Staff and Governing Bodies*, London: Secretary of State for Education.

DES/WO (1991a) *National Curriculum Physical Education Working Group Interim Report*, London: DES.

DES/WO (1991b) *Physical Education for Ages 5–16: Proposals of the Secretary of State for Education and the Secretary of State for Wales*, London: DES.

Dewey, J. (1931) *The Way Out of Educational Confusion*, Cambridge, MA: Harvard University Press.

Dewey, J. (1938) *Experience and Education*, New York: Macmillan.

Dewey, J. (1988) *Human Nature and Conduct*, Vol. 14 of *The Middle Works, 1899–1924*, ed. J.A. Boydston, Carbondale, IL: Southern Illinois University Press.

Eisner, E. (2003) 'Educational connoisseurship and educational criticism: An arts-based approach to educational evaluation', in T. Kellaghan and D.L. Stufflebeam (eds), *International Handbook of Educational Evaluation*, Dordrecht: Springer, pp. 153–66.

Eisner, E. (2004) 'The roots of connoisseurship and criticism: A personal journey', in M. Alkin, *Evaluation Roots*, London: Sage, pp. e1–7.

Ennis, C.D. and Chen, A. (1993) 'Domain specifications and content representativeness of the Revised Value Orientation Inventory', *Research Quarterly for Exercise and Sport* 64: 436–46.

Evans, J. (2012) 'Physical education as porn', *Physical Education and Sport Pedagogy*, I First, 1–15.

Evans, J. (2014) 'Neoliberalism and the future for a socio-educative physical education', *Physical Education and Sport Pedagogy*, 19(5): 545–58.

Evans, J. and Davies, B. (2008) 'The poverty of theory: Class configurations in the discourse of physical education and health (PEH)', *Physical Education and Sport Pedagogy*, 13(2): 199–213.

Evans, J. and Davies, B. (2014) 'Physical education plc: Neoliberalism, curriculum and governance. New directions for PESP research', *Sport, Education and Society*, 19(7): 869–84.

Evans, J., Davies, B. and Penney, D. (1996) 'Teachers, teaching and the social construction of gender relations', *Sport, Education and Society*,1(2): 165–83.

Ferry, M. and McCaughtry, N. (2013) 'Secondary physical educators and sport content: A love affair', *Journal of Teaching in Physical Education*, 32: 375–93.

Fletcher, S. (1984) *Women First: The Female Tradition in English Physical Education*, London: The Athlone Press.

Foucault, M. (1985) *The Use of Pleasure*, New York: Vintage Books.

George, N. (1985) 'Introduction', in N. George, S. Banes, S. Flinker and P. Romanowski (eds), *Fresh: Hip Hop Don't Stop*, New York: Sarah Lazin Books.

Greene, M. (1995) *Releasing the Imagination: Essays on Education, the Arts, and Social Change*, San Francisco, CA: Jossey-Bass Publishers.

Greene, M. (2001) *Variations on a Blue Guitar: The Lincoln Center Institute Lectures on Aesthetic Education*, New York: Teachers College Press.

Greene, M. (2008) 'Philosophical insights from Maxine Greene', Presidential address, AERA, New York City.

Hill, M.L. (2009) *Beats, Rhymes and Classroom Life: Hip Hop Pedagogy and the Politics of Identity*, New York: Teachers College Press.

HMSO (Her Majesty's Stationery Office) (1988) *Education Reform Act*, London: HMSO.

Hodgson, J. and Preston Dunlop, V. (1995) *Rudolf Laban: An Introduction to His Work and Influence*, Plymouth: Northcote House.

Humberstone, B. (1993) 'Equality, physical education and outdoor education: Ideological struggles and transformative structures?', in J. Evans, *Education, Equality and Physical Education*, Lewes: Falmer Press, pp. 217–32.

Humphreys, M. and Hyland, T. (2002) 'Theory, practice and performance in teaching: professionalism, intuition and jazz', *Education Studies*, 28(1), 5–15.

Jeanes, E.L. and De Cock, C. (2005) 'Making the familiar strange: A Deleuzian perspective on creativity', paper for Creativity and Innovation Management Community Workshop, 23–4 March, Oxford.

Jonzi D. (2015) 'Hip-Hop Theatre: recognition without permission', *TEDxWarwick*, 7 May. Available at TEDx Talks youtube.com/watch?v=g10orKvya5o.

Kessel, A. (2016) *Eat Sweat Play: How Sport Can Change Our Lives*, London: Pan Books.

Killingbeck, M. (2016) 'Moving to the Midway Model: The longer-term development of dance education', in D. Kirk and P. Vertinsky (eds), *The Female Tradition in Physical Education: Women First Reconsidered*, London: Routledge, pp. 96–104.

Killingbeck, M. and Whitehead, M. (2015) 'Observation in PE', in S. Capel and M. Whitehead (eds), *Learning to Teach Physical Education in the Secondary School: A Companion to School Experience*, London: Routledge, pp. 58–66.

Kirk, D. (1992) *Defining Physical Education: The Social Construction of a School Subject in Post-War Britain*, London: The Falmer Press.

Kirk, D. (2010) *Physical Education Futures*, London: Routledge.

Kolb, D. (1984) *Experiential Learning*, Englewood Cliffs, NJ: Prentice Hall.

Laban, R. (1988) *Modern Educational Dance*, 3rd ed., rev. by L. Ullmann, Plymouth: Northcote House.

Lawson, H.A. (1986) 'Occupational socialization and the design of teacher education programmes', *Journal of Teaching in Physical Education*, 3(1): 3–15.

Leather, M. (2018) 'Outdoor education in the National Curriculum: The shifting sands in formal education', in P. Becker, B. Humberstone, C. Loynes and J. Schirp (eds), *The Changing World of Outdoor Learning in Europe*, Abingdon: Routledge, pp. 179–93.

Levy, D.L. and Byrd, D.C. (2011) 'Why can't we be friends?', *Journal of the Scholarship of Teaching and Learning*, 11(2): 64–75.

Low, G. (2008) 'Metaphor and education', in R.W. Gibbs Jr (ed.), *The Cambridge Handbook of Metaphor and Thought*, Cambridge: Cambridge University Press, pp. 212–31.

Lynch, S. and Curtner-Smith, M.C. (2019) 'You have to find your slant, your groove: One physical education teacher's efforts to employ transformative pedagogy', *Physical Education and Sport Pedagogy*, 24(4): 359–72.

McGregor, G. and Mills, M. (2006) 'Boys and music education: RMXing the curriculum', *Pedagogy, Culture and Society*, 14(2): 221–33.

McLaren, P. (2009) 'Critical pedagogy: A look at the major concepts', in A. Darder, M. Boltondano and R. Torres (eds), *The Critical Pedagogy Reader*, 2nd ed., Abingdon: Routledge, pp. 61–83.

Myerson, J. (2005) *Not a Games Person*, London: Yellow Jersey Press.

Newlove, J. and Dalby, J. (2004) *Laban for All*, London: Nick Hern Books.

Ofsted (Office for Standards in Education) (2004) *Outdoor Education: Aspects of Good Practice*, HMI 2151, London: Ofsted.

Ogg, A. and Upshal, D. (1999) *The Hip Hop Years: A History of Rap*, London: CH4 Books.

Penney, D. (2002) 'Gender policies', in D. Penney (ed.), *Gender and Physical Education: Contemporary Issues and Future Directions*, London: Routledge, pp. 103–22.

Pickard, A. Risner, D. and Pakes, A. (2016) 'Editorial', *Research in Dance Education*, 17(2): 63–6.

Pope, M. and Gilbert, J. (1983) 'Personal experience and the construction of knowledge in science', *Science Education*, 67(2): 193–204.

Randall, L. and Robinson, D.B. (2016) 'An introduction to social justice in physical education: Critical reflections and pedagogies for change', in D. Robinson and L. Randall (eds) *Social Justice in Physical Education: Critical Reflections and Pedagogies for Change*, Toronto: Canadian Scholars Press, pp. 1–13.

Robinson, K. (2014) 'Teaching is an art form, teachers are artists!', World Innovation Summit for Education (WISE), 22 August, available at: https://www.youtube.com/watch?v=Jd9zlxuNDFg (accessed 25 January 2021).

Robinson, K. (2020) 'Teaching is an art form, Suzy Barry interviews Sir Ken Robinson (Rosie Clarke)', *School News Australia*, available at: https://www.school-news.com.au/news/vale-sir-ken-robinson-teaching-is-an-art-form/ (accessed 25 January 2021).

Rose, C.E. (2018) 'What really goes on: Exploring a university-based critical hip hop pedagogy teacher education course', unpublished doctoral thesis, Teachers College, Columbia University.

Sansom, A. (2007) 'Rudolf von Laban', in J. Kincheloe and R.A. Horn Jr (eds), *The Praeger Handbook of Education and Psychology*, Westport, CT: Praeger Publishers, pp. 231–9.

Smith-Autard, J.M. (2002) *The Art of Dance in Education*, London: Bloomsbury.

Stark, D. (2017) 'An interview with Nathan Vincent, crochet artist who transforms the medium in unexpected ways', *Huffingham Post*, 6 December.

Stidder, G. (2007) 'Outdoor and Adventurous Activities in secondary schools and the development of subject knowledge amongst trainee physical education teachers in south-east England', *Physical Education Matters*, 2(3): 34–40.

Sykes, H. (2011) *Queer Bodies: Sexualities, Genders and Fatness in Physical Education*, New York: Peter Lang.

Thomson, R. (2014) 'Resource: KS4/teaching choreography as Key Stage 4 through Laban theory', *Dance Matters*, 69(Summer): 14–19.

Thorburn, M. (2018) 'Reconstructing Dewey: Habit, embodiment and health and well being', *British Journal of Educational Studies*, 66(3): 307–19.

Thorburn, M. and MacAllister, J. (2013) 'Dewey, interest, and well-being: Prospects for improving the educational value of physical education', *Quest*, 65(4): 458–68.

Vertinsky, P. (2009) 'Transatlantic traffic in expressive movement: From Delsarte and Dalcroze to Margaret H'Doubler and Rudolf Laban', *The International Journal of the History of Sport*, 26(13): 2031–51.

Vertinsky, P. (2015) 'Reconsidering the female tradition in English physical education: The impact of transnational exchanges in modern dance', *The International Journal of the History of Sport*, 32(4): 535–50.

Villanueva, G. (2020) 'You must learn: Sampling critical hip hop pedagogy in communication education spaces', *Pedagogy, Culture and Society*, online accessed 30 July 2020.

Ward-Hutchinson, B. (2009) 'Teaching from the outside in: Finding meaning in movement', *Journal of Dance Education*, 9(2): 52–60.

Wolgemuth, J.R. and Donohue, R. (2006) 'Toward an inquiry of discomfort: Guiding transformation in "emancipatory" narrative research', *Qualitative Inquiry*, 12(5): 1022–39.

Youdell, D. (2011) *School Trouble: Identity, Power and Politics in Education*, London: Routledge.

Zagerman, J.M. (2018) 'Using song lyrics in teaching an undergraduate statistics course', unpublished doctoral thesis, University of New England.

10 Bringing the physical education curriculum to life for all children and young people

Paul Sammon and Ian Roberts

Major questions addressed in this chapter are:

- What is the purpose of a physical education curriculum with which you are familiar?
- Does the curriculum provide meaningful and inspiring learning experiences for all children and young people?
- To what extent are all children and young people challenged and supported to achieve their full potential in physical education?

Abstract

This chapter considers how the physical education curriculum can be constructed to equip all children and young people with the necessary knowledge, skills and values to lead active lifestyles, a key aim of the National Curriculum for Physical Education. A primary intention is to advocate physical literacy as the aspirational intent of the physical education curriculum to help prepare all children and young people to lead active lifestyles. Further, the chapter argues for a broad and balanced curriculum offer, where all children and young people are challenged, engaged, included and inspired to achieve their full potential in physical education.

Introduction

In this chapter, we consider how the physical education curriculum can be constructed to help equip all children and young people with the necessary knowledge, skills and values to lead active lifestyles, a key aim of the National Curriculum for Physical Education (DfE, 2013). A primary intention is to advocate physical literacy, which can be described as 'the motivation, confidence, physical competence, knowledge and understanding to value and take responsibility for engagement in physical activities for life' (IPLA, 2017), as the key aim of physical education and to discuss some of the implications of adopting this particular aim. We also consider the importance of providing authentic, meaningful and high-quality learning experiences in physical education through a broad and balanced curriculum offer, where all children and young people are supported and challenged to achieve their full potential. Finally, we provide a detailed example of how teachers might plan a physical education curriculum so that it is child-centred and focuses primarily on developing learning, rather than on teaching the activity content.

The purpose of physical education

In the UK, the Association for Physical Education (afPE) advocates that physical education 'involves both *learning to move* (i.e. becoming more physically competent) and *moving to learn* (e.g. learning through movement, a range of skills and understandings beyond physical activity, such as cooperating with others)' (Harris, 2020, p. 4). While the concept of *learning to move* highlights the subject's unique position within the school curriculum of prioritizing physical development (Harris, 2018), it is contended by Bowler *et al.* (2020) that this idea risks treating the body and mind as separate entities. The second concept, *moving to learn* emphasizes physical education's undoubted potential to nurture a wide range of life skills, yet Kirk (2010) argues that this simultaneous pursuit of diverse learning goals has led to inconsistency with regards to the subject's specific purpose. We further propose that having multiple aspirations can result in a lack of clarity on physical education's uniqueness in the school curriculum of helping to prepare children and young people for active lifestyles. That said, there are repeated claims that the subject has remained largely unsuccessful in motivating young people (and adults) to adopt active lifestyles (Armour, 2010; Cale *et al.*, 2016; Carse, 2015; Haerens *et al.*, 2011). This is problematic considering physical education's relatively low status and increased marginalization in the school curriculum, when compared with core subjects such as English and Mathematics. For instance, research conducted by the Youth Sport Trust in England has revealed 38 per cent of secondary schools have cut timetabled physical education for 14–16-year-olds since 2012, with examination pressures, additional time for core subjects and staffing cuts cited as key factors (Youth Sport Trust, 2018). In primary schools, despite the ring-fenced PE and Sport Premium funding which has been allocated by the UK government since 2013, the situation is arguably worse, with the 'outsourcing' of curriculum physical education to external providers common practice. Consequently, many children experience a poor quality and narrow physical education experience delivered by adults other than teachers, who, Harris (2018) suggests, often lack the pedagogical knowledge and skills to successfully meet their needs.

McClennan and Thompson (2015) advocate that physical education is the most effective means of developing pupil attitudes, values, knowledge and understanding for lifelong engagement in society. More specifically, it is argued that physical education must provide learners with the necessary knowledge and skills to prepare them for a lifetime of physical activity (Heidorn, Weaver and Beighle, 2016). This argument links closely with the concept of physical literacy defined earlier, which Dudley (2015) explains should be viewed as an umbrella concept encompassing the knowledge, skills and values related to taking responsibility for purposeful movement across the life course. Moreover, physical literacy is viewed by UNESCO (2015) as one of three core aspects of inclusive quality physical education, underlining its importance in supporting children and young people to adopt active lifestyles. There is a wealth of evidence demonstrating that a focus on physical literacy in schools can have many cognitive, physical, psychological and social benefits. For example, research shows that the most effective physical activity interventions on cognitive development are curriculum physical education programmes which promote physical literacy (Alvarez-Bueno *et al.*, 2017). It has also been reported by Sport England (2019) that developing physical literacy can lead to more active, happier and resilient children and young people.

In providing a justification for adopting physical literacy, Taplin (2011) proposes that it is based on a strong philosophical platform and will help teachers in their planning and teaching of physical education. Physical educators, however, need to have a clear understanding of what physical literacy is (and is not) and their specific role in its development. Physical literacy is not about teaching children and young people to play sport, nor is it a teaching strategy, but rather it is an inclusive concept with each individual on their own, unique journey. Consequently, *every* child and young person should have the opportunity to develop their physical literacy during school physical education. Whitehead (2010) suggests that attributes such as confidence and motivation need to be carefully nurtured alongside the development of knowledge and physical competence, as part of a well-planned and progressive physical education curriculum. Thus, if the aspiration, or intent, for a curriculum is to develop physical literacy, then inclusion must be at its heart, underpinned by adaptive teaching in a caring and supportive learning environment.

The increased focus on schools' curriculum offer and the subsequent impact on learning in the recently revised Education Inspection Framework in England (Ofsted, 2019) has presented teachers with an excellent opportunity to reflect on how their pupils will engage with the curriculum. According to this framework, 'good intent' (i.e. the knowledge and skills to be developed at each stage) has the following four features. It is:

- Ambitious for all pupils
- Broad and balanced

- Coherently planned and sequenced
- Successfully adapted, designed and developed for pupils with special educational needs and disabilities (SEND) (Ofsted, 2019).

When considering these four features, it is important for teachers to carefully examine whether their physical education curriculum intentions reflect the overarching school curriculum philosophy. Furthermore, is the curriculum sufficiently flexible, broad and balanced to support all pupils to develop relevant knowledge and skills and ultimately achieve success? In the next section, we hope to answer these questions by explaining how teachers can effectively plan and implement a physical education curriculum.

Planning and implementing a physical education curriculum

When planning a physical education curriculum, there are a number of questions that need to be considered. These include whether the curriculum reflects statutory requirements and how does whole school curriculum planning translate into coherent and progressive sequences of learning both within and between Key Stages? It is also important to consider to what extent school senior leaders and governors can clearly articulate how physical education fits into the wider planned learning experience for children and young people. We now introduce five key principles (Specific, Pedagogy, Assessment, Content, Extending) which collectively we have labelled the SPACE acronym, and explain how these principles can be employed to help design a physical education curriculum.

Specific

The first key principle is to ensure that the curriculum is specific to a particular school setting. There is a global intention that schools provide a broad and balanced curriculum, but how that is implemented varies from school to school, depending on a range of factors, some of which are related to pupils' needs, and some around interpretation of guidance and the priorities of the school-based decision-makers. Schools must plan and implement their curriculum provision to reflect their own unique context and circumstances. Yet, it is important to stress that the curriculum has a profound impact on what children and young people will get out of their educational experience (Spielman, 2019). Indeed, we argue that what, and how, pupils learn can profoundly affect the rest of their lives, and this applies to physical education along with all other aspects of the school offer. The potential curriculum content in physical education is vast, so the manner in which schools manage coverage varies. As outlined earlier, one potential aspiration is to develop a physically literate generation of young people, who possess the knowledge, skills and values to lead active lifestyles when they leave formal education. Consequently, teachers must create a physical education curriculum that is both specific to their school context, but also aspires to provide all pupils with access to relevant content that will enhance their life chances.

Pedagogy

The second key principle to consider when planning and implementing a physical education curriculum concerns pedagogy, which is often described simply as the act of teaching. In other words, how teachers teach the curriculum content to their pupils. The European Commission (2008) identified that innovative learning theories and new perceptions of physical education need to be considered, evaluated and implemented in order to make the subject meaningful for children and young people in the twenty-first century. Metzler (2011) claims that historically when planning physical education curricula, the 'organising centre' has predominantly been activity content, which then becomes the key factor in determining how to teach. Typically, this has resulted in teachers concentrating on the development of their pupils' technical skills in different activity areas, such as athletics, games and gymnastics, over short units of learning. Despite concerns that this multi-activity approach allows insufficient time for pupils to develop their knowledge and skills, especially in the context of achieving health-related outcomes (Armour and Harris, 2013; Kirk, 2010), the approach remains dominant in physical education circles. One suggestion for this continued dominance is that many teachers are themselves products of a multi-activity approach and go on to replicate it in their own practice. Furthermore, it is sometimes argued that designing the curriculum in this manner affords pupils breadth of experience across a wide range of different activities and also prevents boredom (Sammon, 2019). However, drawing on Kirk (2012), we firmly believe that planning a curriculum which is a mile wide, but an inch deep, fails to allow sufficient time to master concepts and consequently results in a poor learning experience for many children and young people in physical education.

Pedagogical models or 'models-based practice' provide an alternative approach to curriculum design that moves away from a multi-activity approach. It is claimed that pedagogical models, such as Teaching Games for Understanding, Sport Education, Co-operative Learning and Health-Based Physical Education provide an evidence-informed framework, or blueprint, for teachers to design local curricula in order to facilitate the achievement of specific learning outcomes (Bowler and Sammon, 2020; Casey and MacPhail, 2018; Haerens *et al.* 2011; Kirk, 2010; Metzler, 2011). The foundations of such design specifications include a central theme and key learning goals, closely aligned with subject content and teaching strategies. Each model has a number of distinct critical features to guide teaching and learning and to support the achievement of the specific learning goals. Despite warnings that some pedagogical models are too complex to implement well, Casey and MacPhail (2018) have endorsed their potential to augment practice in physical education, such as promoting learning across multiple domains.

Assessment

The third key principle we propose when planning physical education curricula is about the contested area of assessment. There is much debate around what constitutes effective assessment practice in physical education, but essentially it should help all children and young people 'to become competent, confident, creative and reflective movers' (Physical Education Expert Group, 2014, p. 2). When reflecting on assessment practice, a number of key questions to consider include whether it matches the purpose of physical education, is embedded throughout the curriculum and the way in which it reveals learning. More specifically, if we propose that developing physical literacy is our main goal as physical educators, then it is important to plan clear learning intentions, or outcomes, linked to the National Curriculum for Physical Education (NCPE) (DfE, 2013) and create developmentally appropriate and sequenced learning activities which will support our learners to achieve this goal. Indeed, working back from the NCPE end of Key Stage statements and aligning incremental outcomes is essential.

Hay and Penney (2013) suggest that adopting a life-wide approach to curriculum, pedagogy and assessment is critical for developing a life-long learning orientation. Thus, it is vital to ensure that there is sufficient breadth and depth when assessing learning in physical education. This may be achieved by providing authentic contexts for all children and young people to demonstrate their learning across three broad domains such as: *Head* (cognitive and creative skills), *Heart* (attitudes and behaviours) and *Hands* (physical skill or motor development), as advocated by afPE in the UK. These domains offer a starting point in curriculum design, especially in terms of providing an overview of the knowledge and skills to be learned, before then aligning both success criteria and appropriate content in order to best facilitate attainment of the respective learning intentions. Alternatively, some teachers may wish to plan their assessment in physical education to reflect whole school core values such as commitment, creativity, empathy, honesty and resilience, to name but a few examples.

Unlike summative assessment, which assesses pupils' knowledge and skills over a period of time, Assessment for Learning (AfL), or formative assessment, refers to any activity that guides learning (Wiliam, 2018). In other words, one might suggest that the primary function of AfL is to *improve*, rather than merely *prove*, learning. Consequently, AfL should be embedded in everyday practice to both continuously inform teaching and to improve pupil learning. Drawing on the work of Wiliam (2018), this will specifically involve employing strategies such as clarifying and sharing learning intentions with pupils, checking for understanding through questioning, providing specific feedback that moves learners forward and encouraging pupils to support each other's learning. Indeed, we argue that centrally involving pupils in the assessment process is essential for them to gain a sense of ownership over their learning and also in developing their understanding of concepts.

Content

With the key learning goals, pedagogy and assessment strategies established, the fourth principle when planning curricula for physical education involves deciding on the actual content. We recommend that this should start with the youngest age group in the specific school context, consider the threshold concepts independently from the other year groups and then begin to make connections between the learning outcomes. The National Curriculum for Physical Education (DfE, 2013) is clear and succinct in the expectations for children at the end of each Key Stage. For example, at Key Stage 1 (KS 1):

> Pupils should continue to develop fundamental movement skills, become increasingly competent and confident and access a broad range of opportunities to extend their agility, balance and co-ordination, individually and with others. They should be able to engage in competitive (both against self and against others) and co-operative physical activities, in a range of increasingly challenging situations.

> (DfE, 2013, p. 1)

The effective attainment of the National Curriculum end of Key Stage expectations will provide evidence that learners have developed the expected knowledge and skills for the respective stage of their education. Frapwell (2015) further suggests that the end of Key Stage expectations can be broken down into learning concepts and mapped across the three domains described earlier i.e. *Head, Heart* and *Hands* (see Table 10.1), although he does stress that they

Table 10.1   Learning concepts for KS 1

Hands – Physical (psychomotor abilities)

- Develop fundamental movement skills
- Become increasingly competent and confident and access a broad range of opportunities
- Extend agility, balance and co-ordination, individually and with others
- Engage in competitive (against self and others) and co-operative physical activities in a range of increasingly challenging situation

Head – Thinking (cognitive skills)

- Able to make simple decisions and be aware of what they need to do to improve
- Be creative when using and developing skills and tactics in simple sequences and activities

Heart – Situational (socio-emotional adaptations):

- Able to engage in competitive (against self and others) and co-operative physical activities in a range of increasingly challenging situations
- Keen to participate in activities and clubs both in school and in the wider community

Table 10.2   Learning and teaching outcomes for KS 1

I can copy steps and actions with some control and co-ordination	I can stop/catch/strike a ball with control and accuracy	I can copy individual and whole body movements with some control and co-ordination
I can link individual and whole body movements together	I can pass a ball to someone else and receive a ball when moving	I can link individual and whole body movements together
I can watch others work and choose actions	I can take part in sending and receiving activities with a partner	I can watch others work
I can recognize how to move in space and I can talk about ways to keep healthy	I can talk about exercising, safety and short term effects of exercise	I can recognize and negotiate space and I can handle small and/or low apparatus safely

should be viewed as 'interwoven categories, reflecting the integrative or relational nature of learning and progress' (p. 54).

Vignette: Constructive alignment' in establishing learning and teaching outcomes

Table 10.2 shows an example of the learning and teaching outcomes that we have created through the breaking down, and sequential interpretation of, the attainment target. Frapwell (2015) refers to this cross-referencing process as 'constructive alignment'. We would then align this into unit intentions and lesson outcomes/content. So, for example, we suggest that 'copying steps and actions with some control and co-ordination' could be best taught through the area of dance in a physical education programme at KS 1. These outcomes will obviously be co-constructed with others, such as children 'linking individual and whole body movements together' or 'comparing and improving performances with previous ones'.

What must be stressed is that these outcomes should be established prior to deciding the content or context through which they will be taught, and not the other way round. Indeed, we advocate that this process is conducted sequentially when planning curricula for each Key Stage in your particular school context.

Alongside the Key Stage attainment target, previously referred to, the National Curriculum for Physical Education recommends that all pupils should be taught to do the following:

- master basic movements including running, jumping, throwing and catching, as well as developing balance, agility and co-ordination, and begin to apply these in a range of activities;

- participate in team games, developing simple tactics for attacking and defending;
- perform dances using simple movement patterns. (DfE, 2013, p. 1)

Teachers must ensure that a variety of carefully selected activities are offered, but the real alignment happens when unpacking the learning outcomes to create unit foci.

Unit activity selection

In Table 10.2, we propose that column one would be the learning intentions met through Dance-type activities, column two through Multi-Skills/Games-based activities and column 3 through the area of Gymnastics and Athletics-type activities. Once all of the learning and teaching outcomes, or intentions, have been established for a year group and/or a Key Stage, the challenge is to consider the most suitable content to support and challenge all pupils to achieve those outcomes. The integration of the curriculum is of paramount importance and these outcomes would constantly connect with other units and activities. This will enable teachers to plan units which sequentially align to create a dedicated scheme of learning across the year/Key Stage. Figure 10.1 illustrates how a Key Stage 1 unit focused on developing fundamental movement skills has been designed in this way. The unit shows from right to left, what the learning outcomes are for the unit, the type of activities selected to meet those criteria, and the learning objectives. These have been deliberately aligned into the three learning domains, but the connections must not be ignored.

A unit of learning would be developed for each block that sits within the curriculum map, and these units would be integrated sequentially into year wide schemes of learning, rather like a jigsaw. Figure 10.2 shows how this might look in practice with a scheme of learning for Year 1, where the unit from Figure 10.1 is the first area of learning in the Autumn term.

The planning process is repeated for each year group in turn and must consider progression and coherence, with concepts and themes revisited and built upon over time. Each scheme of learning aligns to create an integrated curriculum map, where connections can be made both vertically and horizontally, and the learning concepts can be effectively developed.

Extending

The fifth key principle when planning curricula for physical education involves extending the offer so that all children and young people can further develop their knowledge and skills. Some areas to reflect on include how to promote out-of-class learning opportunities, how inclusive is the extra-curricular or enrichment programme that is offered and how to embed cross-curricular links with other areas of the school curriculum. We argue that if physical education is to be effective in preparing children and young people to lead active lifestyles, then they must be taught how to be active out of class. Consequently,

Figure 10.1 Example of Key Stage 1 Games/FMS Unit

Key Stage	1	Overaching theme for 'unit of work':	Area of activity: Games/Fundamentals	
Year group	1			

Session	Learning objectives (what they will learn) — INTENT	Learning activities (how we will teach this) — IMPLEMENTATION	Learning outcomes (what we will see/hear) — IMPACT
Physical (Active learning or doing)	To develop control and co-ordination in large and small movements and handle equipment effectively	Activities that involve sending and receiving a ball by rolling, throwing, bouncing. Aiming at a target,	I can stop/catch/ strike a ball with control and accuracy
Thinking (Cognitive)	To move confidently in a range of ways, safely negotiating space and try new activities	Activities that encourage experimenting and trying out a variety of ways including a bounce, and movement with and without the ball	I can pass a ball to someone else and receive a ball when moving
Situational (Social and emotional)	To play co-operatively, taking turns with others, follow instructions involving several ideas or actions. They work as part of a group and understand and follow the rules	Throwing and catching activities requiring increasing control and sending a ball to partner / target	I can take part in sending and receiving activities with a partner

Additional notes:
Resources: Cones, variety of balls, bean bags, hoops, thrown down spots/markers
Links to other topics: Being safe with equipment. Working with a partner. Counting and key word vocabulary

Figure 10.2 Scheme of learning example

		PE Scheme of Learning **Key stage: 1** **Year Group: 1**
Considerations/ rationale for programme		In Year 1, the children build upon the foundations set through the achievement of their Early Learning Goals for physical development in EYFS. They will begin to learn Fundamental Movement skills that will support their learning in all PE units of work as they progress through the school as well as build a foundation of skills such as the ability to thrown and catch as well as to strike a ball with different implements. They will be challenged to learn sample vocabulary such as 'teammate' and 'opponent'. The children should also use these sessions to identify what is good about theirs or a friend's performance and identify simple steps to improve their performances. PE lessons will afford them the chance to work independently or in groups. Gymnastics and Dance sessions allow the children the chance to copy and remember actions and moves as well as improve their control and spatial awareness. Children will also learn the basic shapes and different ways to travel high or travel low. Throughout all learning, the children should be active and display enthusiasm and motivation.

Hour (based on 2 x 1hr sessions per week)	**Autumn**		**Spring**		**Summer**	
Hour 1	Fundamental Movement Skills	Throwing & Catching	Dance - copy and repeat 6 basic actions in sequence	Gymnastics - basic shapes & High/Low travelling	Multi - Skills	Bat & Ball Skills
Hour 2						

teachers should signpost opportunities for physical activity both throughout the school day and also beyond the school gates. Research (Bauman *et al.*, 2012; Biddle *et al.*, 2015) has highlighted the positive influence active parents have on their children's activity levels and illustrates the importance of teachers working closely with families and their local community to support the adoption of active lifestyles.

We firmly believe that a well-planned, inclusive and embracing extra-curricular programme has the potential to consolidate and extend the knowledge and skills that are being developed in physical education. However, it must be stressed that all children and young people should be able to access these learning opportunities in the extended curriculum, and not just a minority of already physically competent individuals. To this end, we recommend that the focus of any extra-curricular programme should be on motivating and inspiring all pupils to lead active lifestyles, through offering a rich diet of different activity types (i.e. individual, leadership and team) and contexts (i.e. recreational and competitive), which are regularly reviewed in consultation with all stakeholders.

Finally, physical educators need to work closely with other colleagues in school to ensure that opportunities for cross-curricular learning are initially embedded in the curriculum and subsequently realized. We envisage that engaging in this collaborative work will help to provide a more cohesive educational experience for all children and young people. Some specific examples of this extended learning across the curriculum could involve pupils performing a song to movement during Music lessons, comparing heart rate changes in Science and exploring health and physical activity trends in different countries as part of the Geography curriculum.

Conclusion

In this chapter, we have considered how the physical education curriculum can be constructed so that *all* children and young people receive an enjoyable, meaningful and memorable learning experience. More specifically, the development of physical literacy has been positioned as a key aim to help equip learners with the necessary knowledge, skills and values to lead active lifestyles. We have stressed the importance of physical education as part of a broad and balanced school curriculum, especially given its potential to enhance children's health through movement contexts. At a time when there are serious concerns for the well-being of children and young people in our society, we argue that this could not be more critical.

References

Alvarez-Bueno, C., Pesce, C., Cavero-Redondo, I., Sanchez-Lopez, M., Martínez-Hortelano, J.A. and Martinez-Vizcaino, V. (2017) 'The effect of physical activity interventions on children's cognition and metacognition: A systematic review and metaanalysis', *Journal of the American Academy of Child and Adolescent Psychiatry*, 56(9): 729–38.

Armour, K. (2010) 'The physical education profession and its professional responsibility…or…why "12 weeks paid holiday" will never be enough', *Physical Education and Sport Pedagogy*, 15(1): 1–13.

Armour, K. and Harris, J. (2013) 'Making the case for developing new PE-for-Health pedagogies', *Sport, Education and Society*, 65(2): 210–19.

Bauman, A.E., Reis, R.S., Sallis, J.F., Wells, J.C., Loos, R.J., Martin, B.W. and Lancet Physical Activity Series Working Group (2012) 'Correlates of physical activity: Why are some people physically active and others not?' *The Lancet*, 380(9838): 258–71.

Biddle, S., Mutrie, N. and Gorely, T. (2015) *Psychology of Physical Activity: Determinants, Well-being and Interventions*, 3rd ed., London: Routledge.

Bowler, M., Newton, A., Keyworth, S. and McKeown, J. (2020) 'Secondary school physical education', in S. Capel and R. Blair (eds), *Debates in Physical Education*, 2nd ed., London: Routledge.

Bowler, M. and Sammon, P. (2020) 'Health-based physical education: a framework for promoting active lifestyles in children and young people Part 1: Introducing a new pedagogical model for health-based physical education', *Physical Education Matters*, 15(3): 60–63.

Cale, L., Harris, J. and Duncombe, R. (2016) 'Promoting physical activity in secondary schools: Growing expectations, "same old" issues?' *European Physical Education Review*, 22(4): 526–44.

Carse, N. (2015) 'Primary teachers as physical education curriculum change agents', *European Physical Education Review*, 21(3): 309–24.

Casey, A. and MacPhail, A. (2018) 'Adopting a models-based approach to teaching physical education', *Physical Education and Sport Pedagogy*, 23(3): 294–310.

DfE (Department for Education) (2013) 'National Curriculum in England: physical education programmes of study', available at: https://www.gov.uk/government/publications/national-curriculum-in-england-physical-education-programmes-of-study (accessed 25 January 2021).

Dudley, D.A. (2015) 'A conceptual model of observed physical literacy', *The Physical Educator*, 72(5).

European Commission (2008) *EU Physical Activity Guidelines: Recommending Policy Actions in Support of Health-Enhancing Physical Activity*, Brussels, European Commission.

Frapwell, A. (2015) *A Practical Guide to Assessing Without Levels*, Worcester: Association for Physical Education.

Haerens, L., Kirk, D., Cardon, G. and De Bourdeaudhuij, I. (2011) 'Toward the development of a pedagogical model for health-based physical education', *Quest*, 63: 321–38.

Harris, J., (2018) 'The case for physical education becoming a core subject in the National Curriculum', *Physical Education Matters*, Summer: 9–12.

Harris, J. (2020) 'Association for Physical Education Health Position Paper', available at: https://www.afpe.org.uk/afpe-2020-health-position-paper/ (accessed 7 September 2020).

Hay, P and Penney, D. (2013) *Assessment in Physical Education: A Sociocultural Perspective*, London: Routledge.

Heidorn, B., Weaver, G. and Beighle, A. (2016) 'Physical activity and physical education: A combined approach', *Journal of Physical Education, Recreation & Dance*, 87(4): 6–7.

International Physical Literacy Association (2017) 'Definition of physical literacy'. Available at: https://www.physical-literacy.org.uk/ (accessed 7 September 2020).

Kirk, D. (2010) *Physical Education Futures*, London: Routledge.

Kirk, D. (2012) 'What is the future for physical education in the 21st century?' in S. Capel, and M. Whitehead (eds), *Debates in Physical Education*, London: Routledge, pp. 220–31.

McClennan, N. and Thompson, J. (2015) *United Nations Quality Physical Education (QPE): Guidelines for Policy Makers*. Available at: https://unesdoc.unesco.org/ark:/48223/pf0000231101 (accessed 1 September 2020).

Metzler, M.W. (2011). *Instructional Models for Physical Education*, 3rd ed., Scottsdale, AZ: Holcomb Hathaway.

Ofsted (2019) 'Ofsted Inspection Framework'. Available at: https://assets.publishing.service.gov.uk/government/uploads/system/uploads/attachment_data/file/801429/Education_inspection_framework.pdf (accessed 1 September 2020)

Physical Education Expert Group (2014) 'Guidance on Assessment: National Curriculum'. Available at: http://www.afpe.org.uk/physical-education/guidance-on-assessment/ (accessed on 25 January 2021).

Sammon, P. (2019) 'Adopting a new model for Health-Based Physical Education: The impact of a professional development programme on teachers' pedagogical practice', PhD thesis, Loughborough University, https://doi.org/10.26174/thesis.lboro.8299685.

Spielman. A. (2019) 'Education inspection framework 2019. Inspecting the substance of education', London: OFSTED. Available at: https://www.gov.uk/government/consultations/education-inspection-framework-2019-inspecting-the-substance-of-education (accessed 25 January 2021).

Sport England (2019) 'Active Lives: Children and Young People Survey Academic Year 2018/19'. Available at: https://www.sportengland.org/know-your-audience/data/active-lives#report_archiveaccess_%20the_data (accessed 1 September 2020).

Taplin, E. (2011) 'Physical literacy: An introduction to the concept', *Physical Education Matters*, 6(1): 28–30.

UNESCO (2015) 'Quality Physical Education (QPE): Guidelines for policy makers', Paris: UNESCO.

Whitehead, M. (2010) *Physical Literacy Throughout the Lifecourse*, London: Routledge.

Wiliam, D. (2018) *Embedded Formative Assessment*, 2nd ed., Bloomington, IN: Solution Tree Press.

Youth Sport Trust (2018) 'Research finds whistle being blown on secondary PE'. Available at: https://www.youthsporttrust.org/news/research-finds-whistle-being-blown-secondary-pe (accessed 7 September 2020).

Part 4

Making it real

Teaching and learning in authentic contexts and, therefore, making the curriculum meaningful in real-life contexts, can be very important in encouraging young people to engage with their learning. Chapter 11 begins this Part by considering the benefits of experiencing subject content through a variety of situations and the limitations to understanding when 'perfect' situations are used. Relating to the National Curriculum, the author discusses how teaching with real-world examples helps to develop problem-solving skills in mathematics, enquiry skills for English, science, geography and history. Chapter 12 continues the theme of authenticity by considering the role and purpose that a quality Forest School education has within the National Curriculum. It discusses the contribution Forest School can make to the holistic development of a child, to the curriculum and to enquiry-based learning. Following this discussion, Chapter 13 notes the complex heterogeneity that characterizes mainstream classrooms in the United Kingdom and that requires novel teaching and learning approaches to bring the curriculum to life at a time of many socio-political tensions. This intricate context is characterized by a growing number of students who are competent in two or more languages. The author focuses on strategy-based instruction, but within a social constructivist understanding of learning through collaboration, to provide generalist teachers with the skills necessary to develop their multilingual awareness and promote multilingual literacies.

11 Real-world contexts and teaching

Mieka Harris

Major questions addressed in this chapter are:

- How real are the real-life examples we provide students with to help explain or justify why they are learning something? Do they involve perfectly rectangular rooms that need regular shaped furniture, journey planning on traffic-free roads or plants growing in a garden that has a constant temperature?
- Does contextual teaching only sit within certain subjects of the National Curriculum?
- Is there time in a school day to teach about real-world applications of the National Curriculum?

Abstract

This chapter considers the benefits of experiencing subject content through a variety of contexts and discusses the limitations to understanding when 'perfect' situations are used. Where real-life examples cannot be easily identified or used, the chapter discusses the strategy of exploring the wider practical applications of the curriculum knowledge to develop subject contextualization. This includes examining what cross-curricular learning actually means, the use of manipulatives to create practical lessons and the role of alternative learning environments. Using real-life examples develops skills beyond the subject-specific ones and helps students create a more realistic understanding of the world; such examples do, however, mean that answers are not always 'nice and neat', and so the chapter also offers strategies to address this.

Introduction

Replicating real-world examples in the classroom can be tricky, but it is not impossible. By using a context, the lesson feels less contrived or simulated and more like an opportunity to explore the application of knowledge. Students learn to see why their subjects are useful in a variety of environments and can therefore relate more to the purpose of learning it. Many of us, as teachers, try to replicate real life in the classroom, fitting it into a single lesson and making sure the learning objectives for that lesson in the sequence of learning are met. However, in doing so, we are forced to make changes or assumptions as to what would actually happen outside the school grounds and, before we know it, we have created an artificial situation which the students will see right through!

This chapter begins by outlining the components of authentic learning in context, goes on to describe some of the benefits of such learning, and offers a number of practical strategies for designing authentic learning activities.

Components of contextual teaching and learning

In order to help students relate their learning to the real world, Johnson (2002) identified eight components of a contextual teaching and learning theory:

1   Making Meaningful Connection
2   Doing Significant Work
3   Self-Regulated Learning
4   Collaborating
5   Critical and Creative Thinking
6   Nurturing the Individual
7   Reaching High Standard
8   Using Authentic Assessment

However, as teachers, we need to know what all these different elements look like in the classroom and how to enable the students to identify the appropriate skills. Once teachers are committed to contextualized teaching, and accept that lessons can and should go off in tangents, then the possibilities of bringing the real world into the classroom to enhance curriculum learning are endless.

Benefits of experiencing subject content through a variety of contexts

Despite the recent reconstruction of the GCSEs in a large number of subjects, the real test of understanding is still whether students know how to use their knowledge when faced with a situation in any environment that calls for it to be used. This is exemplified by Bransford *et al.* (1990) in their analysis of the scene from the *Raiders of the Lost Ark*, where Indiana Jones has to match the weight of a golden icon so that he can remove it. They outline that there needs to be a baseline understanding of mathematics/science (weight and density), however, that on its own is not sufficient. The situation also needs to be considered in order to make a successful swap. So a knowledge of something is not enough; students need to identify that the knowledge is appropriate as well as know how to apply it when faced with an unfamiliar scenario.

Students need to see their learning as adding to a toolbox; it is about having the right tools for a situation and knowing how to use them. By experiencing the same content but in different contexts, students can both acquire and assimilate understanding, which then makes it more accessible to them for future use. Meeting new knowledge in a context it is designed to be used in helps students create links for themselves and therefore appreciate when and how they can apply their existing knowledge. This is widely recognized as the vertical transfer of knowledge, where an individual acquires new knowledge or skills by building on more basic information and procedures (Seel, 2012). Thus, it enables students to have strategies for working on real-world problems.

Contextual learning develops skills in students beyond the subject-specific ones; these are often referred to as key skills and processes or twenty-first-century skills. In preparation for the workplace, students need to be flexible thinkers rather than only having procedural competence (Hoyles *et al.*, 2010). By working on non-routine problems, students are forced regularly to critically evaluate the approach they are taking, and justify why they have selected a particular strategy. Repetitive textbook questions, whilst they have their uses and can be very effective in procedural variation, do not allow students to develop their reasoning for an approach. This also means that they do not have to articulate their methodology rationale, and so do not have an opportunity to develop their speaking and listening skills. Working on unfamiliar tasks allows students to evaluate the best communication strategy, whether written or verbal. It will see students use a combination of technical, lexical and everyday language which develops their understanding of subject vocabulary and also an appreciation of the wider applications of it; variances on a word should be recognized alongside the use of technical words so that students can create links between them all and therefore will have the ability to undertake vertical transfer of their knowledge. Working collaboratively on such tasks then cements the use of vocabulary, as well as developing skills on how to work with other people. Numerous articles and research papers have explored different learning styles, however, for contextualized learning Costa and Kallick's (2009) 'Habits of Mind' are more relevant. Rather than attempting to identify a particular learning style, they consider a variety of skills that successful learners should master, such as listening, persistence, creating questions, taking responsible risks and managing impulsivity. All of these are required in problem-solving scenarios and are transferable skills to non-classroom environments.

Posing real-life problems means that there may not be a 'nice and neat' solution, which is discussed further in the chapter. The main advantage to this is that students can be creative – there are no limits to their initial thinking. They can then think realistically and start to impose some practical and realistic parameters on how to approach the task. The more students work on these types of tasks, the more self-regulated and independent learners they become; they realize that at some point they will have to make decisions, as there are set timeframes to work on the problem. This is, therefore, just like a workplace situation, and so it helps students create a more realistic understanding of the world they are growing up within. Bransford *et al.* (1990) put forward an integrated approach to teach both thinking and content knowledge simultaneously. Within this they emphasize the importance of having subject-specific knowledge and being able to apply it appropriately in a given situation.

The creativity is also beneficial to us as teachers, as working on non-routine problems combines retrieval practice and interleaving in one go! Students will be digging into their 'toolbox', using content from both recent and older topics as they feel necessary. This also helps them to make connections between the different subject elements, as well as across subjects. Having a secure understanding of these connections and their applications also helps the students feel more confident in their knowledge. Eventually this confidence develops into taking risks and accepting that it's fine to hit a stumbling block as they know they have the skills to work around it.

Construction of knowledge in authentic learning experiences

Lave and Wenger (1991) formalized situated learning theory, which emphasizes that there should be clear connections to workplace situations and opportunities provided to apply knowledge in authentic experiences. They identify learning as a socio-cultural phenomenon, suggesting students learn better when they are part of a community of practice. This concept is furthered by Holmes *et al.* (2001), who introduce the term 'communal constructivism'; a combination of constructivism, social constructivism and the suggestion that everyone has an active responsibility to support the learning and development of all in their group. Using authentic experiences where students work collaboratively will naturally provide opportunities to develop such key skills and processes.

The fundamental element of social constructivism is that students construct their own knowledge, through a range of experiences in a social context. To help develop the ability to vertically transfer knowledge, students need opportunities and the freedom to work on tasks which may appear arbitrary but actually require a deep thought process to consider whether they could apply any of their existing knowledge. Aligned with this approach to the construction of knowledge is the REACT theory for teaching and learning (Crawford, 2001): Relating, Experiencing, Applying, Co-operating and Transferring. These five elements are identified as 'contextual learning strategies' and act as guidelines for creating learning experiences that optimize understanding and application. The 'Relating' element involves setting new concepts in contexts that are familiar to students so that they can immediately link their learning to an area of their prior knowledge. Through this, subject vocabulary, definitions and concepts can develop alongside each other when set in contexts, rather than one being a prerequisite for another. It is important to remember here that 'real life' also needs to be age-relevant, so that students have an informal understanding of it within which to work. Using mortgages, for example, to contextualize percentages in mathematics will be of limited use, as students may not be familiar with the concepts and therefore are trying to work on two unfamiliar themes at the same time. Being able to experience learning, through practical demonstrations, manipulatives or trips, allows students to be directly involved in the construction of both their knowledge and understanding; learning by discovery, to use the constructivist term. Although a video or virtual simulation can support this to an extent, it is still a fairly passive form of learning and so, where possible, students should be able to try or experience something for themselves. This connects with the Applying part of the REACT theory, where students need to be aware of how the skill or knowledge will actually be of use to them. Co-operating entails the skills used in collaborative learning, and links back to the earlier point about students developing key processes, such as communicating and reasoning, which will help in their own construction of knowledge. The ability to transfer knowledge is the connecting element in the REACT theory, and underpins contextualized learning itself.

Alongside the collaborative element, the revision of Bloom's taxonomy saw the introduction of metacognition in the knowledge dimension (Anderson *et al.* 2001). This built on the original 'conceptual knowledge' element of the taxonomy, and promotes thinking about both the self and wider application of knowledge. This synthesizes well with the cognitive dimension of the taxonomy, and promotes an understanding of appropriate contextual knowledge use.

Bloom's taxonomy was first created in 1956 and identified three categories of areas of learning in education: (1) cognitive – mental skills (knowledge); (2) affective – growth of feelings/emotions (attitude – self); and (3) psychomotor – manual or physical skills. In terms of the 'cognitive' category, Bloom's hierarchy (revised) is a framework of six levels of thinking that can be very useful for teachers in designing tasks, preparing questions for discussion with students, and providing feedback on students' work. In the bullet list below, the first term is from the original taxonomy, and the second from the revised version:

- Level I Knowledge/Remembering: This is the lowest level that requires recall only of basic facts and concepts.
- Level II Comprehension/Understanding: This means understanding that is evidenced by describing, comparing, interpreting and organizing of facts.
- Level III Application/Applying: This is problem solving in new contexts by applying new techniques, knowledge and rules.
- Level IV Analysis/Analyzing: This means investigating information and identifying causes by making inferences and supporting generalizations with evidence.

- Level V Synthesis/Creating: In the revised hierarchy 'Creating' has been re-ordered as Level VI and 'Evaluating' as Level V. Compiling and combining information in a new way and/or a new pattern.
- Level VI Evaluation/Evaluating: This is the highest level and requires defending opinions and views through making judgements about the validity of ideas in relation to set criteria.

Authentic learning experiences therefore support the scaffolding created through the taxonomy and push students to develop and apply their higher-order thinking skills. Linking this taxonomy and the wider benefits that contextual learning has on developing key processes in students suggests that the teaching strategy should be set within the constructivist paradigm.

Teaching and learning therefore have to be student-centred, focusing on outcomes and the development of both skills and knowledge. Enquiry-based learning is possible across all subjects, where a problem or question is posed and the onus is placed on the student to consider different lines of enquiry and identify questions relating to it. By the very nature of being away from their usual learning routines, students are more receptive to learning; they have the opportunity to think differently, arguably more creatively. This style of learning may be delivered under a different name in different subjects. Mathematics often refers to problem solving, where the method is not immediately obvious and there may or may not be a discrete answer. English and History will talk about enquiry skills, but then so will some Arts subjects. Science and Geography may label it as critical thinking, whereas PE might discuss tactical thinking. Regardless of the name, they all have the same principle at heart – to help students think independently and creatively about how to develop and apply their knowledge.

In setting up these authentic learning experiences, so that students can see how their knowledge is used, it is equally important to give students the opportunity to reflect on the task. This can take a variety of formats, from a peer discussion to a written self-assessment, but allocating the time in a lesson to stop and think about just how much they've done and achieved really cements the construction of knowledge process. It also raises their confidence in their understanding, which has the domino effect of them feeling more confident to tackle unfamiliar tasks in the future. However, it should be noted that students themselves may not initially be able to identify the variety of skills they have used and the links in their learning when reflecting; therefore the teacher may need to lead this discussion when first using authentic learning experiences to model how to critically analyze the approaches used and the wide range of knowledge involved. Gradually, students will be able to recognize where and how they use different skills in different situations, and will ultimately start to make the connections themselves. This then leads to a deeper understanding of their knowledge as students will have the ability to join up their thinking both within a subject and across subjects, enabling them to vertically transfer their knowledge to any situation.

So for learning experiences to be authentic, apart from being student-centred, they must be relatable, open-ended and active. Across the subjects, the tasks that lend themselves to these experiences may be labelled 'open-ended', 'goal-free', 'low threshold, high ceiling' or 'real world'; however they are branded, they all give students the opportunity to explore ideas, try things out and construct their own knowledge and understanding.

Challenges in using examples that are 'not nice and neat'

If subject content is not taught or reviewed in a context, then students may well not develop adaptive reasoning skills. They may therefore not be able to transfer their knowledge vertically between different contexts, but instead compartmentalize it to one specific use in one specific situation. Without the awareness of how to use their knowledge, the knowledge itself becomes devalued and the students may fail to commit it to their long-term memory. This also applies to using 'perfect' situations, such as designing a garden that is perfectly rectangular. In such situations, students are artificially applying their knowledge, and while this does still have some benefit, it will not help them to use their understanding realistically. If they see at first glance that it is a perfect situation, there is no drive to dig deeper and challenge any of the content. This will then limit how they can use their knowledge and also reduce the opportunity for them to develop their key skills and processes, as discussed previously. Students also need to feel free to explore possible options, try something and, if it does not work, then try something else. As de Bono (2004, p. 166) famously said, 'If you never change your mind, why have one?' It also means that students will not develop coping strategies when they meet a stumbling block, or even fail. Resilience is an important skill to acquire and improve, and students need to learn that there should not be a negative connection between not having an immediate success and their personal confidence.

Problem-orientated learning can be problematic, but only if we let it. It is important to build in discussion time at the start of a problem-solving exercise, so that students can really think about the problem. Ensure students are encouraged to think of counter-examples, and not just obvious ones – go extreme! This is really important if they are to understand how to transfer their learning from the classroom to the real world, as they will need to be aware of limitations and wider possibilities. It really helps the students too if we ask them to phrase their challenges as questions. Listen in while they are having the discussion so that you can capture some of their ideas. Once this 'free thinking' time has ended, take the opportunity to review some of the challenges to help validate their approaches to the task. Select a few of them and set these as the parameters to work within for this lesson. This involves the students directly in the learning process while setting a framework for the problem to still be worked on. By creating and using these questions, students become partners in their learning and are then already engaged in the challenge of answering them (Kahn and O'Rourke, 2005).

However, the creation of these questions cannot be managed, and a teacher needs to feel comfortable with this. It is possible to steer students in a particular direction, but it is important that they feel confident to explore a problem in a way they feel is appropriate. One strategy is to take an initial 3–5 minutes and invite students to write possible entrance points to the task as exploratory questions on the whiteboard; at the end of this free thinking time a teacher can review them and, as a class, decide perhaps on three that will be the ones to be investigated. If the task has been set up as a goal-free problem though, students should be allowed to continue working on it whichever way they have decided, as that forms part of a teacher's evaluation of the task. With the first few instances of real-life learning, if the freedom is too much for the students, then a writing framework could be used to help scaffold their thinking and create an appropriate strategy.

As already alluded to, working on real-world problems is more successful if students can work collaboratively. While there are numerous advantages to groupwork, including informal peer learning, it also does have challenges. Discussions cannot be controlled, therefore the expectations need to be clearly established so that students know and understand how to work with the autonomy they have been granted. This in itself replicates a real-life scenario and so students need to develop these skills, however, they will need guidance initially on how to use the responsibility effectively. Boaler (Accessed 2020) builds on the work of Cohen, creating 'Complex Instruction' as a format to help upskill students in how to work collaboratively whilst simultaneously providing a structure for teachers to help manage it. The strategy involves creating equity among members of the group, delegating authority and promoting a 'group learning' mentality. One way to achieve this is through the use of well-defined roles, where the contribution of each member to the outcome of the task is clear and therefore everyone feels valued.

Supporting real-life learning

Outlined below are a number of strategies that encourage learning in real-life, authentic contexts. The first relates to learning across the curriculum.

Strategy 1: Cross-curricular learning to contextualize

One of the first steps in the lesson planning process should be to identify links with other subjects; you should also allocate some lesson time so that students can think about this too for themselves. Promote abstract thinking here so that students can really appreciate just how transferable the knowledge and skills are; similarities between science and geography investigations, fractions used in maths and music or analysis of a poem and a historical document. Related concepts can be explored through thematic problems, identifying similarities and differences. Perhaps the phrase 'curriculum integration' suggests more synthesis than 'cross-curricular'; Fogarty (1995) determines 10 levels of curriculum integration, moving from fragmented, connected and nested within single disciplines, to sequenced, shared, webbed, threaded and integrated across several disciplines, and finally to a position where the curriculum is immersed and networked within and across learners. Contextual teaching sits within all subjects of the National Curriculum and there are natural opportunities to form connections across children's academic life and create a more holistic understanding of their knowledge.

Next, we move to strategies to scaffold learning in practical lessons.

Strategy 2: The use of manipulatives to create practical lessons

Using manipulatives, whether concrete or virtual, can support the scaffolding process in students' understanding. For some subjects, such as maths and science, it can make abstract concepts more relatable; for subjects that are naturally more practical, they help cement understanding. Both of these reduce the cognitive load pressure on students, and therefore help transfer their learning to the longer-term memory. The role of 'paper' should not be underestimated as a manipulative – it can be folded to make a quick model, cut up to show a layout or used to create a chain of reasoning for the group's thinking. As the use of manipulatives replicates the real-world situation, it helps create an authentic learning experience. Again, students should have freedom over the manipulatives; their use should not be compulsory, and neither should the way they are used, so as not to stem creativity.

Finally, we look at the ways in which alternative sites around a school can be used as environments for learning.

Strategy 3: Exploring alternative learning environments

There are numerous spaces within a school site that can be used throughout the day, including outside areas. Just by taking the learning into a different environment, it immediately changes the situation and provides a change in context. Not only can this help contextualize a task, but it can also promote an increased confidence in students to work on it, possibly in a different or more creative way. Trips to local or national places and institutions are also very beneficial, and will often have thematic sessions or resources available. However there can be additional costs associated with this, as well as the organization logistics.

Vignette: Creation of an integrated curricular learning resource for use in a museum

A group of trainee teachers from the University of Bedfordshire worked with The Higgins Bedford to create an integrated curricular resource for students to use in the museum. By spending time in the museum and thinking creatively about how concepts from a variety of subjects could be taught, the trainee teachers not only felt confident using The Higgins Bedford but also had more contexts to take back to the classroom in which to set the learning.

The trainees began by exploring museum education and understanding the connection between Museum Generic Learning Outcomes, as set by Arts Council, and Bloom's taxonomy. They then thought creatively about language that promotes intrigue before selecting some key objects within the museum around which to structure the different sections of the resource. Once the objects were chosen, the trainees identified a large number of questions that could be asked of the object to elicit both information and context. This then enabled a key question to be created with sufficient supporting information available to help students explore ways to answer it. The questions were open and curriculum-integrated in their approach, such as, 'Why am I important?' so that pupils could think creatively and draw on different subjects to formulate an answer. The trainees created a set of teacher notes to support the resource, which contained more information and points for differentiation as well as curriculum-integrated follow-up activities for the classroom.

This structure of starting with an object or photograph and creating questions can be used for any activity or environment, as it helps identify links within and between subjects and therefore begins to form a context around it.

Conclusion

So we might ask what it is that creates memories. Psychologists might talk about environment, educationalists might discuss cognitive load theory whereas students might say doing something different; contextualized learning combines all three! By using real-world contexts, students can instantly see how their knowledge can be applied and have a more creative experience in the learning of it. Alongside this, it helps develop integrated skills that transcend specific subjects and are akin to workplace behaviours and requirements. Working on real-life problems that are open-ended promotes confidence and enquiry. As Leat (2017, p. 4) outlines, learning should be 'driven by questions and curiosity' and using non-familiar routines promotes this. Seeing their learning in context helps students make connections and decompartmentalize their knowledge, thus increasing their confidence in its application.

In order to set up situations where students can think creatively, teachers also have the opportunity to plan more creatively. They can both take risks too in the lessons, albeit calculated ones to some extent, and really get embroiled in problem solving. It may take longer than one lesson, it may be more noisy than a normal lesson and it may even be in a different space for the lesson, but this is all part of the fun of the experience! As teachers, we need to let go and give students the opportunity to try things and work out for themselves whether it will be successful or not; knowing that we have that trust in our students will spur them on to think creatively and try something new. Whilst simulated experiences do have some value, there is nothing like having a go at a real-world problem; there may not be a nice, neat answer and in fact there may not even be a definite answer, but that is alright. It is the application of knowledge and development of key skills that are the main outcomes of such tasks. Seeing students think realistically about how they can use the knowledge teachers have taught them is incredibly rewarding; teachers know the students truly understand what they have been taught and they know why they learnt it.

References

Anderson, L.W. (Ed.), Krathwohl, D.R. (Ed.), Airasian, P.W., Cruikshank, K.A., Mayer, R.E., Pintrich, P.R., Raths, J., & Wittrock, M.C. (2001). A taxonomy for learning, teaching, and assessing: A revision of Bloom's Taxonomy of Educational Objectives (Complete edition). New York: Longman.

Bloom, B. and Krathwohl, D.A. (1956) 'Bloom's taxonomy'. Available at: http://www.bloomstaxonomy.org/Blooms%20Taxonomy%20questions.pdf (accessed 27 February 2020).

Boaler, J. (No date) 'How complex instruction led to high and equitable achievement: The Case of Railside School'. Available at: https://nrich.maths.org/content/id/7011/nrich%20paper.pdf (accessed 25 January 2021).

Bransford, J.D., Vye, N., Kinzer, C. and Risko, V. (1990) 'Teaching thinking and content knowledge: Toward an integrated approach', in B.F. Jones and L. Idol (eds), *Dimensions of Thinking and Cognitive Instruction*, Hillsdale, NJ: Lawrence Erlbaum, pp. 381–413.

Costa, A. and Kallick, B. (2009) *Learning and Leading with Habits of Mind: 16 Characteristics for Success*, Alexandria, VA: Association for Supervision and Curriculum Development.

Crawford, M.L. (2001) *Teaching Contextually: Research, Rationale, and Techniques for Improving Student Motivation and Achievement in Mathematics and Science*, Waco, TX: CORD.

de Bono, E. (2004) *How to Have a Beautiful Mind*, London: Random House.

Fogarty, R. J. (1995) *The Mindful School: How to Integrate the Curricula*, French's Forest, NSW: James Bennett Publishers.

Holmes, B., Tangey, B., FitzGibbon, A., Savage, T. and Mehan, S. (2001) 'Communal constructivism: Students constructing learning *for* as well as *with* others', in Proceedings of Society for Information Technology and Teacher Education (SITE) 2001 Conference, Orlando, FL, 5–10 March 2001. Available at: https://www.cs.tcd.ie/publications/tech-reports/reports.01/TCD-CS-2001-04.pdf (accessed 27 August 2020).

Hoyles, C., Ross, R., Kent, P. and Bakker, A. (2010) *Improving Mathematics at Work: The Need for Techno-mathematical Literacies*, London: Routledge.

Johnson, E.B. (2002) *Contextual Teaching and Learning: What It Is and Why It's Here to Stay*, London: Sage.

Kahn, P. and O'Rourke, K. (2005) 'Understanding enquiry-based learning', in *Handbook of Enquiry and Problem-based Learning: Irish Case Studies and International*

Perspectives, No. 2, Galway: Centre for Excellence in Learning and Teaching, AISHE Readings.

Lave, J. and Wenger, E. (1991) *Situated Learning: Legitimate Peripheral Participation*, Cambridge: Cambridge University Press.

Leat, D. (2017) *Enquiry and Project-Based Learning: Students, School and Society*, Abingdon: Routledge.

Seel, N.M. (2012) *Encyclopedia of the Sciences of Learning*, New York: Springer.

12 How can Forest School education enhance children's curricular experiences?

Perry Knight

Major questions addressed in this chapter are:

- How can teachers ensure children have opportunities to explore different environments that both enrich and sustain their learning?
- How does Forest School promote active engagement and enrich learning outcomes?
- How do you facilitate opportunities for Forest School?
- How do teachers reconcile the demands of the English National Curriculum with personal beliefs of enriching a child's education with Forest School practice?
- How far does the National Curriculum reflect the ethos of Forest School principles?
- How can the impact of Forest School education be measured in relation to its contribution across curriculum areas?

Abstract

This chapter takes the view that children have the innate ability to construct their own sense of the world. If knowledge can be socially constructed through physical and symbolic learning, a child has the ability to construct meaning from reality. Social construction is developed through evolving activity in which children can identify, select and develop learning strategies that enhance their ability to retain and transfer knowledge to differing environments. The chapter acknowledges Forest Schooling as a style and format of outdoor learning that enriches the child developmentally, psychologically and socially.

An effective engaging curriculum will have a profound and long-term effect on how children learn and how they enjoy the process of their learning. Forest School curricula have the power to transform concepts of learning for children and place the child on a successful lifelong trajectory. The chapter illustrates the discussion with a recent study in which a primary school has adopted the principles of Forest School in all its curriculum areas and throughout every Year group. It identifies the impact Forest School Education has had on children's progress and attainment; their social communication; and holistic development.

Introduction

'Forest School' is not a new concept, but is based on a philosophical ideal based on the fundamental respect for children, in which children have a right to play; to access the outdoors; to access risk; and the right to experience a healthy range of emotions, through the challenges of socialization and interaction. In doing so, children can then start to build resilience and creative engagement with their peers and to have opportunities to fulfil their potential (Forest School Association, 2020). The Forest School concept was introduced into the United Kingdom in the 1990s, during which time centres were established, usually to provide extracurricular activities for children. However, its origins stem from the open-air culture, 'friluftsliv', or free air life, which developed from a way of life in Scandinavia (ibid.). The Forest School Association (2020) has defined 'Forest School' not only as this way of life, but as incorporating a child-centred learning process that offers holistic growth and development of a child. Research has demonstrated that regular Forest School experiences develop confidence and self-esteem through hands-on experiences in a natural setting. The child is in control and facilitates his/her learning in a natural setting through play, exploration and supported risk taking (ibid.; Knight, 2009; Tori, 2011).

Underpinning values

Forest Schools are based on values that not only support the ethos, but consider the rights of a child. They provide unique opportunities for sensory and learning experiences in which the child creates their own voice, curriculum and social learning experience. Its values state that all children are:

- equal, unique and valuable
- competent to explore and discover
- entitled to experience appropriate risk and challenge
- entitled to choose, and to initiate and drive their own learning and development
- entitled to experience regular success

- entitled to develop positive relationships with themselves and other people
- entitled to develop a strong, positive relationship with their natural world

(www.forestschoolassociation.org)

The ethos is grounded in an entitlement, rather than a set of competences and, therefore, can be seen to place children at the heart of their own development and learning experience. This is a powerful concept that goes beyond the notion of enriching a curriculum. If knowledge is socially constructed through the physical and symbolic learning that Forest School offers, then the child has a unique ability to construct its own meaning from its reality. Burr (2007) considers that children can socially construct an evolving activity in which they can identify, select and develop their own learning experiences. As a result, children have the ability to transfer meaning to a variety of environments, using each to enrich and develop experiences. The entitlements Forest School offers promote and sustain such concepts.

Forest School's curriculum framework

Forest School provides a framework for an effective and developmental curriculum. Children have opportunities to take ownership of their learning within a relatively risk-free environment with an enhanced understanding of the delights and wonders of the outdoors. In many ways, it removes the children from the confines of the classroom and places them in the context of a natural environment promoting the following characteristics:

- The development of self-esteem and self-confidence. The understanding of risk and the participation in outdoor activities provide opportunities for children to plan; challenge themselves as learners and participators; and socialize through play. As a result, they are developing effective tools for communication and using these to participate in a range of inclusive activities.
- A curiosity and fascination with the environment. Forest School has the ability to develop escapism from some of the pressures children face in their day-to-day lives. The natural environment a Forest School offers promotes new understanding of the outdoors and appreciation of the natural world. Forest School allows children, and adults, to discover the excitement and wonder such an environment offers.
- A respect and knowledge of the natural world. This respect stems from a deep understanding of the natural world and the different habitats that are created in it. It provides opportunities for children to experience and participate in nature, to access its risks and understand the reality of the world we live in.
- Learning in all curriculum areas. The Forest School provides an extension and enrichment to the curriculum we offer as teachers. It touches on all aspects of the curriculum providing a natural resource that cannot be found in textbooks and classroom-based activities.

The principles of Forest School provide a framework for a holistic curriculum that enables children to develop transferable skills. It offers an environment to allow children to develop strategies to problem solve through communication and physical activity. The concept of child-initiated learning forms a close collaboration between the child and the adult. It is evident across all age phases that child-led activities promote curiosity and questioning, allowing the child to make decisions through enquiry and self-direction. Such can be defined as an emergent curriculum that develops a close relationship between the concepts of a child's prior knowledge, influencing new individual and social learning experiences. An effective curriculum will provide a profound and long-term effect on how children learn and how they enjoy the process of their learning (Stacey, 2009). In brief, the Forest School curriculum has the power to transform concepts of learning for children and place the child on a successful trajectory for lifelong learning.

Vignette: Application of the Forest School principles

A primary school, with a forest area attached to it, has mapped its entire curriculum offer against the Forest School principles. All Year groups are time-tabled weekly to use the forest area in which they have opportunities to explore and discover this area; manage their own risk in the use of tools and construction activities; and promote well-being, using the space to talk, socialize and reflect on their learning opportunities in the classroom. Other times, it is used as a resource to further learning in a range of subject areas including English, Mathematics and Science, and to construct artefacts that represent different concepts in topic-led work. In this primary school the forest area is not classed as an additional learning environment, but an enhancement of the classroom experience. Teachers reported on the impact Forest School has had on children's learning. Children are more confident in using their new skills and knowledge across curriculum subjects; they have developed closer relationships between peers; and children are able to recognize their learning development and achievement.

Importance of play

As Bullock and Muschamp (2005) clearly state, children are challenged within their learning environment when they learn independently and take responsibility for their own learning. As a child progresses through school and matures, learning develops from effective dyad relationships that offer correction, mutual support, encouragement and guidance, to extended dyad learning relationships that include peers, and group relationships, where the outcome is to form participatory roles within a range of contexts. As children transfer into different learning environments, they need to experience and learn from various physical learning contexts to gain independence of thought. Kozulin (1986), following Piaget (1954) argues that pre-school children are unable to 'decentre'. In other words, they cannot yet understand how others perceive the world, or recognize how their own perceptions and feelings differ from others'. However, at this stage they have the ability to absorb meaning through discovery and play. Play, fantasy and games are important activities for cognitive, motivational and social development (Bronfenbrenner, 1979; Vygotsky, 1978). Play therefore is a powerful source of symbolism. Learning occurs through gesture, play and speech systems. If play is an essential ingredient to the development of learning in early childhood, then it can be used throughout a child's education to foster confidence, participation and turn-taking. The current author would argue that, as a child matures, schools neglect play as an element of learning and, therefore, potentially tame imagination.

Enriching learning in Forest Schools

Forest School offers a unique and powerful solution to the issue of play as it provides a natural classroom which children can explore using the medium of physical activity and language. Children have a 'freedom' not only to develop tools for communication, but to explore educational values and knowledge independent of restrictions that classrooms may create. Literacy is one such concept in which children can transfer their learning between the more traditional and the forest classroom. We know that language is a powerful tool and appreciate the importance of turn-taking; reading body language; and developing empathy towards others. Forest School provides a more natural flow of language through play, socialization and symbolic learning.

Vignette: Development of comprehension of text in a Forest School setting

A brief example of a real-life activity designed to enhance children's comprehension of text in a Forest School setting indicates how such an environment can provide a wealth of opportunities for them to explore, create and, above all, use imaginative learning in a social context. The BFG by the British children's author Roald Dahl captures a range of emotive language and imagery (Dahl, 2007). The concept of dreams was explored in which a class of Year 4s had the opportunity to create their own dream bottles. Children listened to the story being told within a discreet reading circle in the forest area and spoke of ambitions and dreams. They had the opportunity to share their ambitions and consider futures. Using the imagery of the BFG story, the teacher blew the 'dream trumpet' and allowed children to create artefacts from the forest and place them in bottles. Some children identified wildflowers, grasses and twigs to create images representing their dreams. These were then placed into their own dream bottles. Children spoke of unicorns, rainbows and faraway lands. Others considered ambitions of becoming a famous person, future job prospects, and reflection on personal skills, such as confidence. In fact, all children had the opportunity to capture their dreams.

The labelling of the bottles was very important, as children wrote what their dream was on a giant label and used twine to attach it to a bottle. The following day, the teacher used the dream bottles in circle time to continue the discussion of the importance of goals and aspirations.

(Based on a concept developed by students at the University of Bedfordshire)

School children are expected to solve problems that other people have set, so education is viewed as a dialogic process (Mercer and Littleton, 2007; Neisser, 1976). For learning to be successful, a child needs prescribed tools to access what is being taught and to understand how knowledge can be transferred to a variety of contexts to enforce meaning and its realization. Piaget identifies three interwoven processes that contribute to, and detract from, a child's learning: (1) intrapsychic processes; (2) cognitive processes; and (3) repercussions of artificial intelligence (Magnusson, 2001). For learning to develop, it is essential to be able to construct knowledge from perception, thoughts and values, referred to as intrapsychic processes. These are subsequently used to develop learning and intelligence or cognitive processes. A child will then be able to differentiate from knowledge that is taught, and innate knowledge developed from cultural context (ibid.). In order to function, knowledge needs redefining according to the social context in which it is realized. A child pursues two forms of experience: scientific, specialized enquiry; and spontaneous, everyday enquiry (Kozulin, 1986). Therefore, a child can potentially develop knowledge from two discreet planes of enquiry using their natural and structured contexts. The vignette above identifies children's enquiry in which they used a teacher-facilitated activity to construct meaning through experience of collecting artefacts within a non-judgemental and semi-structured setting. This activity considered the development of self and protected the child from the pressures of everyday life to enable the construction of knowledge through imagination and self-perception.

We might conceptualize learning development as a process of internalization (Vygotsky, 1978). This occurs within the concept of a child's 'zone of proximal development', that is, the difference between a child's actual development and a child's potential development. To navigate through the zone an 'expert' can scaffold a task using a process that is developed to enable a 'novice' (or child) to solve a problem, carry out a task or achieve a goal that would usually be beyond them (Cheyne and Tarulli,1999; Woods *et al.*, 1976). Moll and Whitmore (2006) suggest that the zone is language-driven and, within the process, dialogue structures contribute to the child's development. The *magistral* dialogue is asymmetric, using the voice of a teacher (*magistra*), the voice of a child (novitiate) and third, the voice of the subject (authoritative). The authoritative voice contains subject-specific materials, including curriculum content and policy. Alternatively, Socratic dialogue is potentially available to all who participate, allowing mutual enquiry that is guided by the 'expert'. Primary settings operate on two distinct planes of enquiry. Using unstructured and informal dialogue, the teacher will operate using principles of Socratic dialogue, which have the potential to frustrate the recipient. Forest Schooling suggests that these perceived differences will have an impact on a child's learning pathway within their own education. Not only do children need to adapt to continuous new curriculum content, but also to the language structures portrayed by individual teachers across a range of subjects.

Children are exposed to different curricula and learning environments throughout their academic year. For some children, this transfer of new knowledge and situations forms a natural part of their journey. For others, this transfer creates different anxieties and will delay children's acquisition of knowledge. Teachers play an essential part in the development of knowledge through the ways we engage and articulate understanding. It is important, therefore, that teachers should consider:

- which strategies they might use to promote and engage new learning;
- considering the Forest School ethos, how they might use these concepts in the teaching of new knowledge;
- what strategies they might use to launch and enrich new topics using the Forest School as an extended classroom.

Integrating the Forest School concept into the National Curriculum

Forest School provides opportunities for children to develop independence and confidence in their learning. It has the potential to remove barriers and increase self-esteem. The National Curriculum prescribes a framework for the foundations of understanding across a range of core and foundation subjects. It identifies specific aims that develop skills, knowledge and understanding in which children develop new concepts through curiosity, experience and excitement. The Science National Curriculum (DfE, 2015) clearly states that:

> pupils should be encouraged to recognise the power of rational explanation and develop a sense of excitement and curiosity about natural phenomena. They should be encouraged to understand how science can be used to explain what is occurring, predict how things will behave, and analyse causes.

Forest School provides experiences to facilitate such learning and excitement. Its curriculum framework promotes a range of experiential learning opportunities for children to explore first-hand differing habitats, plants and wildlife, and differing textures of pathways. Such enhancement allows teachers to bring to the classroom through experiential analysis, observation and recording. The vignette below details a Year 5 habitat project in which children developed their own variation of teacher-led work. Their learning transformed experientially and from teacher-led to child-led activity that both analyzed and recorded differing habitats in a natural context.

Vignette: Approaching science topics in a forest area

A Year 5 class have been studying habitats as part of their Science curriculum. A focus of this project was the consideration of potentially endangered species and they created an indoor habitat for hedgehogs. The project comprised the children visiting a local hedgehog sanctuary and building shelters for them to hibernate in. Close to the school was a small wooded area to which the teacher took them to complete a field study analysis of the wood. The children began replicating their classroom shelters in the wood using natural resources such as twigs, dried grass and soil. By the end of the field trip, a small 'Hedgehog village' had developed.

Children then visited their shelters over a series of days and recorded any wildlife using their habitats created, and tracked any animal trails in and around the shelters. In addition, they compared different shelters for construction and durability. Evidence for the project was collated through photographs that were proudly displayed around the classroom.

For some children, this removed some of the barriers they faced within the classroom as they had to rely on imagination, rather than first-hand experience. Experiencing the woodland and its resources, they managed to extend their learning opportunities and approached their work with confidence and excitement. Children were able to verbalize their learning; self-select appropriate resources to support their shelters; and evaluate and compare their shelters to others.

Erikson (1995) classifies children as carriers of tradition and concludes that, in order to enhance cognitive ability, schools have much to learn from examining the pedagogy of everyday life. Schools create formal socialization structures that have the potential to tame imagination. The child's role in this is one of 'collector', rather than 'active participator' of knowledge (Engestro˝m, 1987; Erikson 1995). Traditional education models force age, rather than ability, to be the basis for the segregating structures that conduct children through school. Teachers develop their pedagogy through age-related tasks that are differentiated to suit the ability of each individual. Every child has a learning entitlement with the right to be stimulated in a learning manner and immersed in knowledge so that they can develop critical thinking, understanding and problem-solving skills (Copland, 1998). After all, research concludes that children automatically define themselves as learners, and it is the teacher's role to foster and encourage effective learning environments (Moll and Whitmore, 2006). Therefore, it is essential never to underestimate a child's mental capacity (Copland, 1998), and to develop learning contexts, such as those associated with the Forest School concept, in which all can thrive and be active participators.

Forest School begins to break down hierarchical power relationships between teacher and child. Kellet (2010) defines power not as a source, but as knowledge created and controlled by teachers that has the potential to disempower children. The entitlement Forest School offers does not diminish roles and responsibilities; it allows learning to evolve through experience, communication and developing self-esteem. It creates a mutual power relationship, allowing teachers to become facilitators of learning and extending classroom opportunities to the outdoors. Forest School allows children to develop their own 'agendas' for learning through exploration and trial and error.

Forest School promotes an ethos of allowing children to explore and discover in a natural setting. This includes the confidence to take risks through play and emergent learning. For teachers, this raises a number of questions, for example:

* how to prepare children to consider risk and accept challenge in their learning?
* how to ensure children develop transferable skills across a range of contexts?
* in a school setting, what natural resources are available to support and develop experiential learning?

Conclusion

A curriculum provides a framework of skills, knowledge and understanding in relation to specific learning and developmental outcomes. The teacher then makes decisions about pedagogies that provide a foundation to learning through the process of meaningful activities. The critical point here is to allow children to develop their learning identities by making invisible learning visible (Claxton *et al.*, 2011). This then cements learning relationships between the child, the family, peers and the teacher, thus creating a series of dyadic and triadic relationships. The notion of Forest School provides a series of different curriculum models, including the emergent, play-based, progressive and evolving curricula. Each have their own tensions between policy and interpretation. However, each has the potential to provide a child-led, experiential approach to learning.

Forest School provides a powerful tool that both offers and enhances a range of curricula in which children have the opportunity to seek their own experience in all aspects of their learning. Stacey (2009) suggests that children have an 'inborn curiosity' that equips them to explore, thus satisfying children's innate desire to want to learn more. In many ways, they desire opportunities to examine the unexamined. Forest Schools provide a resource for children to deconstruct what they have learnt, and rebuild knowledge and skills in a natural environment through communication, experimentation and experience.

This reconstruction enables children to explore meaning and hypothesize connections in a highly social and naturalistic setting. In this way, Forest Schools move beyond the concept of simply allowing children to access outdoor learning, by providing children with a rich nurturing learning environment that facilitates exciting opportunities for their development, growth and creativity.

References

Bronfenbrenner, U. (1979) *The Ecology of Human Development: Experiments by Nature and Design*, Cambridge, MA: Harvard University Press.

Bullock, K. and Muschamp, Y.M. (2005) 'Learning to love learning. What the pupils think', paper presented at British Educational Research Association Annual Conference, September, Pontypridd.

Burr, V. (2007) *Social Constructionism*, London: Routledge.

Cheyne, J.A. and Tarulli, D. (1999) 'Dialogue, difference and voice in the zone of proximal development', in H. Daniels (ed.) (2005) *An Introduction to Vytgotsky*, Hove: Routledge, pp. 125–48.

Claxton, G., Chambers, M., Powell, G. and Lucas, B. (2011) *The Learning Powered School: Pioneering 21st Century*, Bristol: TLO Ltd.

Copland, D. (1998) *Lessons in Class: A Fresh Appraisal of Comprehensive Education*, Newcastle Upon-Tyne: TUPS Books.

Dahl, R. (2007) *The BFG*, London: Puffin Books.

DfE (2015) 'The Science National Curriculum'. Available at: https://www.gov.uk/government/publications/national-curriculum-in-england-science-programmes-of-study/national-curriculum-in-england-science-programmes-of-study

Erikson, E.H. (1995) *Childhood and Society*, London: Vintage Books.

Forest School Association (2020) 'About us'. Available at: https://www.forestschoolassociation.org/ (accessed 25 January 2021).

Kellett, M. (2010) Rethinking Children and Research, London: Continuum.

Knight, S (2009) *Forest Schools and Outdoor Learning in the Early Years*, 1st ed., London: Sage.

Kozulin, A. (ed.) (1986) *Thought and Language by Lev Vygotsky*, Cambridge, MA: The MIT Press.

Magnusson, D. (2001) 'Individual development: A holistic, integrated model', in P. Moen, G.H. Elder and K. Lüscher (eds), *Examining Lives in Context: Perspectives on the Ecology of Human Development*, Washington, DC: American Psychological Association, pp. 19–60.

Mercer, N. and Littleton, K. (2007) *Dialogue and the Development of Children's Thinking: A Sociocultural Approach*, Abingdon: Routledge.

Moll, L.C. and Whitmore, K.F. (2006) 'Vygotsky in classroom practice: Moving from individual transition to social transaction', in D. Faulkner, K. Littleton and M. Woodhead (eds), *Learning Relationships in the Classroom*, London: Routledge, pp. 131–58.

Neisser, U. (1976) *Cognition and Reality: Principles and Implications of Cognitive Psychology*, San Francisco, CA: W.H. Freeman and Company.

Piaget, J. (1954) *The Construction of Reality in the Child*, New York: Basic Books.

Stacey, S. (2009) *Emergent Curriculum in Early Childhood Settings*, Montana: Redleaf Press.

Tori, D. (2011) 'Place-based education theory and pedagogy', *Children, Youth and Environments*, 21(1): 349–51.

Vygotsky, L. (1978). *Mind and Society: The Development of Higher Psychological Processes*, Cambridge, MA: Harvard University Press.

Woods, D., Bruner, J.S. and Ross, G. (1976) 'The role of tutoring in problem solving', *Journal of Child Psychology and Psychiatry*, 17: 89–100.

13 Using language learning strategies to transform teaching and learning experiences in mainstream classrooms

Mario Moya

Major questions addressed in this chapter are:

- What is the role of home languages (L1) in the development of communicative competence in English (L2)?
- How can transferable language learning strategies (LLS) be used in the classroom to learn English in the context of the National Curriculum?
- Can strategy-based approaches be used to develop learners' autonomy for greater engagement and development of new skills in L2?
- What are the major issues around the pedagogical value of translanguaging and the 'Third Space'?

Abstract

This chapter discusses the way in which learners' ability to understand and convey information can be enhanced if both teachers and learners use their existing linguistic repertoires by tapping into transferable skills to make teaching and learning more creative and relevant. The complex heterogeneity that characterizes mainstream classrooms in the United Kingdom requires novel teaching and learning approaches to bring the curriculum to life at a time defined by many uncertainties. Within this intricate context, which is also characterized by a growing number of students who are competent in two or more languages, such heterogeneity has contributed to refreshing the agenda of languages in the country. At the same time, the role of early second language learning and multilingual literacy practices appears to be slowly resurrecting. In order to provide generalist teachers with the skills necessary to develop their multilingual awareness and promote multilingual literacies, this chapter focuses on increasing subject knowledge and pedagogical competence in a relatively short time following the tradition of strategy-based instruction, but within a social constructivist understanding of learning through collaboration.

Introduction

The constant influx of learners from different cultural and linguistic backgrounds other than English into the English education system has posed different challenges to schools and teachers as they need to deploy a range of resources to support those students and help them succeed. For such multilingual learners there appears to be a linguistic tension produced by two distinct domains of use: while home languages[1] (henceforth L1) are mainly confined to the intimacy of the family group, English is exclusively employed at school and mainly for educational purposes. While learners' L1 have been increasingly encouraged in British schools over the years, some misunderstandings remain regarding their pedagogical value. This is because of a prevalent belief that mixing languages in school inevitably leads to linguistic hybridity, metaphorically described as the 'Third Space', that hampers the development of the learners' communicative competence in L2. Although such concerns are reasonable, they tend to overlook the fact that the emphasis on 'English-only' policies makes the domains of use (home vs. school) even more fragmented, potentially leading to L1 loss. Additionally, concerns about bringing L1 to the school ignore that multilingual learners have a variety of language learning strategies at their disposal that can be retrieved and transferred to L2, allowing these learners to access the National Curriculum, for example, through a combination of actions, such as code-switching or *translanguaging*.

The complex nature of diversity in the classroom can be challenging and problematic for teachers as they need to find effective ways to cater for the varied needs of their students, which is even more difficult if those learners are new to English. However, embracing diversity and using the learners' existing linguistic repertoires as a teaching resource can create purposeful learning communities, infusing the curriculum with novel and creative approaches where all students, regardless of their cultural and linguistic provenance, are equally acknowledged and are given opportunities to develop a growth mindset to thrive.

The role of learners' home languages in the development of communicative competence in English

The use of the learners' L1 when learning English has been the focus of an ongoing debate, resulting in a variety of pedagogical practices in primary and secondary schools. This is partly because of the influence of communicative approaches in the twentieth century discouraging L1 use (Pennycook, 1994) and because of the 'monolingualising nature of the National Curriculum' (Conteh, 2012, p. 39) still prevalent in some schools. So, the proponents of an 'English-only' policy proclaim that learners need to be totally immersed in L2 to guarantee fluency and accuracy (Pacek, 2003) and to access the National Curriculum (DfE, 2011). Others, however, argue that it is impossible to separate the L1 from the learners' identity and cultural background (Auerbach, 1993; Norton, 2000; Ricento, 2005). One reconciling position considers that L1 have a potential to help learners acquire English without asking them to relinquish their linguistic capital. The emphasis on linguistic experience at the level of cognition makes it difficult for these learners to compartmentalize languages and, therefore, any attempts to suppress them for the purpose of school instruction imparted solely in English will invariably delay the learning process or result in utter failure (Martín Martín, 2000). This position argues that multilingual learners tend to link all the languages in their repertoires, the basis of the Linguistic Interdependence Theory (Butzkamm and Caldwell, 2009; Cummins, 2007), which proposes that the underlying proficiency learners have in their L1 allows them to master an additional language much easier and at a faster rate than monolingual learners. Swain and Lapkin (2013) suggest that the principled use of L1 is a legitimate instructional strategy 'to illustrate cross-linguistic comparisons or to provide the meaning of abstract vocabulary items' (p. 123). They also suggest that learners should be permitted 'to use their L1 during collaborative dialogue or private speech in order to mediate their understanding and generation of complex ideas (*languaging*) as they prepare to produce an end product (oral or written) in the target language' (ibid., pp. 122–3). This stage is described as the 'Third Space', discussed later.

Language Learning Strategies (LLS)

The idea that multilingual learners start their schooling in English with no knowledge of the language was long prevalent in many educational settings. Teachers adhering to this belief thought it was desirable, and even necessary, for these learners to spend time 'listening' to the new language before becoming engaged in classroom activities with other peers. During this phase, called 'the silent period', teachers assumed that 'children [were] absorbing the new language and building up their comprehension' (Clarke, 1999). During this period, teachers expected to see whether learners could follow basic spoken and written commands and instructions and produce prefabricated language chunks in English. However, evidence emerging at the beginning of the twenty-first century contradicted the belief that learners remain passive during the silent period (Harris, 2019). For example, Bligh (2014, p. 21) highlights the role of 'mother tongue thinking' as a means of making sense of the learners' new 'community of practice', and notes that learners are not silent, but they are actively making sense of the world internally through their L1, using a wide range of LLS.

LLS have been defined as 'activities consciously chosen by learners for the purpose of regulating their own learning' (Griffiths, 2007, p. 2) or 'specific actions, behaving as former steps or techniques students employ to improve their progress in internalising, storing, retrieving, and using the L2' (Nyikos and Oxford,

Table 13.1   Strategy groups and their domains

Strategy type	Domains
Cognitive	Language manipulation involving reasoning, analysis, and practice
Memory	Retrieval of information stored in the long-term memory
Compensation	Inference processes to compensate for missing knowledge
Communication	Use of compensation techniques in spoken interactions
Metacognitive	Evaluation of one's learning facilitated by reflection and action planning
Affective	Control over emotions, attitudes and motivations
Social	Co-operation with others in the language learning process

Source: Adapted from Oxford (1990).

1993, p. 17). Rubin (1975), a pioneer in the field, used his observations to describe and contextualize LLS in relation to the behaviours of a prototypical good language learner. He concludes that those learners like to communicate with others (communication strategy) and are tolerant and outgoing with native speakers (empathetic strategy). They plan according to a personal learning style (planning strategy) and practise willingly (practice strategy). They have the technical know-how concerning language (formal strategy) and develop an increasingly separate mental system in which they brainstorm ideas in L2 (novelization strategy), while making sense of new words and concepts (semantic strategy). At the same time, although good language learners are methodical in approach, they are flexible and are constantly looking to revise their linguistic understandings (experimental strategy) by testing out hypotheses. While most of the research produced in the 1980s and 1990s produced fuzzy results, and most of the classification of strategies lacked consensus (Cohen and Macaro, 2007), Oxford's (1990) taxonomy became a point of reference. This is summarized in Table 13.1.

Given the number of strategies and their complex nature, Oxford (1990) groups them into two clusters: those related to the immediate use of L2 (cognitive, memory, compensation and communication), which she calls 'direct' and those concerned with the learners' ability for self-regulation (metacognitive, affective and social strategies) or 'indirect'. Responding to some criticisms concerning the currency of LLS, Oxford (2017, p. 11) acknowledges 'the compatibility of learning strategies and concepts such as self-direction and autonomy … and the nexus of autonomy, self-regulation, and strategies'.

Strategy-based instruction (SBI) approaches

The major contribution of LLS to teaching practice has been the notions of autonomy and learner-centredness, which are the foundations of strategy-based approaches. While such concepts were originally discussed by Locke and Rousseau, who were opposed to a content-centred or curriculum-centred education (Noddings, 2018), LLS apply these notions of autonomy and learner-centredness to redefine the role of teachers as facilitators of learning opportunities. Learners are seen essentially as problem-solvers, who are aware of their own needs, deploying an array of strategies to achieve their goals and progress to the next stage in their learning experience (Manyukhina and Wyse, 2019). In this framework, LLS are context-dependent, teachers are not the only source of knowledge and learners, as they acquire more knowledge and skills, become the more knowledgeable ones who can support their peers. Although there are different strategy-based models, the communicative ones are based on dialogic interaction following a socio-constructivist perspective; teaching groups form a learning community where one student learns from another (Norton and Pavlenko, 2019). This is an iterative process and is largely based on the learners' ability to engage with three main skills: (1) metacognition, a higher-order thinking that enables understanding, analysis and control of the cognitive processes (Haukås, 2018); (2) shared cognition, the collective cognitive action from individual group members where the collective activity has an impact on the overall group goals and learning outcomes (Levine, 2018); and (3) action planning, an ability to think about learning goals and decide which strategies are the most effective to achieve those goals (Welsh *et al.*, 2019). Action planning involves the evaluation of learning outcomes and the strategies put into practice and, as a result, this stage promotes reflection (metacognition), thus closing a circuit, enabling the process to start again.

The debate on whether strategies can be taught has dominated the field of language pedagogy for quite some time (Nisbet and Shucksmith, 2017; Oxford, 2017), though the current position appears to favour explicit instruction (Dörnyei, 2005) as LLS are unconscious and learners may not be aware they are using them. Therefore, the explicitness of language strategy instruction (LSI) affects the degree to which learners retain and transfer strategies. In direct or informed LSI, learners are informed of the value and purpose of strategy instruction, are told strategy names and are prompted to use specific strategies on an assigned task. In embedded LSI, learners are presented with materials and activities structured to elicit the use of strategies, but are not informed of the reasons why this approach is being practised. These approaches are examined in the context of three strategy-based instruction (SBI) models in the next section.

Cognitive Academic Language Learning Approach (CALLA)

The most popular instructional models employed during the 1980s and 1990s were the Cognitive Academic Language Learning Approach (CALLA) (Albashtawi, 2019) and the Problem-Solving Process Model (PSM) (Orosco and Abdulrahim, 2018). The CALLA approach is aimed at improving multilingual learners' level of L2 ability to develop academic language skills as opposed to social language use.

The CALLA approach moves through a number of stages where the roles of the teacher and the students reverse. At the beginning of LSI the teacher has the major responsibility. By contrast, the students' responsibility is relatively limited. As the students widen their repertoire of learning strategies, their responsibility increases while that of the teacher's reduces. The students' responsibility progresses so that eventually they can self-assess strategies and use them independently, having previously received feedback.

Problem-solving model (PSM)

The PSM is based on four metacognitive processes: planning, monitoring, problem solving and self-evaluation. Individual strategies are presented within each of these four processes and they are operationalized through either a description of the task that learners perform or a question they ask themselves and use at various stages in their learning (Table 13.2).

Table 13.2 Example of the metacognitive processes involved in the problem-solving model

Planning	
Goal setting	What do I need or want to do?
Think about what I know	What have I learned before?
Prediction	What am I going to hear? What do I need to say?
Selective attention	What are the key words?
Monitoring	
Self-questioning	Am I understanding? Am I being understood?
Using what I know	What might what I already know help me?
Visualization	Am I making a mental picture as I read or listen?
Self-talk	'I can do it!'
Personalization	What does it mean to *me*?
Co-operation	Am I helping my peers and letting them help me?
Problem solving	
Inferencing	Can I make a guess?
Substituting	Can I say it in another way?
Clarification	Do I ask when I don't understand?
Self-evaluation	
Goal-checking	Did I achieve my goal?
Self-evaluation	How well did I do it?
Strategy evaluation	Did the strategy work well for me?

Chamot's SBI model

Chamot's model (2004) consists of three major stages underpinned by the assumption that strategies can be taught. Before the lesson, during the preparation stage, the teacher decides: (1) which strategies to use based on the needs of the group; (2) the type of practice opportunities to give the students; and (3) follow-up activities to consolidate learning. The teacher considers the needs of the teaching group in relation to the complexity of the task and their current ability and then decides on the strategies to teach. In the next stage, the teacher undertakes an initial presentation of the new strategy, including a brief statement about why the strategy is important and how it is expected to assist students. The teacher models the strategy, demonstrating the steps involved in approaching and completing a task. Immediately after, the teacher moves to the practice stage, where learners practise the new strategies in class and are asked to reinforce learning through homework.

The three instructional models emphasize the importance of providing multiple practice opportunities so that learners can use the strategies autonomously, encouraging learners to evaluate how well a strategy has worked, choose strategies to complete a task and transfer them to new tasks.

Translanguaging and the 'Third Space'

In recent times, some schools have been more tolerant in allowing, or even encouraging, multilingual learners to employ their linguistic repertoires in classrooms. Where this is the case, code-switching among multilingual learners is a common feature. While these learners routinely switch between different languages in their everyday social interaction, in educational contexts, especially in the classroom, code-switching was deemed inappropriate or unacceptable, as a deficit or dysfunctional mode of interaction, and in many cases prohibited by policy (Li and Lin, 2019). Hartmann *et al.* (2018) define code-switching as the practice of 'alternating between two or more languages in a single conversation, [which] is a marked feature of multilingual communities' (p. 1615) and this phenomenon, as explained by Talaat (2003), should be considered a source of creativity.

Translanguaging is similar to code-switching in that it refers to multilingual learners shuttling between languages in a natural manner (Canagarajah, 2011). Lasagabaster and García claim that translanguaging is

> a pedagogical strategy ... which fosters the dynamic and integrative use of bilingual students' languages in order to create a space in which the incorporation of both languages is seen as natural and teachers accept it as a legitimate pedagogical practice.
>
> (2014, p. 557)

García and Kleyn (2016) explain that multilingual learners strategically select words, rules, speaking style and pronunciation from their idiolect that includes features of the L1 and English. Chumak-Horbatsch (2019) explains that 'guided by their *translanguaging instinct*, [these students] adjust language boundaries, disrupt linguistic and cultural cues and move beyond and between language varieties, styles, registers and writing systems' (p. 13). According to García and Wei (2014), translanguaging is 'part of a moral and political act that links the production of alternative meanings to transformative social action' (p. 37). They acknowledge that such a welcoming of multilingual language practices in classrooms as a tool for transformative social action is nonetheless controversial, arguing that the controversy points to a general undervaluing of multilinguals' fluid practices in school settings. A translanguaging approach to teaching allows both learners and teachers to draw on their full linguistic repertoires and enables them to engage in a wide range of language practices in the classroom. Additionally, as García-Mateus and Palmer (2017) put it, translanguaging disrupts the normalized instructional assumptions of a monolingual National Curriculum and promotes social justice by affirming the legitimacy of the language practices of multilingual learners, teachers and their home communities. This, therefore, includes the acceptance of code-switching, translation and the use of varieties of vernacular forms of the L1, all of which are often devalued in school. Research shows that, when such aforementioned pedagogical practices are put in place, multilingual learners feel valued, recognized and develop novel dispositions for learning (Durán and Palmer, 2014; Gort and Sembiante, 2015), which may include hybrid forms of L2 or *languaging* in the 'Third Space'.

From the perspective of critical pedagogy, Guitiérrez (2018) introduces the metaphor of the 'Third Space' to refer to linguistic practices that use L1 in formal and informal educational settings to empower multilingual learners and teachers who, by virtue of being a linguistic minority, are often ignored by the monolingual practices of a dominant language and, consequently, their voices are silenced. This metaphor, according to Guitiérrez (ibid.), is akin to Vygotsky's Zone of Proximal Development (Vygotsky, 1980) and describes the social environment for development in which learners begin to reconceive who they are and what they might be able to accomplish academically and beyond. Two of the main features of the 'Third Space' are hybridity and diversity of ethnic, linguistic and educational practices that are not seen as problematic, but rather as important cultural resources in the learners' development (Cole, 1998). In a school context, multilingual learners negotiate what is known, for example, local cultural knowledge and linguistic registers, as they attempt to make sense of their identity in relation to prevailing notions of self and cultural practices. Moya (2020) explains that this perspective looks at the individuals, their identities, their aspirations as well as their own views of the world, acknowledging their linguistic capital as factors contributing to their academic achievement, thus subverting the English-only, one-size-fits-all curricula. Safford (2003) argues that there is a conflict between the celebration of ethnic and linguistic diversity, on the one hand, and the universal model of language development and assessment, on the other. One such practice that tends to ignore the voices of learners coming from linguistic minorities is assessment as it inadvertently curtails the educational success of multilingual learners (ibid.). However, the National Curriculum provides many affordances, particularly through Modern Languages in Key Stage 2, to allow these learners to celebrate their linguistic identity and use translanguaging to bridge home and school. These learning zones, which McKey (2002) also calls 'zones of contact', promote the development of global awareness and understanding, empowering learners to have a voice in school settings that are immanently polycontextual, multi-voiced and multiscripted.

Vignette: Chamot's (2004) revised SBI model in practice

The strategy-based instruction models described above have traditionally followed a cognitive perspective with an emphasis on the role of memory to store and retrieve linguistic knowledge. This is not surprising as most of the research, in fact the agenda of the time, around LLS stated that the role of the mind was like a 'black box'. While it was unknown what happened inside the mind, applied linguists sought to explain language acquisition by using computer terminology such as input, or instances of L2 exposure and output, or instances of production, with information processing occurring between them. Within the cognitive paradigm, there was an assumption that multilingual learners were able to resort to different strategies stored in the long-term memory, which had been internalized because of repeated use and which were, by and large, unconscious. Therefore, the teacher was instrumental in bringing the internalized strategic knowledge and LLS practice to the fore through a careful task design, prompting their conscious use. According to these models, language learning emerges from the learners' engagement with input-rich resources by employing specific strategies that are not explicitly taught, but are taken for granted. However, since a new understanding of learning as a social and situated experience (Lave and Wenger, 1990) taking place in a community of practice (Wenger et al., 2002), contributions from the ethnography of communication have promoted a new understanding of how linguistic practices occur in classrooms. Alexander (2008) emphasizes the need to create interactive opportunities in such environments where dialogue is used as a tool for learning (Mercer, 2000). To exemplify this point, Chamot's (2004) model has been reviewed, incorporating talk as a vehicle for learning. The revised model, presented in Table 13.3, is applied in the context of an English lesson, though it can be used with any other subject in the curriculum. The revised model consists of four stages, namely: presentation, comprehension, assisted practice and reflection, and learners are required to use their L1, if necessary, to discuss how strategies are applied to solve language problems, followed by a reflection on the outcomes of the experience.

Table 13.3 Chamot's (2004) SBI model revised

Stages	Chamot's model (2004)	Stages	Revised model
One	The teacher decides: (a) which strategies to use based on the needs of the group, (b) the type of practice opportunities to give the students; and (c) follow-up activities.	Presentation	The teacher presents the learning outcomes and key LLS for learners to use. L2 is embedded in a context, followed by questions and answers to elicit information, such as type of text, genre and content. Learners are encouraged to work in pairs and, if necessary, use translanguaging for exploratory talk.
Two	The teacher considers the needs of the teaching group in relation to learning tasks.	Comprehension	Learners work in pairs on a focused task assigned by the teacher. For example, the identification of parts of speech, characters, tone and genre, among others. Learners discuss and agree on the strategies to use to work out the meaning of words and structures. They may use think-aloud protocols as part of the exploratory talk in L1 if necessary.
Three	The teacher undertakes an initial presentation of the new strategy, or a combination of strategies, including a brief statement about why the strategy is important and how it is expected to assist students.	Assisted practice	Once the learners have identified key language features such as vocabulary items, grammatical structures, phonological units, etc., they practise their own utterances using different strategies, such as an online translation for vocabulary development and pronunciation model, using chanting, singing or tapping the rhythm of the words to commit the pronunciation to memory, and then assess one another, providing feedback. The L1 is not used in this stage.
Four	The teacher models the strategy using think-aloud protocols, demonstrating the steps involved in approaching and completing the language task. The teacher plans for immediate practice. The students practise the new strategies in class and are asked to reinforce learning through a piece of homework.	Reflection	Learners reflect on their learning experience, recording their views on a journal and tracking their progress using 'I can statements' (e.g., I can understand simple directions to go from Y to Z). They also discuss their performance, providing feedback to one another, and decide on their next learning goals. They keep a record of achievement where they also include future goals. Learners can use their L1 to explain complex situations in L2 with the support of other peers for translation.

The revised SBI model makes overt use of direct strategies, however, the use of indirect strategies is evident throughout the four stages. Learners are engaged in a process of negotiation with peers, discussing alternatives, using metacognition to monitor their learning and regulating their emotions as they contribute ideas for the resolution of tasks, reducing stress and anxiety while increasing participation and sense of belonging. The 'I can' statements also provide learners with tangible evidence of their learning, thus developing their self-esteem, happiness and involvement in lessons, as documented by Moya (2014). The indirect strategies, therefore, are powerful tools to promote self-efficacy, which is a person's beliefs about whether s/he feels s/he can successfully complete a task in a specific context (Bandura, 1997). The revised model contributes to the development of learners' self-efficacy by allowing them to experience success and get constructive feedback from significant others, by observing others succeed who are similar in competences to themselves and by evaluating their own emotional states and their responses to the learning experiences (Bandura, 1977).

Conclusion

For teachers, making a richer and motivating curriculum relevant to all is no mean feat, as they need to harness an understanding of how learners' life experiences can be used to plan creative and engaging lessons. Traditionally, learning has been associated with the active promotion of direct strategies linked to cognition and memory, while the indirect strategies (metacognition, affective and social) have remained largely underestimated. With a renewed emphasis on a learner-centred approach, a more holistic vision of learning has led to the consideration of the funds of knowledge and various skill sets that learners bring to the classroom, as well as the importance of creating the right internal and external conditions to develop more resilient learners with a growth mindset. Interestingly, Dweck (2006) argues that people can be placed on a continuum between two extremes: one that a person is born with fixed amounts of abilities, including intelligence, and that these cannot be changed (i.e., fixed mindset); the other representing the view that everyone can develop their potential further and grow their intelligence or change personal traits (i.e., growth mindset). According to Mercer and Dörnyei, 'a person with a growth mindset would believe that language learning abilities can always be enhanced through *strategic efforts* and that everyone can improve on their base level of abilities' (2020, p. 34). This idea resonates with the importance of cultivating the indirect LLS (metacognition, affective and social) as they have a direct link with the theory of learner attributions (Weiner, 1992) concerned with the various explanations that learners give to reflect on their past successes and failures. In this sense, Mercer and Dörnyei explain that:

> [F]uture willingness to engage with tasks is improved by a learner making 'healthy' attributions, that is, concentrating on factors contributing to their

failures that they can influence and change. That is, future engagement will occur if students feel they have control over their learning outcomes.

(2020, p. 35)

In the example model discussed above, learners exercise their autonomy to identify their next learning goals emerging from peer discussion, where feedback is given as a compassionate practice (Jones and Vari, 2018), followed by an individual assessment of their performance. The use of reflection enables learners to track their progress and this, in turn, can be used as further evidence for teachers to transform the practice of formative assessment and make it more encompassing and fairer, since the learners are in control.

While many teachers have understood the importance of promoting the learners' existing knowledge and skills, there is still some further room to capitalize on the tacit knowledge and skills that multilingual learners possess by encouraging the development of a 'Third Space', the metaphorical place where L2 emerges as a result of the use of LLS, to breach the gap between home and school. This is an example of 'linguistically appropriate practice' (Chumak-Horbatsch, 2019) that calls for teachers to reflect on their teaching beliefs and practices, inviting them to be more linguistically responsive so that they can promote learners' autonomy and self-efficacy for them to grow and thrive in settings where they feel valued.

Taking the discussion in this chapter into account, teachers might choose to reflect on the following questions from their own experience:

1 How do multilingual learners with a limited amount of English in a class approach the learning of subject-specific content?
2 Which strategies do these learners use in order to negotiate learning?
3 How might students be encouraged to use language learning strategies to develop their linguistic capacity to learn another language?
4 How, in your view, can teachers promote the notion of 'Third Space' in their classrooms?

Note

1 According to Moya (2019), 'bilingualism' and 'multilingualism' in England have many implications and are susceptible to many interpretations; therefore, the use of L1 here as a generic terminology includes bilingual, multilingual and plurilingual speakers.

References

Albashtawi, A.H. (2019) 'Improvement of EFL students' academic reading achievement through the Cognitive Academic Language Learning Approach (CALLA)', *Reading Psychology*, 40(8): 679–704.

Alexander, R.J. (2008) *Towards Dialogic Teaching: Rethinking Classroom Talk*, York: Dialogos.

Auerbach, E. (1993) 'Reexamining English only in the ESL classroom', *TESOL Quarterly*, 27(1): 9–32.

Bandura, A. (1977) 'Self-efficacy: Toward a unifying theory of behavioral change', *Psychological Review*, 84(2): 191–215.

Bandura, A. (1997) *Self-efficacy: The Exercise of Control*, New York: W.H. Freeman.

Bligh, C. (2014) *The Silent Experiences of Young Bilingual Learners: A Sociocultural Study into the Silent Period*, Rotterdam: Sense Publishers.

Butzkamm, W. and Caldwell, J. (2009) *The Bilingual Reform: A Paradigm Shift in Foreign Language Teaching*, Tübingen, Germany: Gunter Narr Verlag.

Canagarajah, S. (2011) 'Translanguaging in the classroom: Emerging issues for research and pedagogy', *Applied Linguistics Review*, 2: 1–28.

Chamot, A. (2004) 'Issues in language learning strategy research and teaching', *Electronic Journal of Foreign Language Teaching*, 1(1): 14–26.

Chumak-Horbatsch, R. (2019) *Using Linguistically Appropriate Practice: A Guide for Teaching in Multilingual Classrooms*, Bristol: Multilingual Matters.

Clarke, P. (1999) 'Investigating second language acquisition in preschools: A longitudinal study of four Vietnamese speaking children's acquisition of English in a bilingual preschool', *International Journal of Early Years Education*, 7(1): 17–24.

Cohen, A. D. and Macaro, E. (2007) *Language Learning Strategies*, Oxford: Oxford University Press.

Cole, S. (1998) The use of L1 in communicative English classrooms. [Online] Available: https://jalt-publications.org/tlt/articles/2439-use-l1-communicative-english-classrooms (accessed 29 January 2021).

Conteh, J. (2012) *Teaching Bilingual and EAL Learners in Primary Schools*, London: SAGE Publications.

Cummins, J. (2007) 'Rethinking monolingual instructional strategies in multilingual classrooms', *Canadian Journal of Applied Linguistics*, 10(2): 221–40.

DfE (Department for Education) (2011) *The Framework for the National Curriculum: A Report by the Expert Panel for the National Curriculum Review*, London: Department of Education.

Dörnyei, Z. (2005) *The Psychology of the Language Learner: Individual Differences in Second Language Acquisition*, London: Routledge.

Durán, L. and Palmer, D. (2014) 'Pluralist discourses of bilingualism and translanguaging talk in classrooms', *Journal of Early Childhood Literacy* 14(3): 367–88.

Dweck, C.S. (2006) *Mindset: The New Psychology of Success*, New York: Ballantine Books.

García, O. and Kleyn, T. (2016) 'Translanguaging theory in education', in O. García and T. Kleyn (eds), *Translanguaging with Multilingual Students: Learning from Classroom Moments*, Abingdon: Routledge, pp. 9–33.

García, O. and Wei, L. (2014) 'Translanguaging and education', in O. García and L. Wei (eds), *Translanguaging: Language, Bilingualism and Education*, London: Palgrave Macmillan, pp. 63–77.

García-Mateus, S. and Palmer, D. (2017) 'Translanguaging pedagogies for positive identities in two-way dual language', *Bilingual Education, Journal of Language, Identity and Education*, 16(4): 245–55.

Gort, M. and Sembiante, S.F. (2015) 'Navigating hybridized language learning spaces through translanguaging pedagogy: Dual language preschool teachers' languaging practices in support of emergent bilingual children's performance of academic discourse', *International Multilingual Research Journal*, 9(1): 7–25.

Griffiths, C. (2007) 'Language learning strategies: Students' and teachers' perceptions', *English Language Teaching Journal*, 61(2): 91–9.

Gutiérrez, K. (2018) 'Developing a sociocritical literacy in the Third Space', *Reading Research Quarterly*, 43(2): 148–64.

Harris, R. (2019) 'Re-assessing the place of the "silent period" in the development of English as an Additional Language among children in Early Years settings', *TEANGA, the Journal of the Irish Association for Applied Linguistics*, 10: 77–93.

Hartmann, S., Choudhury, M. and Bali, K. (2018) 'An integrated representation of linguistic and social functions of code-switching', in *Proceedings of the Eleventh International Conference on Language Resources and Evaluation* (LREC). Miyazaki, Japan: European Language Resources Association (ELRA). Available at https://www.aclweb.org/anthology/volumes/L18-1/ (accessed 25 January 2021).

Haukås, Å. (2018) 'Metacognition in language learning and teaching: An overview', in Å. Haukås, C. Björke and M. Dypedahl (eds), *Metacognition in Language Learning and Teaching*, New York: Routledge, pp. 11–30.

Jones, J. and Vari, T.J. (2018) *Candid and Compassionate Feedback: Transforming Everyday Practice in Schools*, London: Routledge.

Lasagabaster, D. and García, O. (2014) 'Translanguaging: Towards a dynamic model of bilingualism at school/Translanguaging: hacia un modelo dinámico de bilingüismo en la escuela', *Cultura y Educación*, 26(3): 557–72.

Lave, J. and Wenger, E. (1990) *Situated Learning: Legitimate Peripheral Participation*, Cambridge: Cambridge University Press.

Levine, J.M. (2018) 'Socially-shared cognition and consensus in small groups', *Current Opinion in Psychology*, 23: 52–6.

Li, Wei and Lin, A.M.Y. (2019) 'Translanguaging classroom discourse: Pushing limits, breaking boundaries', *Classroom Discourse*, 10(3–4): 209–15.

Manyukhina, Y. and Wyse, D. (2019) 'Learner agency and the curriculum: A critical realist perspective', *The Curriculum Journal*, 30(3): 223–43.

Martín Martín, J.M. (2000) *La Lengua Materna en el Aprendizaje de una Segunda Lengua*, Seville: Servicio de Publicaciones de la Universidad de Sevilla.

McKay, S.L. (2002) *Teaching English as an International Language: Rethinking Goals and Perspectives*, Oxford: Oxford University Press.

Mercer, N. (2000) *Words and Minds: How We Use Language to Think Together*, London: Routledge.

Mercer, S. and Dörnyei, Z. (2020) *Engaging Language Learners in Contemporary Classrooms*, Cambridge: Cambridge University Press.

Moya, M. (2014) 'Developing a strategy-based instruction approach to teaching and learning modern languages to train ab-initio PGCE trainees', *Journal of Pedagogical Development*, 4(1): 3–12.

Moya, M. (2019) 'Bilingualism and Multilingualism in Secondary Education (England)', *Bloomsbury Education and Childhood Studies (BECS)* https://doi.org/10.5040/9781350996274.0005

Moya, M. (2020) 'Empowering multilingual learners through critical liberating literacy practices in English-dominated speech communities', in G. Neokleous, A. Krulatz and R. Farrelly (eds), *Handbook of Research on Cultivating Literacy in Diverse and Multilingual Classrooms*, New York: IGI Global.

Nisbet, J. and Shucksmith, J. (2017) *Learning Strategies*, Abingdon: Routledge.

Noddings, N. (2018) *Philosophy of Education*, Abingdon: Routledge.

Norton, B. (2000) *Identity and Language Learning: Gender, Ethnicity, and Educational Change*, London: Longman.

Norton, B. and Pavlenko, A. (2019) 'Imagined communities, identity, and English language learning in a multilingual world', in X. Gao (ed.), *Second Handbook of English Language Teaching*, Bern, Switzerland: Springer International Publishing, pp. 703–18.

Nyikos, M. and Oxford, R. (1993) 'A factor analytical study of language-learning strategy use: Interpretations from information-processing theory and social psychology', *The Modern Language Journal*, 77(1): 11–22.

Orosco, M.J. and Abdulrahim, N.A. (2018) 'Examining comprehension strategy instruction with English learners' problem solving: Study findings and educator preparation implications', *Teacher Education and Special Education*, 41(3): 215–28.

Oxford, R.L. (1990) *Language Learning Strategies: What Every Teacher Should Know*, New York: Harper and Row.

Oxford, R.L. (2017) *Teaching and Researching Language Learning Strategies: Self-regulation in Context*, 2nd ed., London: Routledge.

Pacek, D. (2003) 'Should EFL give up on translation?' Talk given at the 11th Annual Korea TESOL International Conference. Seoul, South Korea. Available at https://koreatesol.org/sites/default/files/pdf_publications/KOTESOL-Proceeds2003web.pdf (accessed 25 January 2021).

Pavlenko, A. and Norton, B. (2007) 'Imagined communities, identity, and English Language learning', in J. Cummins and C. Davison (eds), *International Handbook of English Language Teaching*, Boston, MA: Springer, pp. 669–80.

Pennycook, A. (1994) *The Cultural Politics of English as an International Language*, London: Routledge.

Ricento, T. (2005) 'Considerations of identity in L2 learning', in E. Hinkel (ed.), *Handbook of Research in Second Language Teaching and Learning*, Mahwah, NJ: Lawrence Erlbaum, pp. 895–911.

Rubin, J. (1975) 'What the good language learner can teach us', *TESOL Quarterly*, 9: 41–51.

Safford, K. (2003) *Teachers and Pupils in the Big Picture: Seeing Real Children in Routinised Assessment*, Reading: National Association for Language Development in the Curriculum.

Swain, M. and Lapkin, S. (2013) 'A Vygotskian sociocultural perspective on immersion education: The L1/L2 debate', *Journal of Immersion and Content-Based Education*, 1(1): 101–29.

Talaat, M. (2003) 'Some aspects of creativity in Pakistani English or improvised communication', *Pakistani Journal of Language*, 4(1).

Vygotsky, L.S. (1980) *Mind in Society: The Development of Higher Psychological Processes*, Cambridge, MA: Harvard University Press.

Weiner, B. (1992) *Attributional Theories of Human Motivation: Human Motivation: Metaphors, Theories, and Research*, Newbury Park, CA: Sage.

Welsh, D., Bush, J., Thiel, C. and Bonner, J. (2019) 'Reconceptualizing goal setting's dark side: The ethical consequences of learning versus outcome goals', *Organizational Behavior and Human Decision Processes*, 150: 14–27.

Wenger, E., McDermott, R.A. and Snyder, W. (2002) *Cultivating Communities of Practice: A Guide to Managing Knowledge*, Boston, MA: Harvard Business Press.

Part 5

Learning environment

Teacher trainers', early years teachers' and child and adult learners' perspectives

The significance of the learning environment in facilitating positive attitudes and engagement with learning activities cannot be overestimated. Chapter 14 in this Part takes the important issue of pupil behaviour and its relationship to the wider curriculum, and discusses ways of helping new teachers, teaching assistants and other adults who work in schools to understand the 'bigger picture'. The authors take the view that the learning environment is important in all areas of the National Curriculum, but they place particular emphasis on the way paraprofessionals and developing teachers might think about pupil behaviours in two core areas of the curriculum: Mathematics and English. Chapter 15 moves into the early years to consider how, for the authors, teaching in two contrasting environments for early years education (England and Tanzania) led to them reflecting on the connections between learning environments and teaching pedagogies. They discuss how contrasting physical learning environments in the English and Tanzanian contexts had a direct influence on how adults worked with children and therefore children's opportunities for learning and development. They conclude that environment, and who has ownership of it, can reflect deeply held beliefs about viewpoints of how children learn and what holds value to those in positions of authority. Chapter 16 also draws on its author's experiences and suggests ways in which practitioners can maintain the worth and dignity of children with EAL within the National Curriculum framework so that they never feel ashamed of who they are, the colour of their skin, their home language(s) and culture. Finally, Chapter 17, too, is written from the perspective of one of the authors on the theme of Personal, Social, Health, and Economic (PSHE) programmes. She comments that, while they may have a positive impact on both academic and non-academic outcomes for some young people, lesson content may be potentially damaging to those who are disadvantaged in some way. She discusses ways in which the content of the PSHE curriculum can be inclusive of all learners.

Learning environment

14 Starting to see the 'bigger picture'

Ways of developing professional and paraprofessional understandings of behaviour, curriculum and the learning environment

Steve Connolly and Allyson Goodchild

Major questions addressed in this chapter are:

- What do new teachers and teaching assistants need to know about behaviur in the classroom and how can this be taught?
- What is the relationship between the types of behaviour pupils exhibit in different curriculum areas and the pupil's relationship with that curriculum area?
- How do education students who are working in paraprofessional and professional roles learn to connect theory with practice in order to develop effective learning behaviours in different curriculum areas?

Abstract

This chapter considers the development of a course module entitled 'The learning environment' on an undergraduate Applied Education degree, that sought to introduce students (who were largely, themselves, in teaching assistant or paraprofessional roles) to some of the issues surrounding pupil behaviour in

UK schools. Developing the module led to the identification of three key areas to which both people in these roles, and new teachers, should be introduced. These can be summarized as (1) policy contexts; (2) theoretical and academic views of behaviour; and (3) practitioner knowledge. The first of these areas involves understanding the nature of school behaviour policies and how these fit in with national policies on behaviour and the wider learning environment. The second involves learning about the way that perspectives from psychology and other academic disciplines might inform these policies and subsequent practice. The final area involves examining a range of practitioner approaches to the learning environment, behaviour and behaviour management and the way that these factors influence the curriculum. As well as summarizing key information in these areas, the chapter seeks to explain the ways in which the module might inform practice in schools, in terms of allowing new professionals and paraprofessionals to gain a deeper understanding of pupil behaviour and the contexts (curricular, pastoral and extra-curricular) in which it occurs.

Introduction

I will also be concentrating on the use of positive praise and feedback for students. Directing my attention to the good behaviour in order to give students reinforcement of what is expected, rather than giving students punishments or sanctions for displaying poor behaviour. This should lead to our learning environment becoming a more positive place where students want to be in order to succeed academically.

This is an extract from a report written by an unqualified teacher who is completing an Education degree alongside her full-time job. She has been asked to write a report reflecting on how she thinks her school's behaviour policy is enacted and the extract above comes from the section of her assignment in which she is reflecting on what her roles and responsibilities are in terms of creating a positive learning environment for the children she works with. It may not, at first, seem obvious to have a chapter on behaviour in a book about curriculum, but this student has grasped a very important point; namely that the curriculum that a teacher or school intends to deliver will only have impact if it is delivered within an effective learning environment. In this chapter, the authors want to explore the relationship between curriculum, behaviour and the learning environment by relating their experiences, and the experiences of students, in teaching an undergraduate module entitled 'The Learning Environment'. This module, outlined further below, seeks to encourage students – many of whom are in paraprofessional roles in schools, as teaching assistants or unqualified teachers – to think about this 'bigger picture', i.e., the way that pupil behaviour, the environment and the curriculum are all interconnected. These experiences are offered here not, then as a 'behaviour manual' (as there are plenty of these available to which teachers can refer) but rather as a means of encouraging those who work in classrooms to think about the way that particular areas of the curriculum might require particular types of learning behaviour from pupils and particular types of teaching behaviours from the adults involved.

'The Learning Environment' module

Students on the part-time BA (Hons) Applied Education Studies course are already working in educational settings in a variety of roles such as teaching assistants, cover supervisors, early years workers and unqualified teachers. In the main, they are skilled paraprofessionals who are seeking future career progression into teaching. On completion, many of our graduates apply for an employment-based route to Qualified Teacher Status, or undertake a PGCE course. The 'applied' nature of the course makes explicit links between education theory and students' professional experiences. This connection enables our students to develop their knowledge and understanding of teaching and learning processes while continuing to work which, in turn, improves their professional practice.

The course is designed to provide an understanding of a range of aspects of primary education, including curriculum content and pedagogy, educational theory and professional practice. It introduces students to the importance of research and enquiry within education and gives them the opportunity to carry out primary research in their own setting. The' Learning Environment' module is a relatively new addition to the range of modules offered on the course. While the degree provides plenty of opportunity to learn about teaching English and mathematics, with 120 credits devoted to these two subjects over the four years, student surveys revealed they really wanted support to help them manage the behaviour of the children they are assigned to work with in order to be able to successfully apply their new curriculum knowledge. Our students are often expected to teach individuals with complex needs, run intervention groups in the core subjects or indeed cover teaching sessions at short notice. This can be a source of frustration when behaviour disrupts learning, particularly when learning targets are not met, and continued poor behaviour impacts on their ability to teach effectively. In turn, this can lead to feelings of stress and anxiety especially when they view another colleague managing the behaviour of the same pupil or groups of pupils well. A subsequent course review further highlighted this gap and a timely redesign of the degree programme resulted in this new module being developed.

The learning environment is multi-faceted but is essentially social and in the public domain. Each individual, whether an adult or a child, will interpret and respond to the environment differently through their behaviour. It is easy for a busy paraprofessional to lose sight of this when faced with the core task of teaching, perhaps reaching for behaviour strategies and using rewards and sanctions without fully understanding the rationale behind the behaviours demonstrated and the use of behaviourist approaches. A report for the Sutton Trust (Coe *et al.*, 2014) into what makes 'great teaching' identifies through research the essential components of effective teaching. While teachers' knowledge of the subject and the quality of their teaching are likely to produce the most favourable student outcomes, there is evidence to show that environmental factors, such as establishing a positive classroom climate and effective classroom management, including managing behaviour, are also necessary for effective learning. It might be unsurprising to read this but it can be challenging to enact as part of daily classroom practice, especially when a paraprofessional is called upon to work with a range of pupils in differing contexts within a setting.

With this in mind, the 'Learning Environment' module sets out to introduce students to theoretical principles underpinning the methods and strategies used by schools to manage the learning environment. The aim is to help them understand the rationale behind the decisions that are taken at a school level that they are expected to implement and to build their knowledge and understanding of this important area. Students are introduced to the wider educational policy context and investigate how schools manage behaviour through policy and practice as well as examining the contributory factors that help to create a positive learning environment in settings in order to maximize the learning opportunities for all pupils. The content of the module challenges them to re-evaluate their own thinking about the purpose of behaviour management in supporting learners and they are encouraged to reflect and share their professional experiences in this area.

The two assessment tasks within the module are closely connected. The first, a literature review, provides an opportunity to explore and evaluate the wider body of research and thinking surrounding how best to manage behaviour in an educational setting. The second, a work-based report, builds on this. Students are asked to analyze their school behaviour policy and to consider how aspects of the policy can be observed in the learning environment by providing concrete examples from practice. A fundamental part of this assessment requires them to reflect on their professional responsibilities to create the right conditions for learning for the children they support. This is a powerful piece of learning which helps them consider their role in teaching and fostering positive learning behaviours to help pupils learn effectively.

School policies

In the module students see from the outset that managing behaviour is not incidental to teaching and learning, rather, it is an integral component requiring both planning and reflection as well as attention to the wider environmental factors that may have an impact. Students consider the nature of behaviour policies that operate within their place of work and see how this relates to a range of national policy documents from the DFE, Ofsted and other bodies. Engaging with policy, both in local and national contexts, offers a starting point for students to explore the link between teaching, learning and behaviour more closely and to understand the whole school systems within which they work. Above all, awareness of the policy environment is key to helping both teachers and classroom assistants to achieve consistency.

On occasion, these explorations need to be both complex and nuanced. Over the last 30 years, as part of a wider attempt to deal with underachievement, successive governments have commissioned numerous reports and provided statutory and non-statutory guidance to support schools to promote good behaviour and discipline. A common theme emerging from the reports is that the low-level behaviours, such as calling out, talking, not having the correct equipment, using mobile phones, remain the most frequently cited behaviours seen in schools (DES, 1989; Ofsted, 2006; 2014). In fact, Ofsted (2014) claims that over one hour of learning each day is being lost due to this type of behaviour in English classrooms. Ofsted also raised issues of inconsistent approaches among staff with many simply accepting that low-level disruption was an expected daily challenge they would face. This often resonates with students who witness this type of behaviour in their settings. At the other extreme, the Timpson review of school exclusions highlights how some groups of pupils including boys, children with SEN and children from some ethnic backgrounds, are disproportionately more likely to be excluded from school. There is also wide variability in exclusion rates between schools and in different areas of the country. The report states:

> teachers should be able to focus on helping all children to learn, rather than spending disproportionate time managing poor behaviour. Excellent teaching that challenges and engages children can, itself, provide the backbone to effective behaviour management and promote a classroom environment where all children can progress.
>
> (DFE, 2019, p. 55)

The report goes on to stress the importance of individual schools having clear expectations of behaviour through whole school systems with exclusions being used as and when it is appropriate within a broader supportive framework.

A consistent whole school approach is another common theme within the wider policy guidance. Much of the early research (DES, 1989; DfES, 2005; 2009; Ofsted, 2006) recognizes that good teaching promotes good behaviour, which in turn leads to better outcomes. To achieve this, schools must focus more closely on approaches designed to improve teaching and learning as well as promoting good behaviour. While some of this policy literature is quite dated, there is benefit in students who are working in school examining it and realizing that these systems are the responsibility of all staff. A more contemporary view can be found in Tom Bennett, the government's behaviour tsar. In his independent review of behaviour (2017, p. 6), he places responsibility on school leaders to establish, promote and maintain a school culture, which explicitly demonstrates 'the way we do things around here and the values we hold', which is understood by the whole school community. Furthermore, the latest Ofsted inspection framework (2019) seeks to investigate how leaders and staff create a safe, calm and positive environment and the impact this has on pupil behaviour and attitudes. When discussing ideas about culture, though, we make some effort to problematize it as a concept. It is important for students to consider not only culture within the school but culture outside it as well, alongside the thorny problem of whose culture is being promoted and maintained.

As a minimum, schools are expected to have a school behaviour policy (SBP) in place which 'supports staff in managing behaviour, including the use of rewards and sanctions' (DFE, 2016, p. 3) and promotes good behaviour and discipline. Others take a more holistic view. For example, Chaplain (2016) sees the behaviour policy as being integral to the school climate with values and expectations made explicit. In essence, it should provide any professional working in a setting with a clear and supportive framework to manage behaviour. The policy may include a code of conduct linked to rewards and sanctions, the rights and responsibilities of staff and pupils and systems of support designed to support learning. Above all, the SBP should reflect the school ethos and values and in turn this should be reflected in what can be visibly seen happening within the school. As part of the Learning Environment module, students analyze their own school behaviour policy and consider how it is observed in practice. This is an excellent opportunity for them to understand how the guidance is interpreted by staff and pupils within the learning environment, how this policy can support teaching and learning and the opportunities and challenges this creates. Furthermore, they start to realize the important role they play in taking ownership of this policy as part of their daily practice, and in turn this ownership allows for a more effective delivery of the curriculum.

Theoretical and academic views of behaviour

Many of the students on our course – like many professional teachers – question the need for theoretical knowledge when dealing with pupil behaviour. We often hear students comment about the need to get pupils to behave without ever thinking about the role that theoretical perspectives might have to play in understanding why pupils behave in the way that they do. For us, it is important to make clear the theoretical origins of approaches to behaviour and the establishment of a learning environment, because people who work in schools will often be 'sold' the work of practitioners (see following section) without ever really understanding where these practitioners' work is sited in theoretical terms. Teaching students about this siting allows them to develop a more pluralistic and discerning view of pupil behaviour and how to adapt their practice to deal with it.

Reasons of space do not permit a full analysis of the theoretical and academic perspectives which are used by the 'Learning Environment' module, but to give some insight into what use might be made of such views, we offer the work of three academics here who feature prominently on our course. These are the American psychologist Uri Bronfenbrenner, the father of behaviourism B.F. Skinner, and the English academic Terry Haydn, and they are used in order to explore not only the issues associated with behaviour, learning and the classroom environment, but also to help students establish the relationship between different kinds of theoretical perspective and classroom practice.

Bronfenbrenner's development of ecological systems theory (Bronfenbrenner, 1979), in which he outlines the ecological relationship between individuals and society, is a foundational theoretical perspective which we look at very early on in the module. The theory sets out a range of systems which affect the individual's behaviour, from the microsystem of something like the family module, to the exosystems of local authority policies, to the macrosystems of ideologies and cultures. Here, Bronfenbrenner's work is being used to prompt the student to think beyond the microsystem of the classroom – which they, as a teaching assistant or learning mentor are often very focused on – and towards the other factors that might influence behaviour. This is particularly important from a curricular point of view as there are often mesosystemic factors (such as speaking another language at home) or macrosystemic factors (such as cultural attitudes to the education of girls), which will affect pupil performance in particular curriculum areas like English, Drama or PE.

Skinner's description of *operant conditioning* (Skinner, 1938) also becomes significant later on in the module when discussing the notion of consequences and reinforcers. The idea of behaviour operating on a particular environment and generating consequences is something that often helps students who work in whole class environments understand why groups or individuals behave in particular ways. Many teaching assistants will describe, for example, being involved in English lessons where one student refuses to talk part in oral activities, and the response of the teacher or other students to this refusal operates as a reinforcer for that behaviour. As a consequence, understanding that behaviour allows them to develop different approaches to working with the class so that this kind of behaviour is not reinforced, or at least to be clear about what consequences may result from it.

Finally, the work of Terry Haydn, whose collection of articles and chapters about pupil behaviour in UK schools is used to introduce an element of empirical research to the module, proves invaluable in providing a different kind of academic perspective to student understanding of the learning environment. Haydn's work involves both collation of existing documentary and policy research (Haydn, 2014), empirical research (Haydn, 2015) and guidance for new teachers (Haydn, 2009) and provides students working on the module with an important example of how academic research can influence practice, by both being drawn upon by well-known practitioners (e.g., Bennett, 2017) and also by serving as a model of how research into classroom behaviour might be carried out. Haydn's work makes a direct link between academic and theoretical views of behaviour and classroom practice; as a former History teacher, he is always concerned with what the implications of his research are for the classroom colleague. However, this is grounded in a strong sense that classroom tools (such as his ten-point behaviour scale) need to be tested through research methodologies (Haydn, 2015).

These theoretical and academic perspectives allow students' thinking about the Learning Environment to make more informed decisions about the way that they deliver their curriculum because they lead to a greater understanding of the way that theory and practice are connected, and perhaps more importantly, why particular kinds of behaviour policy are pursued. There are many other perspectives discussed in the module that unfortunately cannot be included here; the work of Jere Brophy (1986), Ivan Pavlov ([1897] 1902) and Ellis and Tod (2015) all feature and all are used to get students to both think about their own practice and the way they use different types of source in their own academic and classroom work.

The role of practitioner knowledge

Students start the module having gained prior knowledge from the practitioners they work with. In an attempt to understand and manage the complexities of behaviour, many will have sought advice from those they perceive as 'knowledgeable' or 'expert'. While observing others is invaluable, it is often difficult to see or for the expert to explain exactly how they achieve the productive learning environment the student witnesses and aspires to, a process the expert will have internalized through their own experiences. Conversely, our students often pick up unhelpful perspectives and advice such as 'they are just attention seeking' or the old adage 'don't smile at them before Christmas'. This type of advice can erode confidence and lead to further confusion. Do I give them more attention or less? If I smile at them, will they behave better or worse? Replacing these questions with more helpful ones such as 'why is this child seeking to control the situation through their attention-seeking behaviour?' or 'how will they react to my negative body language?' requires a reflective approach. A significant aspect of the Learning Environment module then, involves analyzing the work of a number of high profile behaviour experts, whom we term 'practitioners', in order to understand some potential approaches to understanding both the behaviour they see and the advice they are given. It offers students the chance to evaluate and reflect upon practitioner and expert views in order to consider what they could develop into their own practice.

The Learning Environment does not advocate any particular system or practitioner approach, maintaining that it is the paraprofessional's responsibility to work within the guidance provided in the school policy. That said, the module affords them the opportunity to reflect on the strategies adopted by the school, to analyze their origin and their application and to consider how they can be successful in implementing them. To aid this process, we introduce students to a number of well-known expert practitioners including Paul Dix, Sue Cowley, Bill Rogers and Doug Lemov but, rather than encouraging them to implement the strategies and advice they advocate, we ask them to consider the approaches in light of the underpinning theory and how they might work in their own, unique setting.

A good example of this is the expert practitioner, Paul Dix. Dix's bestselling book *When the Adults Change, Everything Changes* (2017) is fast becoming a staffroom favourite. Dix advocates five pillars of practice: consistent, calm adult behaviour; first attention for best conduct; relentless routines; scripting difficult interventions; restorative follow-up. Dix is a great speaker and writer and talks anecdotally about his own experiences as a teacher that professionals can relate to. He provides plenty of practical, useful strategies such as: meeting and greeting pupils at the door, using recognition boards and positive notes home, which settings and professionals can and do adopt. Without proper analysis and deconstruction, such approaches could end up simply being 'quick fixes'. As part of the module, students are encouraged to unpick his approach to managing behaviour and strip it back to the underpinning theory. They soon start to see how the work of the humanist psychologist, Carl Rogers (1951) has implicitly impacted on Dix's approach to behaviour management. In particular, Rogers' concept of unconditional positive regard, whereby a child is shown complete support and acceptance no matter what they say or do, can be seen in some of Dix's key messages such as pupils being shown 'deliberate botheredness' and 'visible kindness' by their teacher. We also ask them to identify where Dix uses behaviourism in a positive way to reward rather than punish. A favourite example explored with the students is the writing of names on the board as a first step on the sanction ladder. After analyzing why the approach is used and how the child on the receiving end of this public sanction might perceive it, we then discuss Dix's alternative, to create a recognition board where names are written when positive behaviours are seen. Most importantly, we ask students to consider these approaches in relation to their own practice within their setting and to consider both the enablers and barriers to using them to support them in developing a positive learning environment.

As a contrast to Dix's humanistic approach, students are also introduced to Doug Lemov. His book, *Teach Like a Champion* (TLAC) (2015), contains 62 strategies that teachers can apply to engage children in their learning. Once again, we encourage students to view his practical ideas through an analytical lens. From the outset they start to see how TLAC is essentially a practical manifestation of Skinner's operant conditioning with the routines and techniques enabling positive reinforcement. For those working in quite ordered environments or teaching subjects such as science and DT, they quickly make the connection and can articulate how such routines lead to better organization and classroom management which in turn leads to better learning. In contrast, other students view some of his strategies as potential inhibitors of learning in curricular areas such as drama where inflexible approaches could stifle creativity.

Further and deeper discussion of practitioners, such as Lemov and Dix, leads to a much wider exploration of both the causes and the implications of the behaviour approaches they advocate. Some students will feel uncomfortable with the way that Lemov's techniques seem deliberately designed to force pupils into accepting certain kinds of cultural norm – a point echoed by Ilana Horn (2015), while others will see Dix's work as not setting strong enough boundaries for pupils. This discussion is significant, because it is the place where the student will begin to see the 'bigger picture' of not only what might and might not work for them in the classroom, but also why certain things might or might not work in their schools, or even in their geographical area.

Affording students the opportunity to compare and contrast different practitioner-led approaches enables individuals to reflect more deeply on their own experiences and consider what they could implement and use in their own practice. Behaviour management is complex and multifaceted. Therefore, encouraging students to engage with a range of perspectives, they start to realize that the strategy should be the end, not the starting point. By adopting a questioning, reflective approach to the behavioural problems they encounter when teaching their subject, they are better placed to choose strategies that will work in the longer term rather than seeking a quick fix that deals with the immediate problem they encounter.

Examples of seeing the bigger picture

The following vignettes come from work-based reports written by students working on the module who are asked to consider the way that their school's behaviour policy (SBP) is enacted in practice. This task gives them the opportunity to consider the theoretical and practical origins of the policy, while at the same time exploring what that looks like. The examples here are offered as a way of showing how the students' understanding of the relationship between behaviour and curriculum has grown through their engagement with the module. This understanding should be something that all new teachers and paraprofessionals should aspire to, as it is likely to make their work in the classroom easier.

Vignette 1: Targeted use of rewards

During my observations, I was able to see praise and reward being used regularly. An example of this was during an English lesson in a Year Five class, where children were completing a creative poem. One child had gone up to the teacher and asked whether their work was 'ok' as they were uncomfortable writing poetry. The teacher smiled and asked the class to stop and listen while he read out the poem. He then explained why he thought this was a good example and what he liked about it. The child was then awarded five merits, a points system that is used within the school to reward good behaviour and work. The child beamed from ear to ear! Within minutes, other children were not only putting up their hand to ask for the teacher's opinion on their work, but some couldn't wait and started to line up by his desk! What was even more interesting was that up until this point, the children appeared to be disengaged and uninterested with the lesson.

(Source: Year 3 BA Student, Learning Environment module – Work-Based Report, unpublished)

This vignette shows an interesting observation about the way that rewards and sanctions might be used specifically in creative or imaginative work. Many teachers and TAs, when setting a creative or imaginative task, will often be presented with disengaged or negative responses. However, in this observed example, the student writing the report realizes that there is a direct relationship between the school's reward system and the type of lesson being taught. This seems obvious in some ways, but for a TA who may often just be told to 'make sure the pupils do this', there is real value in giving them the opportunity to reach this realization for themselves.

Vignette 2: Reflecting on the efficacy of a school behaviour policy

A pupil with attention deficit hyperactivity disorder (ADHD) dislikes taking their medication and therefore can be disruptive within lessons, however, sometimes these behaviours cannot be controlled, especially in lessons such as: English, Mathematics and History as these lessons are more classroom and book work based. In design and technology and physical education, this student thrives as they can move about and be practical ... the whole school approach does not always work for some students, such as some with Special Educational Needs or Disabilities (SEND), who require a more adaptable approach to behaviour. This student receives the majority of their behaviour points during subjects where they have to sit and write for a prolonged period of time or where they have to be more formalized. This is because their attention span cannot cope with this level of intensity and therefore begins to be disruptive.

(Source: Year 3 BA Student, Learning Environment
module – Work-Based Report, unpublished)

Similarly, in this vignette, the student writing the report is reflecting on the efficacy of the SBP in relation to the circumstances of SEND pupils in particular areas of the curriculum. The student is beginning to consider the multiplicity of factors which influence the way that behaviour and learning – a reflection of Bronfenbrenner's ecologies in action – and viewing the limitations of the SBP, albeit in a professional way.

Conclusion

The putting together of the various pieces of the puzzle of behaviour is an important stage in the professional development of the teacher or teaching assistant, where they are beginning to make connections between theory, policy and practice. However, it is important to note that before the professional or paraprofessional can make these connections, they must be exposed to a range of theoretical and practical ideas which allow them to do so. The students studying the 'Learning Environment' module are, in many ways, lucky.

They have a chance to read, discuss and implement the ideas discussed above and more. Not all of their contemporaries will work in schools where senior leaders and other teachers have the time or opportunity to support new teachers or TAs by explaining the origins of their behaviour policies or giving them room to observe how they work. It is clear, however, from the vignettes included above that colleagues in this position will benefit from thinking about these things in both practical and theoretical terms and discussing them with other colleagues. This chance to 'see the bigger picture' can really benefit schools, staff and ultimately pupils, if it is, for example, incorporated into a school's CPD programme, or perhaps facilitated by a study or research group to which these staff are invited. In turn, the understandings gained by such work will help teachers and other staff to develop and deliver a broad and rich curriculum which will benefit all pupils, regardless of circumstance or ability.

References

Bennett, T. (2017) *Creating a Culture: How School Leaders Can Optimise Behaviour*, London: Department for Education.

Bronfenbrenner, U. (1979) *The Ecology of Human Development*, Cambridge, MA: Harvard University Press.

Brophy, J. (1986) 'Classroom management techniques', *Education and Urban Society*, 18(2): 182–94.

Chaplain, R. (2016) *Teaching Without Disruption in the Primary School: A Practical Approach to Managing Pupil Behaviour*, 2nd ed., London: Routledge.

Coe, R., Aloisi, C., Higgins, S. and Major, L. (2014) 'What makes great teaching? Review of underpinning research'. Available at: https://www.suttontrust.com/our-research/great-teaching/ (accessed 8 July 2020).

DES (1989) *The Elton Report: Behaviour and Discipline in Schools*, London: HMSO.

DFE (2016) 'Behaviour and discipline in schools: Guidance for headteachers and staff', Available at: https://www.gov.uk/government/publications/behaviour-and-discipline-in-schools (accessed 8 July 2020).

DFE (2019) 'The Timpson review of school exclusion'. Available at: https://assets.publishing.service.gov.uk/government/uploads/system/uploads/attachment_data/file/807862/Timpson_review.pdf (accessed 8 July 2020).

DFES (2005) 'Learning behaviour: The report of the practitioners group on school behaviour and discipline'. Available at: http://dera.ioe.ac.uk/id/eprint/5494 (accessed 29 August 2019).

DFES (2009) 'Learning behaviour: Lessons learned'. Available at: https://webarchive.nationalarchives.gov.uk/20130321074534/https://www.education.gov.uk/publications/standard/publicationDetail/Page1/DCSF-00453-2009 (accessed 8 July 2020).

Dix, P. (2017) *When the Adults Change, Everything Changes: Seismic Shifts in School Behaviour*, Bancyfelin: Independent Thinking Press.

Ellis, S. and Tod, J. (2015) *Promoting Behaviour for Learning in the Classroom: Effective Strategies, Personal Style and Professionalism*, Abingdon: Routledge.

Haydn, T. (2009) 'Initial teacher education and the management of pupil behaviour: What experiences, resources and interventions do students find helpful?' Paper presented at the 4th ESCalate ITE Conference, University of Cumbria.

Haydn, T. (2014) 'To what extent is behaviour a problem in English schools? Exploring the scale and prevalence of deficits in classroom climate', *Review of Education*, 2(1): 31–64.

Haydn, T. (2015) 'Working to improve classroom climate using a ten point scale and focusing on the development of the classroom management skills of individual teachers', *Creative Education*, 6: 2351–60. doi:10.4236/ce.2015.622241.

Horn, I. (2015) 'What I notice and wonder about "Teach Like a Champion"'. Available at https://teachingmathculture.wordpress.com/2015/04/02/what-i-notice-and-wonder-about-teaching-like-a-champion/ (accessed 25 January 2021).

Lemov, D. (2015) *Teach Like a Champion 2.0: 62 Techniques that Put Students on the Path to College*, 2nd ed., San Francisco, CA: Jossey-Bass.

Ofsted (2006) 'Improving behaviour'. Available at: https://dera.ioe.ac.uk/8537/1/Improving%20behaviour%20(PDF%20format).pdf (accessed 8 July 2020)

Ofsted (2014) 'Below the radar: Low level disruption in the country's classrooms'. Available at: https://www.gov.uk/government/publications/below-the-radar-low-level-disruption-in-the-countrys-classrooms (accessed 8 July 2020).

Ofsted (2019) *School Inspection Handbook*. Available at: https://assets.publishing.service.gov.uk/government/uploads/system/uploads/attachment_data/file/843108/School_inspection_handbook_-_section_5.pdf (accessed 8 July 2020).

Pavlov, I.P. ([1897] 1902) *The Work of the Digestive Glands*, London: Griffin.

Rogers, C.R. (1951) *Client-Centered Therapy; Its Current Practice, Implications, and Theory*, Boston, MA: Houghton Mifflin.

Skinner, B.F. (1938) *The Behavior of Organisms: An Experimental Analysis*, New York: Appleton-Century.

15 Bringing the curriculum to life in the early years

A consideration of the learning environment

Michelle Sogga and Karen Siddons

Major questions addressed in this chapter are:

- What are the limitations and opportunities in the design of your early years learning environment?
- How does the design of your learning environment impact on children and their learning?
- Who has ownership of the learning environment in a setting?
- How does the design of a learning environment influence teaching styles?

Abstract

One of the overarching principles of the Early Years Foundation Stage (EYFS) that should guide practice is the provision of an enabling environment in which children learn and develop. This enabling environment should be responsive to children's individual needs. This chapter discusses how, for the authors, teaching in contrasting environments for Early Years education (England and Tanzania) led to them reflecting on the connections between learning environments and teaching pedagogies. How contrasting physical learning environments in the English and Tanzanian contexts had a direct influence on how adults worked with children and, therefore, children's opportunities for learning and development are examined. The chapter concludes that environment and who has ownership of it can reflect deeply held beliefs about viewpoints of how children learn and what holds value to those in positions of authority.

Introduction

Provision of enabling environments is one of the principles of the Early Years Foundation Stage in England (DfE, 2017). An enabling environment should support children's learning and development, be responsive to their individual needs and enable effective partnerships between practitioners and parents/carers. Walking into an early years setting gives an immediate impression, based on our first perceptions and evaluations of the environment, but a deeper look can identify how others may feel and interact in the space, and the values portrayed by those who have designed it (Gandini, cited in Edwards, Gandini and Forman, 2012, p. 318). Malaguzzi (1984, cited in Edwards, Gandini and Forman, 2012, p. 339) suggested that the 'environment should act as a kind of aquarium which reflects the ideas, ethics, attitudes and culture of the people who live in it'. However, there are often constraints on this. Practitioners may inherit their learning environments: the physical spaces in which they enable teaching and learning, the layout of the space, the resources within it and the furniture provided are often pre-determined by setting leadership, physical and budgetary constraints, and may be outwith the control of the individual practitioner. However, even with these constraints, early years practitioners can make localized environment choices, such as how they arrange furniture, accessibility of resources and the provocations to learning provided. The choices made are driven by knowledge of how children learn and the values and principles that are the practitioner's own. Choices are driven by cultural and historical contexts, the practitioners we work with and those who came before us. Practitioners alter a space, the space alters how we work and so it goes on (Cadwell, 2003).

This chapter considers some of the factors that influence practitioners in the early years setting to use learning environments to bring the curriculum to life, including the interplay between the environment and the practitioner and the impact of the environment on approaches to children's learning and development, based on the authors' own experiences of working within different learning environments. In the discussion we illustrate some of the most important issues through the use of three vignettes, the first from Tanzania, the second from a maintained nursery school in England, and the third from professional home-based care, also in England.

Limitations and opportunities in the design of early years learning environments

Arrangements of the physical space can enable or deter movements, encourage or detract from exploration, support social interaction between children and children and adults, or limit opportunities for social contact. The arrangement of the learning environment directly influences how practitioners work with children, and how the children are able and supported to learn and development. There may be multiple uses to be considered within the space allocated, for example, whether there are places where adults can comfortably sit alongside children as they play in different areas of the environment, or are predominantly sited at a desk, whether children can move freely around the space or if too many tables and chairs in a small space constrict movement, or whether there are spaces for children to be away from adults, enabling autonomous exploration.

The philosophy we choose of how we want to work with children also directly influences how we set up the environment. The learning environment reflects our deeper values and ethos about how we believe children learn, about what we give priority to in children's learning and development, and the value we place on children's experiences during their time with us. The spaces we create, the resources we provide, and where we as adults spend our time, all show children what we give value to, as do the amount of time we spend at tabletop activities in directed tasks, or the opportunities we give to children to participate in child-led play in spaces chosen by the child. We should ask ourselves what choices we are providing to children in the learning environment and if the social sense of the children is reflected in the environment we prepare for them. 'Little children are profoundly at the mercy of grown-ups and of the environment which grown-ups determine, and are always ready to draw in the sensitive feelers which they put out to test the world' (Isaacs, 1938, p. 82).

Understanding our choices within the historical context adds another dimension to the philosophy of our current practices and how we may then develop them. Many of the approaches of the early years pioneers, such as Froebel (1912), Montessori (1912), McMillan (1930) and Isaacs (1932) can be seen reflected in practice today. Understanding the origins of our approach enables us to understand what we do and why we do it, while also offering potential to challenge and justify our choices as we move forward. We are also shaped by our own experiences and it is these experiences in contrasting contexts that encouraged the authors to reflect on their own concepts of the learning environment in relation to their personal philosophies of teaching and learning.

Training nursery school teachers in Zanzibar, 2003–2005

The first vignette comes from the experience of one of the authors of the current chapter in Tanzania. In the Tanzanian context at the time of the vignette (and we must be mindful that this was early in the twenty-first century where these experiences had such a significant impact on one of the author's developing thinking about learning environments), the control rested very much with the teacher, linked to the cultural expectations, views of the child as a passive learner as well as the constraints of the learning environment, where children simply did not have freedom of movement, sitting as they were in rows.

Vignette 1: Training nursery school teachers in Zanzibar, 2003–2005

One of the authors spent two years teaching trainee nursery school teachers in Zanzibar, Tanzania. Many of the nursery school buildings were shared with primary schools, with different age children attending the school at different times on a shift basis. This resulted in many nursery school children, aged 4–7 years old, being taught in classrooms with fixed desks and benches. Teaching styles were predominantly didactic, for example, the teacher would stand at the front of the class using the blackboard to write a line of numbers. Children recited the numbers and wrote them on individual blackboards. In other schools, there was no furniture, but the teacher would still stand at the blackboard, while children sat in rows with their individual blackboards and chalks.

When modelling teaching strategies, the author would adjust the furniture where possible to create large open spaces or would take children outside in the shade. She introduced interactive resources and games where children could move around the space to use the resources and be asked questions to develop their problem solving and thinking, while staying within the teachers' comfort zone of adult-led learning. Parachute games with large pieces of materials, sets of dominoes made from card and word banks were resources teachers were happy to adopt. In some schools, teachers placed boxes of resources at the back of the classroom, and began to introduce the concept of free play with short periods of time during the day where children could self-select their activities and would occupy themselves in purposeful play with their friends.

Reflections on experience

The predominant teaching style at the time in Zanzibar was a didactic 'talk and chalk' approach. The author wondered whether it was the layout of the learning environment that dictated the teaching style, or the understanding of how children learn that influenced the pedagogy and the subsequent design of the learning environment. She also wondered what it was about the cultural context and the role of child in society, reflective of the power dynamics that influenced this approach. These questions highlighted the complexities of reflecting on the origins of learning environment and the connections with individual pedagogies. The images of children sitting in rows were reminiscent of the tiered classrooms of nineteenth-century England. With a learning environment set up in rows, the natural position for the teacher was at the front of the classroom. Children were cramped into benches, so were unable to move freely, and this would appear to be an explanation for the didactic teaching approach. However, even when the environment provided more opportunities for being creative with teaching methodologies, for example, where there was no furniture, the 'talk and chalk' style dominated. This suggested the approach was influenced, not by the environment, but by an understanding of how children learn. Children were viewed as being passive learners by the teachers, the learning environment reinforced this view through a didactic teaching model, and the children consequently became passive learners within the classroom setting. A prescriptive curriculum did not support creativity, with many teachers constrained by their understanding of what they should be delivering, and from their own limited education under the same model. Most nursery teachers had only completed two to four years of secondary education themselves. The interplay between teachers' own education and experiences, their knowledge about how children learn, the cultural values of the time and place, and the design of the learning environment culminated in a particular pedagogic approach.

However, within this context, with contrasting personal educational experiences and different knowledge about how young children learn and different cultural values, alternative pedagogies were possible. Making more creative use of the space and introducing some basic resources, hand-made using locally sourced materials, enabled a change in pedagogy, active learning, collaborative learning and a greater flexibility in the approach. Professional dialogue opened up new ways to deliver the curriculum, with teachers seeing that the same learning could occur in different ways. This was not embraced by all teachers, as it not just challenged ways of working, but ways of believing. Teachers, who themselves had received a limited education and were used to passive modes of learning, were able to re-create modelled lessons, but struggled to adapt the approaches to different situations. A change in physical environment, and a change in teaching methodologies also required changes to beliefs about how young children learn and the role of the teacher in this. Those teachers who embraced the changes noticed the impact on the young children they worked with; children who were more independent, children who were able to use and apply their learning across different contexts. Early years practitioners rarely work in silos, but as part of larger and often multi-agency teams. Each individual and each professional will bring their personal as well as their professional values and beliefs to the setting, influenced by their own experiences and their education and training. Without a shared philosophy of how young children learn in a context, the learning environment and the subsequent impact on children's learning and development are likely to be muddled and potentially conflicting.

Early Years settings across England

This second vignette is in stark contrast to the learning environment described in the example from Tanzania, and is currently common in many early years settings across England. Learning environments where children are able to move freely, to make independent choices, where autonomy is encouraged and where adults are there to scaffold and extend children's thinking in sensitive ways, are encompassed within the principles of the EYFS. It is clear that different cultural expectations as well as practitioner values and beliefs about how children learn are reflected in the environmental design and consequently have different outcomes in terms of what and how children learn and develop.

Vignette 2: Maintained nursery school in England

A large maintained nursery school with several large and smaller rooms is set up into a range of learning areas. Dry sand, wet sand and water are situated near each other, with equipment available on open shelves with templates, so children can help themselves to resources and know where to return them. Children are able to move between areas, so they can explore the properties of different materials. The dough making, snack area and home corner are close to each other, so children can take their snack into the home corner, or can follow a written and pictorial recipe book to make their own dough, which they can then take to use in their imaginative play in the home corner. Children can move freely between inside and outside. Outside there is a large garden with a mixture of hard surfaces and grass, a large sand pit, a mud kitchen, loose parts resources, wheeled toys, woodwork and areas set up for imaginative play. Adults are interacting with children with focus activities, which children choose to come to as they are planned around their interests. Other adults interact with children in their child-led play, using sustained shared thinking to develop the children's ideas, modelling language and promoting children's curiosity.

Historical influences on development of early years settings in England

Froebelian philosophy has influenced many early years settings within the UK. While Froebel himself changed his approach to the use of the gifts and occupations, initially with the agency lying with the child, then with more specific guidance, then returning to more open-ended use (Liebschner, 1992), resources which can be used creatively in open-ended ways are at the root of many early years learning environments. For Froebel, there was a significant emphasis on the aesthetics of the materials produced to support learning, where play with the blocks supported ideas of creativity, enabling children to make connections between their inner world of feelings and ideas, and the outer world of experiences and objects. Providing quality resources places children at the heart of the setting, demonstrating they are valued and this is a key principle of the Reggio Emilia approach (Edwards, Gandini and Forman, 2012). Importance and status are also given to the learning environment itself, by recognizing the value of the resources and caring for them. Similarly, the Malting House School of Susan Isaacs had a carefully thought-out learning environment, designed to encourage curiosity and investigation (Isaacs, 1938), reflecting the philosophy of her approach. Open plan and zoned learning environment lay-outs, where children can maintain eye contact with a care giver, can support children to maximize use of safe and supported space (Liempd, Oudgenoug-Paz and Leseman, 2020). A carefully planned environment reflects the values and beliefs of the practitioners who have designed it, recognizes the role of the learning environment in supporting children's learning and development and acknowledges children's agency within the environment.

The nursery garden, as exemplified in the vignette above, was also a key tenet of the Froebelian approach, as the garden was an environment where children could make sense of their world. The focus on the outside and natural environments enabled an understanding of the connectedness of learning and the interrelationships between living things (Tovey, 2013). McMillan shared this view, identifying outdoor environments as fundamental and citing them as such; the 'garden is the essential matter' (McMillan, 1930, p. 2). Children here are encouraged to choose freely available resources autonomously, with a focus on self-directed learning and a recognition that play develops sym-bolic thought and abstract thinking. A view of the child as an independent learner, a focus on creativity and exploring interrelationships requires an environment that supports this approach. An environment that is full of choices, open-ended resources and time and freedom to explore those resources enables children to be independent, creative and critical thinkers. It has been found that more natural outdoor environments can also have positive impacts on adults' perception of children as strong and competent, as well as supporting adults to be more creative in their pedagogies (Maynard, Waters and Clement, 2013). Practitioners show their values through the place they give to the outdoors in their practice; whether it is a central part of their approach, or an add-on space where children can 'let off steam'. The value given to the outdoor learning space by adults will be reflected in the impact on children's learning and development outdoors: a place where children flourish with curiosity and creativity, develop and learn holistically, or a focus on physical development and not much else.

In contrast to Froebel's approach, the Montessori learning environment is more highly structured. Rather than open-ended resources, a Montessori learn-ing environment has tasks, which while children can select them independently, are carefully structured to enable a set outcome. So what does this say about the philosophy that drives the creation of this more structured learning envi-ronment and the process children will negotiate as they experience it? It is important to remember that originally Montessori worked with children with learning disabilities, who benefitted from a more structured approach to teach-ing with clear outcomes. Approaches to teaching and learning are socially and culturally situated. The symbiotic relationship between philosophy of teaching and learning and the learning environment is a challenging and thought-pro-voking one. The way resources are organized and presented, used and mod-elled by adults to demonstrate their 'pedagogical goals', and made accessible to children in rigid or flexible ways can inhibit or facilitate learning and develop-ment opportunities (Daniels, 2016, p. 29).

Influence of learning environment on children and their learning

The topics considered so far are intrinsically linked with issues of control of the learning environment. Put any of us into a new and unfamiliar environment and we can feel less safe, less secure. We have a need to have some control over our environments and we are often uncomfortable in an environment which is not our own. Many of us may resist change to our environments because we feel more secure with the familiar. The question arises here of where the children are in this. When adults design learning environments, when adults decide where the sand or water trays are located, where children sit for stories or where they store their bags and coats, they are already imposing their own structure and therefore controls on children's play. Where spaces are designed by adults, there is a question about whether this is so that we can have some control over children's behaviour and actions within the space (Fashanu, Wood and Payne, 2020).

Within Froebel's kindergarten, this issue was resolved to some extent with each child having their own individual plot in the garden, surrounded by the communal garden (Froebel, 1912). Isaacs was also an advocate for the ownership of children over their learning environment. Inspired by the Froebelian approach, children at the Malting House School had their own plots in the garden and had their own resources, to enable them to learn respect for the possessions of others (Isaacs, 1932). A Montessori-influenced setting may take a contrasting approach, with adult-prepared materials, which may simplify the options for children, enabling children to make limited choices, complete specific tasks independently and return the resources ready for the next child, however, this is a different form of independence to that described in the Froebelian approach. If resources can only be used in limited ways, they are less likely to support creativity and critical thinking. There will be fewer opportunities for children to explore the interconnectedness and relationships between their inner thoughts and feelings and outer experiences. Yet Montessori's focus on child-sized furniture, clearly displayed resources and freedom of movement between the inside and outside, still suggests a child-focused philosophy.

This raises challenges for a modern early years setting. There are questions about how much control should rest with children and how much with adults, whether we have the autonomy to find the balance and the support to manipulate it to work for the participants within the setting, and how adults can ensure that each individual has ownership of the environment where they may spend a substantial part of their time. In early years settings in the UK, some of the approaches to support children's ownership of the environment may be easily implemented. A place to store coats and bags labelled with a photo of the child; a special place to keep their special things; resources that are freely available so the children can make choices about where to play and what to play with; flexibility in the routines of the day so children have extended periods of time to become deeply involved in their learning; places where children can display their own work; consultation about which new resources are bought; collaboration about proposed changes to the environment; adults who scaffold rather than scold when children transport resources from one place to another including between inside and outside. There are questions to ask about adults in the settings here: whether they believe in the rights of the child; in the autonomy of children; adults who trust children to lead their own learning; who listen and respect the voice of the child; who trust in the responsibility of children. And what of those adults who do not share this philosophy, what of the adults who govern the space more tightly, whether their children will seek out the peripheries of the space to follow their own interests and discourse regardless (Fashanu, Wood and Payne, 2020).

Froebel encouraged children to learn from the environment around them, but also to care for the environment. If resources were damaged, children were responsible for repairing and returning them so as to learn the consequences of their actions (Liebschner, 1992). If children are given a sense of ownership of their space, this can support the development of children's rights as well as their responsibilities. Claxton and Carr (2004) recommend 'potentiating environments' as having the most impact on children's learning and development, as these environments enable shared activity, the co-construction of learning, with ownership and power within the environment shared between adults and children. Maynard, Waters and Clement (2013) suggest that this may be easier in an outdoor environment, where adults are relieved of some of their own perceptions of teacher control that they associate with being inside. Children, when consulted, are capable of evaluating their own learning environments to support improvements to have a positive impact on their learning and development (Chen and Wang, 2018; Muela *et al.*, 2019). Reflection on our own need to be in control of situations, environments and children is essential if we are to address this within our developing personal and professional practice.

Professional home-based care in England

In current times, the approach to early years education in the area of Reggio Emilia in Italy can be seen to embody the connectedness between the understanding of how children learn and the learning environment. The environment is given primary importance as the 'third educator'. Buildings created around a central piazza, a meeting place which represents the importance of relationships and dialogue, illustrates an approach based on collaborative learning and problem solving with learning spaces designed to support this approach (Edwards, Gandini and Forman, 2012). The needs of the child are paramount in shaping the environment, within an approach that has a particular focus on children's rights, which can also be seen in the third vignette about home-based care. The Reggio Emilia approach also recognizes how the space reflects the culture and history of each centre as well as valuing each individual, a criterion worthy of consideration within the diverse and often unique spaces of early years provision in the UK and further afield in Tanzania. However, the philosophy of Reggio Emilia has its roots in a particular place and time and cannot simply be transplanted to other locations and points in the timeline. Some of the principles, however, can be. There is a focus on an environment that interests children and challenges them, enabling them to explore through first-hand experiences and develop their interests over extended periods of time. Education is viewed as a shared process, where teachers journey alongside the children, co-constructing knowledge, while focusing on developing children's metacognitive skills, through creating and inventing, supporting children to learn to think rather than to merely gain explicit knowledge. Teachers in Reggio Emilia do not follow a named theory or curriculum, but use their pedagogical understanding to support a range of approaches. 'Learning and teaching should not stand on opposite banks and just watch the water flow by; instead they should embark together on a journey down the river' (Malaguzzi, 1998, cited in Hall *et al.*, 2010, p. 31). In many ways the vignette about home-based care reflects many of the principles of practice in Reggio Emilia.

Vignette 3: Professional home-based care in England

A small group of children in a non-biological family grouping work together, in a playful exchange, to replicate the actions of their adult carers. Their adult carers are both familial parents/carers and early years childcare professionals within a home-based setting. Their environment is familiar to them, they know where things belong, they know where they left things and they have strong relationships with the people they meet on a daily basis. They have a routine bound only by their needs which flows with flexibility as their needs change and reform, their learning is supported by the discrete but significant changes that create nuances within their day. They share an indoor environment and an outdoor one, have free and easy access between the two, they have ownership of space and resources and the support of a partnership of collaborative care and a small group of peers. They learn with and from each other and understand their role in protecting and preserving play, space and resources. This small grouping of children is extended at either end of the day when older 'siblings'/children join them. Their learning continues, they take a different role, they experience a different type of relationship, they are exposed to more possibilities within their play, they gain support through challenge and develop resilience together with an alternative more able other. These children are cared for by a childminder working in her own home, they experience home comforts while they learn and are afforded contact with older children that they may not have within their own home. The childminder works closely with the child's parents/carer to scaffold flexible opportunities for children to learn and develop in a home based environment. Learning looks very different here to learning in a nursery school.

Ownership of the learning environment in a setting

While in many ways the vignette about home based care may mirror many of the principles of practice in Reggio Emilia, all early years providers in England need to follow statutory guidance which can also have an impact on practitioners' understanding of how young children learn, thinking about what children should be taught and the type of environment that is needed to meet those requirements. Since the introduction of Desirable Learning Outcomes (SCAA, 1996), there has been increasing focus on what and how children should learn in the early years. The Early Years Foundation Stage, which applies to children from birth to the end of the Reception Year in Primary Schools, was first introduced in 2008, however, it is not a curriculum. Grenier (2019) identifies that whereas practitioners once had the Curriculum Guidance for the Foundation Stage (QCA, 2000), we now have a statutory framework which sets out the standards that should be met, and Development Matters (Early Education, 2012) and Early Years Outcomes (DfE, 2013), which both list sets of developmental outcomes that children are expected to achieve.

There is a danger here that some practitioners, whichever type of setting they work within, may simply teach to these developmental outcomes, ignoring the needs of the child and the possibilities of the environment they have access to. They could plan the environment and philosophy around these outcomes in a prescriptive manner, so that practitioners can tick off when children have achieved them, lessening the possibility for consolidation of learning and working with the child's interests. Ofsted (2017) suggested in Bold Beginnings that this may be the approach taken in some contexts resulting in a decreased focus on learning. However, this document itself suggests a narrowing of the early years curriculum with a focus on learning to read as the 'core purpose' of a child's Reception year; the last year of the EYFS and the first year of primary school (Ofsted, 2017, p. 7). Combined with the introduction of a baseline assessment, not based on observational assessment, but focusing on easily measurable attributes, there could be an increased danger of practitioners teaching to narrowly defined parameters in a prescribed manner. This could lead to both a limited pedagogy and a limited learning environment, questioning the philosophy and ethos of practitioners and the impact of enabled environments. Ofsted (ibid.) identified that many practitioners were confusing the curriculum (what they should be teaching) with their own pedagogical approach (how they should be teaching) and philosophy. Starting with values and beliefs about how young children learn could help to limit or erase this confusion, ensuring the learning environment is created in a way that reflects positive pedagogical values and beliefs, identifying the opportunities and impact for learning and development.

Linking decisions about learning environments with children's learning needs

There is an important question for early years practitioners about what they should be teaching and what influence this has on the learning environment.

Grenier (2019) suggests that one aspect practitioners should be focusing on is supporting the development of children's metacognitive and executive function skills. This would certainly fit with the pedagogical approaches advocated by a Froebelian or Reggio Emilia-inspired approach, where there was a focus on open-ended resources, children being able to select resources that provided them with a level of challenge or comfort, and opportunities for creativity and critical thinking supported by adults and others. A focus on rich, purposeful, first-hand experiences would also be important. Goswami (2015) suggests that children learn like adults, but with less experience than adults, they need a range of rich and diverse experience-dependent learning opportunities to support their cognitive development, create new connections and strengthen existing neural pathways through multi-sensory experiences. Children need opportunities to learn through their active engagement with the environment, with sensory-motor learning enriched by communication, pretend play and interaction with adults and others. This will support children to develop their knowledge base, working memory, metacognition and self-regulation (ibid.). Language and social interactions are key to this, therefore we need to consider learning environments that enable children to develop language in meaningful contexts and through social interactions. Dubiel (2018) identifies that practitioners should be developing a 'responsible ECE pedagogy', focused on early childhood specialism and expertise, resting on the principles and values that practitioners have as educators.

Conclusion

We conclude with the issue of how the design of the learning environment influences teaching styles and some important questions to ask ourselves:

- In doing so, should we identify what is important, to us, the children, the families we work with and the communities they inhabit, together with what we believe about the role of children in society?
- Should we begin with what we want children to leave our setting with (irrespective of what the guidance says they should learn): what perception we want them to develop about play and learning, about risk and challenge, about opportunity and possibility?
- Should we question and evaluate how can we create, manipulate and design our physical spaces and resources to enable children to leave us autonomous and resilient? Only through evaluation and reflection can we develop a principled approach where the learning environment reflects our values as early years practitioners, but where our values are also visible in the learning environment.

Settings, teams and individual practitioners may feel bound by the physical building or the managerial or historically determined pedagogy of their early years provision but by determining the non-negotiable fundamentals of high-quality early years provision, the process of evolving change should become easier. Once a new ethos has been forged and established, other elements of practice should emerge to create possibility and opportunity within the working spaces of settings, for both children and adults. Creating useable, purposeful and creative spaces collaboratively with children will teach practitioners what is the most important aspect for the individual child or collective children. Harnessing tools, such as Clark and Moss's Mosaic Approach (2011), opens a window for us into the child's developing experiences and curiosity. The Mosaic Approach, founded on the principles of participatory appraisal, relevant to the Tanzanian vignette and the Reggio Emilia approach, relevant to both the English nursery school and childminder vignettes, supports a collaboration towards listening to children and valuing their voices as co-constructors of meaning. Through the process of co-constructing, all participants should embrace the potential for both teaching and learning, in fact, we could posit the terminology here as learning and teaching, because without a mind open to change and therefore learning, there is little possibility of harnessing the outcomes of co-construction. The learning environment for us as adult practitioners may present limitations that children see as possibility, we will never know this if we choose not to co-construct understanding. Our perceptions cannot and should not be shared across the world, there can be contrast and comparison that identify, sometimes stark, differences around pedagogy, philosophy and environments but they are not transportable. Elements may be borrowed, shared and adapted, knowledge may be disseminated and supported, ethos and beliefs may be shaped and carved to support a child-centred experience but culture and history underpin the most fundamental foundations of practice. We seek to take elements and blend them with cultural values to create a new meaning, to begin a new history, where children shape their environments and so their learning, driving the cohesion between environment and possibility, easing the blend between past, present and future in a similar way to how we value past learning, present learning and the learning yet to happen.

References

Cadwell, L. (2003) *Bringing Learning to Life: The Reggio Approach to Early Childhood Education*, New York: Teachers College Press.

Chen, H. and Wang, X. (2018) 'Children's evaluation of the physical environment quality in kindergarten: a case study from China', *International Journal of Early Childhood*, 50: 175–92, https://doi.org/10.1007/s13158-018-0219-7

Clark, A. and Moss, P. (2011) *Listening to Young Children: The Mosaic Approach*, London: National Children's Bureau.

Claxton, G. and Carr, M. (2004) 'A framework for teaching learning: The dynamics of disposition', *Early Years*, 24(1): 87–97, doi:10.1080/09575140320001790898

Daniels, K. (2016) 'Exploring enabling literacy environments: Young children's spatial and material encounters in early years classrooms', *English in Education*, 50(1): 12–34, doi:10.1111/eie.12074

DfE (Department for Education) (2013) *Early Years Outcomes: A Non-Statutory Guide for Practitioners and Inspectors to Help Inform Understanding of Child Development Through the Early Years*, London: DfE.

DfE (Department for Education) (2017) *Statutory Framework for the Early Years Foundation Stage*, London: DfE.

Dubiel, J. (2018) 'Responsible early childhood pedagogy'. Available at: https://early excellence.com/latest-news/press-articles/responsible-early-childhood-pedagogy/ (accessed 15 June 2020).

Early Education (2012) *Development Matters in the Early Years Foundation Stage*, London: Early Education.

Edwards, C., Gandini, L. and Forman, G. (eds) (2012) *The Hundred Languages of Children: The Reggio Emilia Experience in Transformation*, 3rd ed., Oxford: Praeger.

Fashanu, C., Wood, E. and Payne, M. (2020) 'Multilingual communication under the radar: How multilingual children challenge the dominant monolingual discourse in a super-diverse, Early Years educational setting in England', *English in Education*, 54(1): 93–112, doi:10.1080/04250494.2019.1688657

Froebel, F. (1912) *Froebel's Chief Writings on Education*, London: Arnold.

Goswami, U. (2015) 'Children's cognitive development and learning', Cambridge Primary Review Trust. Available at: https://cprtrust.org.uk/wp-content/uploads/2015/02/COMPLETE-REPORT-Goswami-Childrens-Cognitive-Development-and-Learning.pdf (accessed 15 June 2020).

Grenier, J. (2019) 'What happened to curriculum in the early years?' *Impact: Journal of the Chartered College of Teaching*. Available at: https://impact.chartered.college/article/what-happened-to-curriculum-early-years/ (accessed 15 June 2020).

Hall, K., Horgan, M., Ridgeway, A., Murphy, R., Cunneen, M. and Cunningham, D. (2010) *Loris Malaguzzi and the Reggio Emilia Experience*, London: Continuum.

Isaacs, S. (1932) *The Nursery Years: The Mind of the Child from Birth to Six Years*, London: Routledge and Kegan Paul.

Isaacs, S. (1938) *Intellectual Growth in Young Children*, London: Routledge and Sons.

Liebschner, J. (1992) *A Child's Work: Freedom and Guidance in Froebel's Educational Theory and Practice*, Cambridge: The Lutterworth Press.

Liempd, I., Oudgenoug-Paz, O. and Leseman, P. (2020) 'Do spatial characteristics influence behavior and development in early childhood education and care?', *Journal of Environmental Psychology*, 67: 1–12, http://dx.doi.org/10.1016/j.jenvp.2019.101385

Maynard, T., Waters, J. and Clement, J. (2013) 'Child-initiated learning, the outdoor environment and the "underachieving" child', *Early Years*, 33(3): 212–25, doiI:10.1080/09575146.2013.771152

McMillan, M. (1930) *The Nursery School*, London: J.M. Dent and Sons.

Montessori, M. (1912) *The Montessori Method*, New York: Frederick A. Stokes Company.

Muela, A., Larrea, I., Miranda, N. and Barandiaran, A. (2019) 'Improving the quality of preschool outdoor environments: getting children involved', *European Early Childhood Education Research Journal*, 27(3): 385–96, doi:10.1080/13502 93X.2019.1600808

Ofsted (2017) *Bold Beginnings: The Reception Curriculum in a Sample of Good and Outstanding Primary Schools*, Manchester: Ofsted.

Qualification and Curriculum Authority (QCA) (2000) *Curriculum Guidance for the Foundation Stage*, London: DfEE.

SCAA (School Curriculum and Assessment Authority) (1996) *Desirable Outcomes for Children's Learning on Entering Compulsory Education*, London: DfEE.

Tovey, H. (2013) *Bringing the Froebel Approach to Your Early Years Practice*, London: Routledge.

16 Culturally responsive approaches for children with English as an Additional Language (EAL) in the English National Curriculum

Reflections from personal experiences

Malini Mistry

Major questions addressed in this chapter are:

- To what extent/how should the National Curriculum be adapted for children with English as an Additional Language (EAL)?
- How can the voices of children with EAL inform de-centred thinking to support planning to meet their learning needs from a culturally-responsive approach?

Abstract

There is a plethora of information associated with strategies that can be used to help meet the learning needs of children with English as an Additional Language (EAL). But very often these are short-term and superficial in nature. This chapter will draw on the experiences of a number of young people known to the author as well as the author's own recollections of her experiences as a child with EAL, to suggest ways in which practitioners can maintain the worth and dignity of children with EAL within the National Curriculum framework so that they never feel ashamed of who they are, the colour of their skin, their home language(s) and culture.

Introduction

There is a plethora of information associated with strategies that can be used to help meet the learning needs of children with English as an Additional Language (EAL). But very often these are short-term and superficial in nature. The curriculum in England is regulated and there is a tension between the emphasis on performance and standards against that on child-centred approaches. In order better to meet the learning needs of children with EAL, practitioners need a well-informed, culturally responsive approach to pedagogy in their classrooms (Gay, 2010). In turn, this requires an understanding of how children learn that is rooted in a model compatible with cultural responsiveness. One such model is that of Vygotsky's (1978) socio-cultural theory that can be used to underpin ways in which practice can be adapted to ensure that children with EAL are included in learning in classrooms and schools.

This chapter begins with a brief discussion regarding what the term 'children with EAL' is intended to convey, and the fundamentals associated with 'culturally responsive' pedagogy and of a socio-cultural view of the learning process. It continues by problematizing assumptions that close adherence to the current regulated National Curriculum (NC) framework in England will necessarily suit the learning needs of all children with EAL. Subsequently it will offer readers an insight into the perceptions of a number of learners with EAL known to the author of this chapter, also with EAL, in terms of her experiences of provision and practice, working alongside native English speakers. These perceptions include the attitudes of others towards her, especially when, from time to time, language was a temporary barrier to interactions within the constraints of the National Curriculum.

Definition of English as an Additional Language (EAL)

The term 'English as an Additional Language' (EAL) is used to describe children who are learning English in addition to their home language(s) (Mistry and Sood, 2015). These children could also be familiar with the use of two or three other languages in addition to English. It needs to be remembered that EAL is not synonymous with 'bilingual', as these children have different language learning needs. Bilingual children are fluent speakers in two languages, but English could be the third or more language for children with EAL. Most importantly, children with EAL do not form one heterogenous group (ibid.) and therefore the different subgroups contained within the umbrella term of EAL need consideration, as this has an impact on provision and practice. This is particularly relevant at the present time especially with the diversity of languages and cultures in England as a result of increasing migration.

Rationale for a socio-cultural model of the learning process

To enable learners with English as an Additional Language in schools from an increasingly diverse range of cultural backgrounds to achieve academically, it is important to adopt pedagogy that is responsive to, and respectful of, them as culturally situated. To underpin this approach, practitioners need a model of learning that encompasses this view of the learner. For this reason this chapter adopts a socio-cultural lens (Vygotsky, 1978) through which to view such pedagogy. Use of this lens enables a focus on the agency of the teacher as a mediator of learning who should acknowledge the learner's cultural situatedness (Kozulin, 2003) if school learning is to be as successful as it might be. It also focuses attention on the predominant value systems and social practices that characterize the school settings in which the learning of those with EAL is acquired.

Pedagogies for school learning should be responsive to the frames of reference that learners with EAL bring from home to their school learning. The distinctiveness in Vygotsky's (1978) work that underpins this claim lies in his explanation of human learning that couples a focus on culture as a context in which learning takes place, with an assumption that a special mental quality of human beings is that they can mediate their actions through language, signs, symbols, tools, and so on that they acquire in interaction with others. In the social environment in which young people are reared, there are 'differences and similarities in communities' practices and traditions', including different 'configurations of routine ways of doing things in any community's approach to living' (Rogoff, 2003, p. 3). It is obvious, therefore, that when the home cultures of learners in any one school vary widely, the tools and frames of reference they appropriate for learning language and other communication tools that they acquire outside the school may well also vary to a significant degree.

Learning process

Vygotsky (1978, p. 57) proposed that there are two planes where the learning process takes place:

- the interpersonal, that is the ' between the people' plane,
- the intrapersonal, within the individual, as s/he thinks about and reflects on new concepts and learning and appropriates new skills, for example, language and knowledge.

Both cognitive development, for example, in language and literacy acquisition, and social development are seen as mutually facilitative (Glynn *et al.*, 2006) and depend on the presence of mediators, for example, teachers in schools who can prompt and guide the use of cultural tools, such as language and literacy. In schools, learners expand their understanding and use of cultural tools, not only through observing mediators model language structure and usage, but also by participating in learning conversations on the interpersonal plane.

One of the concepts for which Vygotsky's (1978; 1981a; 1981b) work is well known is that of the 'zone of proximal development' (ZPD) to explain the process of learning in a social context: the ZPD comprises the next steps in learning and the range of knowledge and skills that learners are not ready to learn on their own but can learn in interaction with more informed and experienced others. The role of the more-skilled adult or peer mediators working in this zone is to support learners to participate in activities in which they are as yet unable to participate on their own and to provide safe contexts for interactions with others. The degree to which teachers-as-mediators of language and other learning are sensitive and responsive to learners' existing culturally based language-related frames of reference can be highly significant to language learning and cognitive achievement (Wearmouth, 2017).

The need for culturally responsive pedagogy

From a socio-cultural perspective there are some important reasons why pedagogy in schools should be responsive to the cultural backgrounds of learners:

- Children learn to speak, think, read and write within their own cultural contexts. Their frames of reference for doing these things come from these contexts. Teachers need to create a means to mediate learners' own cultural contexts and the school cultural context (Bishop *et al.*, 2014; Wearmouth *et al.*, 2011).
- Language learning and its context are interrelated. The act of language learning has meaning within a context. Teachers need to create the safe spaces in which these acts can be understood (Sleeter, 2011; Wearmouth, 2017).
- It is important to facilitate learners' sense of personal agency in learning and achievement, as well as the opportunity for participation on the interpersonal plane (Rogoff, 2003) and interaction through talk (Littleton and Mercer, 2013), in language-related activities alongside more skilled mediators. This may well include siblings and/or parents and families.
- It is essential to acknowledge 'learning to think' as a 'function of appropriating speech-based concepts through cultural practice' (Smagorinsky, 2011, p. 14) in which learners engage with different communities (Wearmouth and Berryman, 2009; Wenger, 1998) at home and school. 'Mind' cannot be seen as located entirely inside the head. Language learning therefore involves transactions within culturally structured social and natural environments of which learners are a part (Wearmouth *et al.*, 2011).

Issues in the National Curriculum for children with EAL

Since the introduction of the National Curriculum (NC) in 1988, there have been several revisions encouraging the move from a more factual way of learning to actually encouraging the understanding of knowledge and more recently, mastery of knowledge, especially in the core subjects. The NC framework suggests a range of skills and knowledge that is expected to be taught through given subjects. However, there is a difference between the culturally responsive, socio-cultural view of how children learn and the conditions that need to be put in place to encourage learning, as well as meeting the demands of the NC in terms of what needs to be taught by certain stages. More importantly, the demands on all staff to ensure that children have an understanding of concepts in core subjects by the end of each Key Stage can override the child-centred approach to learning. For example, many early years settings focus on learning opportunities that promote understanding and the skills associated with early reading and early numeracy in an attempt to address the concerns of Key Stage 1 teachers in relation to maths and English skills. Furthermore, Key Stage 1 teachers are under pressure to ensure that children achieve a required standard in the core subjects by the end of Year 2. This pressure with regard to accountability may override the ideology of how children learn best.

Potential outcomes of disjunction between home and school contexts

The way in which a lack of understanding of learners' backgrounds by teachers can feel threatening and can lead to feelings of discomfort, anxiety or exclusion is illustrated by the real-life experiences of the learner with EAL outlined in vignette 1.

Vignette 1: Influence of dialect

Shona was a child with EAL and started school with some understanding of English, certainly enough to get by. She enjoyed going to school and liked her teacher who was kind to her. Her family were aware of phonics and supported the consolidation of key words that were being learned at home. After a few months, some of Shona's pronunciation of key words used to cause amusement at home as per the following conversation:

Shona: What tume is bedtime?
Dad: What do you mean?
Shona: You know, what tume do I have to go?

This caused confusion for both Shona and her dad. A few days later Shona was picked up from school by her dad. Her dad heard her class teacher say to the children 'OK, children, it's home tume so don't forget your book bags', at that point Shona's dad realized the word 'tume' meant time and the different accent and dialect of the teacher caused amused confusion at home. This vignette highlights the impact of accent and how dialect can illustrate different pronunciation of words which children consider as accurate.

Reflection on vignette 1

Vignette 1 illustrates how the positioning of Standard English pronunciation in the curriculum requires serious consideration. All teachers experienced in teaching children with EAL may well know that they can pick up on inappropriate words not suitable for classroom use much more easily than other words. The question here is how to address this issue without discouraging children to talk openly and confidently.

In addition, the cultural background of children with EAL needs consideration in relation to their language learning. This is because contextual understanding can vary for the same words in different languages. Here, the importance of talk as part of learning is crucial in enabling children with EAL to hear and apply the English language appropriately, regardless of their first language.

Vignette 2: Importance of respect for other languages

Vignette 2 focuses on the experiences of 'Presha', who has EAL, has gone through Early Years provision and is currently in a primary school in England.

Presha was born in Greater London, and a decision was made by her parents shortly after her birth that her mother would work from home as much as possible to enable her to spend time with her child while she was very young. Immediate family on both sides were also involved with Presha as much as possible in the first two years of her life. Presha was surrounded by family, who all spoke Gujerati and English fluently and switched between languages easily and regularly, therefore Presha was used to hearing words and sentences in both languages on a daily basis. Sometimes she would also be exposed to family conversations in Swahili. Presha did not start speaking until she was 22 months old, and initially the family were worried that all she was doing was making sounds until then. Between 22 months and 2 years Presha's speech began to rapidly increase from sounds to words in small sentences, alongside the constant mimicking of words and sentences used by the adults around her. The impact of this was that all adults in the family became more aware of how and the type of language they used in front of Presha to ensure that they were good role models, as very often Presha would say, 'but bapa said' or 'foi said' or 'daddy said'.

At about 3 years of age, Presha found the transition to nursery difficult because she was not used to socializing with other children in a different environment and without her mother. Although Presha was a child with EAL, she knew enough English words and phrases to get by, however, in the nursery she would use names and phrases in Gujerati that she did not know in English.

For example, Presha was asked one Monday if anything nice had happened at the weekend to which she replied: 'Ma, Bapa, and Foi came to see me.' The nursery teacher asked her several times who these people were, to which Presha was confused and kept repeating the same thing. At the end of the session the nursery teacher asked Presha's mother who these people were, to which the reply was that 'these are her grandmother, grandfather and aunty on her dad's side of the family'. In the Gujerati culture, like many other cultures, first names are not used for family and relatives as a mark of respect. There are also different names for aunts and uncles depending on which side of the family they are positioned, which makes it very clear for a person who understands Gujerati who the different people in a child's life are. For a monolingual nursery practitioner, it was challenging to understand the different words Presha used as part of her regular speech, as well as the contextual and cultural aspects of Presha's home background. This is understandable, considering not many teachers or teacher trainee students can speak two languages fluently and code switch between them, illustrating that different language learning is not perceived to be a priority in England. Furthermore, differences in English language accent and dialect also require consideration as they have an impact when trying to teach phonics.

Transition to full-time school in a reception class was also challenging for Presha as she frequently asked when it was time to go home because she was not used to being without her mother for so long. This in turn affected her willingness to learn and take part in social activities as Presha was more used to being surrounded by adults in the home setting than other children. From a spoken English language perspective, Presha was well spoken and pronounced her sounds clearly, which in turn was attributed to her positive role models at home, although she would often discuss the events of the school day at home in a mix of both Gujerati and English. However, in the reception class, she was very often quiet and tended to allow others to go first before following them. She did not dominate conversations and would only talk to the quieter children in the class. Perhaps one reason for this could be that Presha did not feel threatened by the quieter children in the class in terms of judgements being made about her spoken English. The message here is that teachers need to be aware of the fact that quieter children with EAL could be having conversations in play or with other children because they do not feel judged in terms of their English spoken ability, which is illustrated by the following case study:

Presha really enjoyed playing with all the toys that her reception class had. The class was lucky in that it was an open plan, two form entry with both classes having different resources and a shared outdoor area that children were able to freely move between. One reason for Presha's enjoyment was because she did not have a large range of toys at home and therefore she would maximize all opportunities in play. Presha knew full well that if she stood still long enough when other children went off to choose their learning, she would hear the teacher say, 'and you can go and play'. Presha's class teacher expressed a concern to her mother that perhaps Presha did not understand what was going on in the class generally. Presha's mother told the reception class teacher that her child did understand but was choosing not to understand because she liked all the toys and resources that were available to her. This situation went on for another few weeks and the teacher again said to Presha's mother that nothing seemed to have changed. The mother advised the teacher to go around the corner so that she could see and hear a conversation between Presha and their mother in English without being seen at the end of the school day. The conversation went along the lines of:

Mother: Was school good today?
Presha nodded.
Mother: What did you do?
Presha: Played.
Mother: Anything else?
Presha shook her head to imply no.
Mother: Ohh, look out of the window over here, what do you see?
Presha: A cat by the tree.
Mother: Tell me why you think there is a cat by the tree.
Presha: The cat is trying to climb the tree because it wants to catch the birds because it is hungry and wants to eat them.

The mother then signalled for the class teacher to appear in front of her child. The teacher was amazed that Presha understood so much English and was able to formulate answers in full sentences with the appropriate use of English terminology. After that day, Presha had limited opportunities for play at her convenience as her teacher no longer said 'you can go and play' when she stood still for periods of time pretending not to understand what was asked of her.

As Presha progressed from reception to Year 1, she again found the transition hard because the environment changed from a play-based approach to a formal structure of learning in all subjects. Because of the emphasis on English and Maths, Presha soon began to change her play habits at home. Previously in play at home she was happy to mark make and write, but after she started Year 1, she would refuse to do any form of reading and writing at home – all she wanted to do was play with her toys if they did not involve writing. She would not even use pencils and crayons because these tools implied some form of writing. For Presha, transition into Year 2 and above was much easier because the same formal approach to all subject learning took place. As Presha progressed through the primary sector, she assimilated into the school culture and expectations, and today her spoken language fluency in English has overtaken her language fluency in Gujerati and Swahili.

The message here is that an emphasis on the English language at school may suggest to the child that other languages are unimportant, and therefore they may not use them unless encouraged to do so by the elders of the family.

Reflection on vignette 2

Key points from the example above are that:

- Children with EAL already have 'funds of knowledge' (Moll *et al.*, 1992; Gonzalez, Moll and Amanti, 2005).

- They also have language skills and can be more capable of understanding than they are given credit for.
- It is important to carry out discreet observations of children with EAL in play in order to gauge their understanding of English.

The example illustrates some of the major pedagogical challenges that can arise when the language-related activities and practices of the school differ substantially from those in learners' homes and communities, and where teachers have little or no understanding or appreciation of those home and community activities (Glynn *et al.*, 2006). From a socio-cultural understanding of mind, and in order that all learners from increasingly diverse cultural backgrounds make progress in their language and other learning, it is essential that schools 'teach to and through the strengths' (Gay, 2010, p. 31) of their students by 'using the cultural knowledge, prior experiences, frames of reference, and performance styles of ethnically diverse students to make learning encounters more relevant to and effective for them'.

It is important for monolingual teachers to try to develop culturally responsive thinking to help better understand their children with EAL (ibid.). Without this approach, children with EAL could be overlooked, or, worse still, ignored, in the hope that they will eventually assimilate into the English language and culture and therefore no extra effort is worth being made. Perhaps one reason for this kind of perspective is a lack of opportunities to work with children who have EAL after leaving university, or an alternative view is if teachers are monolingual themselves, then they may not appreciate the different language skills a child with EAL can bring to their class.

Swanwick (2019, p. 83) argues that the construction of knowledge is 'a social activity on many levels'. Language is 'the most powerful cultural tool in the human repertoire for making sense and sharing experience'. Humans learn through action that, importantly, is mediated by language as the most 'ubiquitous, flexible and creative of all the meaning-making tools available' (Mercer and Littleton, 2007, p. 2). Swanwick goes on to discuss the so-called 'dialogic theory of learning', based on putting into classroom practice the work of Vygotsky (1978). Classroom teaching based on this theory of learning focuses on ways in which teachers and learners share activities for the purpose of co-constructing knowledge. In 'dialogical meaning-making', the learner is seen to play an active role in constructing personal understanding through the process of dialogic interchange (Bakhtin, 1981; 1984). Applying Alexander's (2006) list of essential features of effective dialogic teaching to approaches appropriate for including children with EAL, we might include:

- teachers and learners with EAL addressing learning tasks together, listening to each other and considering alternative viewpoints;
- learners articulating ideas without fear of embarrassment about being wrong, and giving each other mutual support;
- teachers and learners building on their own and others' ideas and linking them into coherent lines of thinking;

- teachers, as the more knowledgeable others, planning dialogic teaching with particular goals in view.

From this perspective, all learners are active, all think about their learning, and have views and feelings about it.

Assessment concerns for children with EAL

One of the issues for children with EAL in relation to the NC is that assessment figures 'can be misleading' because the results of any assessments carried out in English could be lower than the academic ability of the child, due to the fact that the test was not conducted in their first language (Hutchinson, 2018, p. 7). Therefore, assessments carried out initially may not indicate a true reflection of a child's capability until they have overcome the English language barrier. This implies that assessment data gained for children with EAL could be an inaccurate perception of their ability, hence leading to misconceptions (ibid.). Therefore, it can be argued that alternative forms of assessment should be used with children with EAL in addition to the criteria-based norm, such as observations and assessments through the use of play.

Hutchinson has also noted that because the EAL group is so heterogeneous, it means that children's language ability in this group is very varied, from non-speakers of English to complete fluency. However, Mistry and Sood (2020) have implied that understanding learners' level of language proficiency and comprehension is vital for all those working with children with EAL. Without this knowledge, provision could be misaligned to children's needs which could mean that they fail to make sufficient progress. Furthermore, Mistry and Sood (ibid.) emphasize that just because children with EAL may not be fluent in the English language, this does not mean that they have no understanding of language or of what is going on around them.

Vignette 3: Consideration of valid assessment of children with EAL
Keya was a new arrival into a Year 2 class with Punjabi as her first language. She had some basic understanding of English and would generally copy or follow the children in the class. She was a little reserved by nature in front of adults but was more open with her peers. Through play and other group work tasks, her teacher had observed her making progress, not only with her spoken English and understanding, but also her confidence. However, when it came to the Year 2 standard assessment tasks (SATS) at the end of the year, Keya achieved a much lower mark than what she was capable of. Although Keya had made huge progress since her arrival into the setting, the criteria on the tests were not a fair reflection of her ability, so at first glance it could be assumed that she was one of lowest performing children in the year group

in terms of her ability. Her teacher found this very frustrating because SATS are a snapshot of performance at one point in time rather than evidence of the learning journey that Keya had undergone. According to the criteria in the tests, there is no way of showing how much Keya has improved in confidence, or how she is beginning to make connections in her learning, or the fluency and comprehension she has in her home language, or the fact that she is more than capable of adding and subtracting while playing snakes and ladders with her peers.

Reflection on vignette 3

This vignette demonstrates that showing the progress of children with EAL is not always straightforward when the goal is to meet the National Curriculum criteria. Perhaps there also needs to be some consideration of teacher judgements as supporting evidence especially for children with EAL.

Another challenge in relation to the National Curriculum is that formal testing happens at set points within the academic year, so what does this mean with regard to the outcomes of children with EAL who are new arrivals after the tests have taken place? Here teacher judgements are essential to evidence a child's learning journey which perhaps is more evident in the early years. Indeed, it is clear that snapshot judgements are not always fair in terms of assessing the true ability of individual children, therefore, a consideration could be not just assessing a child's English language proficiency – but with the help of parents/carers, also trying to assess a child's language proficiency in general, so that assumptions are not made about the child's language skills (Mistry and Sood, 2010).

Culturally responsive approaches in practice

In the previous section there was discussion about some of the challenges a monolingual teacher may experience when working with a child with EAL. In this section the focus is on the perceptions of an EAL teacher with regard to the benefits and challenges they may experience when working with children with EAL.

Vignette 4: A culturally responsive teacher's pedagogy

The author of this chapter was born in England and started school not being able to speak any English, therefore, she understands exactly how children with EAL may feel in the classroom and how they may be treated throughout the English schooling system, especially when assumptions were made about her lack of ability to understand anything. These kinds of assumptions led the author to be reserved and withdrawn through much of her education, which was in direct contrast to the way in which she behaved with her family and friends. After she secured a job as a primary school teacher, her head shared with her that one reason that she stood out above the other candidates was because of her multilingual ability and the fact that as a former child with EAL in the English educational system, she would be better placed to help meet the needs of the children with EAL in her class.

On reflection, the author never asked children with EAL to speak only in English in the classroom. She actively encouraged the use of home languages, but she was also aware of what certain words in Bengali and Hindi meant, so the children were more cautious of trying to pretend that they did not understand. Key words were also used instead of English at times to help children such as 'give this to your ama (meaning mum)'. In addition, she made sure that not only was she visible at the beginning and the end of each school day, she made the effort to meet and greet all parents, even if they did not speak English just to say 'Hello' or 'Good morning', which then progressed to asking 'Are you well?'. Over time, some of the parents began responding to her with 'Morning' or 'Hello' which felt like a huge achievement for the school. This in turn had a positive effect on the children because they began to realize that their teacher would happily engage with their parents at the end of the school day to share successes as well as any issues that had occurred.

In terms of planning provision and opportunities, the author knew from her personal experience that there was no point in shouting at children to make them learn. Instead, she used her early years experience and knowledge to create learning opportunities that encouraged children to work together in different ways. For example, in every year group in a primary school in which the author taught, she always had a home corner linked to the current topic which was changed termly. The home corner was used as an learning activity to promote talk, which really benefited the children with EAL who like all children, at times thought that if they were not seen, then they were not heard.

On reflection, the author's multilingual knowledge and different cultural background supported the school's relationships with the parents and the wider community. The head teacher shared with the author that it was important for the school to employ staff with a range of different languages so that children with EAL could be better supported. The different cultural background of the author in comparison to the other monolingual teachers made her different to the norm and did make her feel like an outsider, but it was the opposite with the parents and the children of her class.

Reflection on vignette 4

Clearly encouraging the participation and scaffolding of the learning of all young people in classrooms, enabling social participation, and responding to the variety of communication needs of learners with EAL through classroom dialogue can be challenging. A serious constraint of working within the National Curriculum is that some teacher trainees, support staff and teachers have none or very limited experience of working with children who have EAL. This lack of experience can make adults feel anxious about meeting the needs of children with EAL especially if they lack confidence in applying knowledge of language learning theory to practice. Just as in the example of the culturally-responsive teachers above, Swanwick (2019, p. 94) advocates a focus on 'translanguaging', 'that is, teachers' mindful use of sign, spoken, and written languages that promotes inclusivity and engagement and is supportive of language and curriculum learning' and draws on the language repertoire of learners in individual classrooms. This may involve switching between languages and so on to check comprehension, and introduce new concepts and vocabulary. There are provisos in this approach, of course. According to Swanwick (2019, p. 98), translanguaging will enhance learning and language development of EAL learners if:

1 it is embedded within an inclusive and additive language context;
2 the diverse language repertoires of individuals are recognized and nurtured;
3 practitioners have the bilingual skills and agility to lead and respond to translanguaging practices that enhance language development and learning.

The way forward: useful strategies

Today, there are a number of sources where teachers and support staff can access a range of resources to support children with EAL in the classroom. The Bell Foundation has sponsored a number of research projects that support better outcomes for children with EAL. In addition, the National Association for Language Development in the Curriculum (NALDIC) (2020) has a range of advice and resources on their website that supports learning for children with EAL for both early years and primary sectors of education in all subjects.

In Table 16.1, the author of this chapter depicts a range of strategies that have been successful in supporting practice from her own personal experience of working as an early years and primary teacher as well as working in a university.

The strategies suggested in Table 16.1 can be applied to any context or topic and any year group. In addition, schools would love to employ staff who speak the languages of their children's communities, but this can only take place if adults are bilingual in the first place. This implies that there needs to be a greater focus on learning an additional language in schools from an earlier age to ensure that there is a healthy respect for children who speak different languages.

The most important way forward is, first, to know the child well, and second, for the practitioner to be secure in their knowledge and understanding

Table 16.1   Strategies to support culturally responsive practice for children with EAL

Strategy	Application for children with EAL
Use of play	• Had a home corner/area set up linked to the topic of the term, then would use this as a speaking and listening activity as well as other group tasks that required children to collaborate and problem solve • Sometimes it would also be used as part of golden time whereby children were free to actually play
Use of games and board games	• A stock of games were kept to support literacy and numeracy skills (Scrabble™, guess who, snakes and ladders, bingo, etc.) which were used to support specific skills and also to encourage collaboration and team work
Scribing children's thoughts	• During discussions, children's ideas could be scribed therefore taking the emphasis away from being forced to write
Problem-solving challenges	• Setting up a problem and encouraging different groups to offer solutions to different parts of the problem that did not always need to be written
Using stimulus for writing	• Flipping learning around so that a creative project or task would take place first and then using the creation and discussions to form the basis of writing (rather than doing a piece of writing and drawing a picture at the end of it)
Modelling tasks	• Allowing children to have a go initially, then modelling tasks/conversations so that children with EAL have something to link their thinking to
Making time to work with children	• Always working with a group and listening into their conversations which gives the practitioner a better insight into the children's knowledge and understanding
Observing children	• Especially in play or in free choice/golden time when children can assume that they are not being assessed
Joining in	• Join in with children's play or their activities as they thrive on their teacher joining in

of how children learn. Finally, it is important to have a sound awareness of how children learn language. By combining knowledge of all three, teachers are in the best place to meet the learning needs of their children with EAL because the answer is not to have a range of temporary, short-term strategies, rather more long-lasting interventions that have a positive impact on outcomes.

Conclusion

In summary, this chapter shares the scenarios of learners and personal reflections from the experiences of a teacher with EAL to help the reader gain an understanding of some of the needs of children with EAL. This in turn will support practice and provision and more importantly, give teachers the confidence to take risks in trying out different strategies for children with EAL that are long-term and cognitively challenging in nature to help improve these children's learning outcomes.

References

Alexander, R. (2006) *Towards Dialogic Teaching*, 3rd ed., New York: Dialogos.

Bakhtin, M.M. (1981) *The Dialogic Imagination: Four Essays by M. M. Bakhtin*, ed. M. Holquist, trans. C. Emerson and M. Holquist, Austin, TX: University of Texas Press.

Bakhtin, M.M. (1984) *Problems of Dostoevsky's Poetics*, ed. and trans. C. Emerson, Minneapolis, MN: University of Minnesota Press.

Bishop, R., Berryman, M. and Wearmouth, J. (2014) *Te Kotahitanga: Towards Effective Education Reform for Indigenous and Other Minoritised Students*, Wellington, NZ: NZCER

Gay, G. (2010) *Culturally Responsive Teaching: Theory, Research and Practice*, New York: Teachers' College Press.

Glynn, T., Wearmouth, J. and Berryman, M. (2006) *Supporting Students with Literacy Difficulties: A Responsive Approach*, Maidenhead: Open University Press/McGraw Hill.

Gonzalez, N., Moll, L.C. and Amanti, C. (2005) *Funds of Knowledge: Theorizing Practices in Households, Communities and Classrooms*, Mahwah, NJ: Lawrence Erlbaum Associates.

Hutchinson, J. (2018) *Educational Outcomes of Children with English as an Additional Language*, Cambridge: The Bell Foundation.

Kozulin, A. (2003) 'Psychological tools and mediated learning', in A. Kozulin, B. Gindis, V.S. Ageyev and S.M. Miller (eds), *Vygotsky's Educational Theory in Cultural Context*, Cambridge: Cambridge University Press, pp. 15–38.

Littleton, K. and Mercer, N. (2013) *Interthinking. Putting Talk to Work*, London: Routledge.

Mercer, N. and Littleton, K. (2007) *Dialogue and the Development of Children's Thinking*, London: Routledge.

Mistry, M. and Sood, K. (2010) 'English as an Additional Language: Challenges and assumptions', *Management in Education*, 24(3), 1–4.

Mistry, M. and Sood, K. (2015) *English as an Additional Language in the Early Years: Linking Theory and Practice*, London: David Fulton.

Mistry, M. and Sood, K. (2020) *Meeting the Needs of Young Children with English as an Additional Language: Research Informed Practice*, London: David Fulton.

Moll, L., Amanti, C., Neffe, C. and Gonzalez, N. (1992) 'Funds of knowledge for teaching: Using a qualitative approach to connect homes and classrooms', *Theory into Practice*, 32(2): 132–41.

National Association for Language Development in the Curriculum (NALDIC) (2020) *The National Subject Association for EAL*. Available at: https://naldic.org.uk/ (accessed April 2020).

Rogoff, B. (2003) *The Cultural Nature of Human Development*, Oxford: Oxford University Press.

Sleeter, C. (2011) *Professional Development for Culturally Responsive and Relationship Based Pedagogy*, New York: Peter Lang.

Smagorinsky, P. (2011) *Vygotsky and Literacy Research*, Boston, MA: Sense Publishers.

Swanwick, R. (2019) 'Dialogic teaching and translanguaging in deaf education', in H. Knoors and M. Marschark (eds), *Evidence-based Practices in Deaf Education*, Oxford: Oxford University Press, pp. 81–107.

Vygotsky, L. (1978) *Interaction Between Learning and Development*, trans. M. Cole, Cambridge, MA: Harvard University Press.

Vygotsky, L.S. (1981a) 'The genesis of higher mental functions', in J.V. Wersch (ed.), *The Concept of Activity in Soviet Psychology*, New York: M.E. Sharpe.

Vygotsky, L.S. (1981b) 'The instrumental method in psychology', in J.V. Wersch (ed.), *The Concept of Activity in Soviet Psychology*, New York: M.E. Sharpe.

Wearmouth, J. (2017) 'Employing culturally responsive pedagogy to foster literacy learning in schools', *Cogent Education*, 4(1), doi:10.1080/2331186X.2017.1295824

Wearmouth, J. and Berryman, M. (2009) *Inclusion as Participation in Communities of Practice*, Palmerston North, NZ: Dunmore Press.

Wearmouth, J., Berryman, M. and Whittle, L. (2011) 'Shoot for the moon! Students' identities as writers in the context of the classroom', *British Journal of Special Education*, 38(2): 92–9.

Wenger, E. (1998) *Communities of Practice: Learning, Meaning and Identity*, Cambridge: Cambridge University Press.

17 How can we ensure that young people and their Special Educational Needs are included in Personal, Social, Health and Economic (PSHE) lessons?

Philippa Smith, Janice Wearmouth and Karen Lindley

Major questions addressed in this chapter are:

- Do PSHE co-ordinators generally write the guidance for children with SEND? Or is it left to the SEND team to deliver?
- Is the content often too generic for children who do not cope well with generalizations, for example, children with autism?
- Are teachers sufficiently trained to include sensitive content in classrooms where there are children with additional needs?
- Are students with mental health issues considered by all staff in PSHE lessons?
- Are students with physical disabilities or long-term illnesses considered by all teaching staff?

Abstract

This chapter is written from the perspective of an experienced secondary special educational needs co-ordinator (SENCo). She notes how well-delivered

Personal, Social, Health and Economic (PSHE) programmes can have a positive impact on both academic and non-academic outcomes for pupils. However, provision for young people with special educational needs and disabilities (SEND) in PSHE lessons can be sporadic and largely dependent on the teacher providing the course. In the SENCo's experience, outcomes can be beneficial to some, but may be potentially damaging to those who are disadvantaged in some way. She discusses ways in which the content of the PSHE curriculum can be inclusive of all learners.

Introduction

Curriculum guidance from the Personal, Social and Health Education (PSHE) Association (PSHE, 2019a) states that PSHE education is a school subject through which learners develop the knowledge, skills and attributes they need to keep themselves healthy and safe, and prepared for life and work. This chapter takes the view that thoughtful, well-delivered PSHE programmes can have a positive impact on both academic and non-academic outcomes for pupils. However, 'well-delivered', if this term is intended to be inclusive of all learners, may not be realized in practice unless attention is paid to the needs of the most vulnerable and disadvantaged, including children with special educational needs and disabilities (SEND).

The chapter is written from the perspective of a special educational needs co-ordinator (SENCo), experienced in secondary mainstream schools. It begins by outlining the most recent national guidance on the PSHE curriculum for school leaders and PSHE lead teachers, and notes how outcomes can be beneficial to some, but may be potentially damaging outcomes to those who are disadvantaged in some way. Provision can be sporadic and largely dependent on the teacher providing the course. The chapter goes on to discuss the content of the PSHE curriculum, the extent to which it can be inclusive of all types of learners, and the issue of how to ensure a fair and even programme is offered to children with SEND.

National Guidance on PSHE

Updated National Curriculum guidance related to PSHE from the Department for Education that has come into effect in September 2020, states:

> PSHE is a non-statutory subject. To allow teachers the flexibility to deliver high-quality PSHE we consider it unnecessary to provide new standardised frameworks or programmes of study. PSHE can encompass many areas of study. Teachers are best placed to understand the needs of their pupils and do not need additional central prescription.
>
> However, while we believe that it is for schools to tailor their local PSHE programme to reflect the needs of their pupils, we expect schools to use their

> PSHE education programme to equip pupils with a sound understanding of risk and with the knowledge and skills necessary to make safe and informed decisions.
>
> (DFE, 2020)

As a result of this guidance, schools can design and deliver the PSHE curriculum based on the 'needs' of their institution. Over a long period, however, there have been concerns raised about the consistency of provision partly as a result of this status that continues to be non-statutory. The 2013 Ofsted PSHE report found that 40 per cent of schools' PSHE education was 'not yet good enough' (Ofsted, 2013). The experience of the aforementioned SENCo resonates with this report. Often the course may be taught by staff in their capacity as class tutor and can be treated as a 'tick box' exercise. The question that should be posed here is that, if the PSHE curriculum is responsible for educating students in areas as important as health, well-being and relationships, why the course content is not more prescriptive in order to ensure all children in every setting are receiving high-quality education. This of course includes students with additional needs. Keeping the curriculum open-ended and, potentially, undifferentiated can create a number of issues for these children which contravene and damage, rather than take into account, their specific and individual needs.

PSHE education should contribute to schools' statutory duties outlined in the Education Act 2002 and the Academies Act 2010 to provide a balanced and broadly based curriculum and is essential to Ofsted judgements in relation to personal development, behaviour, welfare and safeguarding. The relationships and health aspects of PSHE education have been compulsory in all schools from September 2020.

Under Section 78(1) of part 6 of the 2002 Education Act, England, the curriculum for a maintained school or maintained nursery school satisfies the requirements of this section if it is a balanced and broadly based curriculum which:

1 promotes the spiritual, moral, cultural, mental and physical development of pupils at the school and of society;
2 prepares pupils at the school for the opportunities, responsibilities and experiences of later life.

The PSHE curriculum is intended to meet the above requirements whilst helping pupils to develop the knowledge, skills and attributes they need to manage life's challenges and make the most of life's opportunities. As the National Curriculum provides little to no content for schools in this area of the curriculum, the PSHE Association was established as the national body for PSHE education in England, providing advice and support to a network of over 25,000 teachers and other professionals working in schools nationwide. The Association is an independent charity and membership association, established as the official national PSHE subject association by the Department for Education in 2007.

The PSHE Association states that there is evidence to show that PSHE education can address teenage pregnancy, substance misuse, unhealthy eating, lack of physical activity, emotional health and other key issues. An effective PSHE programme can also tackle barriers to learning, raise aspirations, and improve the life chances of the most vulnerable and disadvantaged pupils (PSHE Association, 2019a). It is therefore in a school's best interest to ensure that the programme it provides is thorough and effective. The range of topics that should be covered as part of the broader PSHE education should be relevant and appropriate to the targeted key stage.

In the new framework, most of PSHE education became statutory for all schools from September 2020 under the Children and Social Work Act 2017. This includes Relationships Education at Key Stages 1 and 2, Relationships and Sex Education (RSE) at Key Stages 3 and 4, and Health Education in both primary and secondary phases. The Department for Education published Statutory Guidance for Relationships Education, Relationships and Sex Education (RSE) and Health Education in June 2019. This sets out what schools *must* cover from September 2020 (though not all they *should* cover as part of broader PSHE education). The statutory content sets out learning opportunities for all Key Stages and cover a number of themes that include relationships, sex education (for secondary-aged learners), and health and well-being. This updated edition of the PSHE Association Programme of Study for PSHE education will support schools to provide a comprehensive programme that integrates, but is not limited to this statutory content. A broader PSHE programme should also cover economic well-being, careers and enterprise education, as well as education for personal safety, including assessing and managing risk (PSHE Association, 2019b).

Guidance for school leaders and PSHE lead teachers

Understandably, not all topics are accessible to children with special needs, an issue that is well considered and addressed by the PSHE Association. Supporting teachers responsible for PSHE programmes and those working with pupils with special educational needs and disability (SEND) is a key part of their work. They have prepared an updated comprehensive planning framework for children with SEND (Key Stages 1–4). This framework states that students will be offered the opportunity to do the following:

- experience taking and sharing responsibility;
- feel positive about themselves and others;
- reflect on their perceptions and experiences;
- develop the understanding, language, communication skills and strategies required to exercise personal autonomy wherever possible;
- carry out or take part in daily personal living routines;
- make real decisions (with support where necessary so that they can act upon them);

- take part in group activities and make contributions;
- develop and maintain positive relationships and interactions with others;
- recognize and celebrate their achievements and successes.

It covers themes including self-awareness; self-care, support and safety; managing feelings; changing and growing; healthy lifestyles and the world I live in. These topics cover the statutory requirements for students in a more inclusive manner. While an excellent resource, the framework is, however, a separate plan appropriate for teaching a specialist group. However, many maintained schools do not have the resources to teach smaller groups during PSHE sessions. As schools often use non-specialist PSHE teachers, such a programme would need to be incorporated into the wider programme for all pupils. The Association has acknowledged the reality for many schools and has therefore included a clause which states that, in mainstream schools, the framework can be used as a resource for teaching learners who experience difficulties in learning by 'using the strand' that matches the topic in the Programme of Study that 'is being taught to the rest of the class', and 'using the learning outcomes' in the framework to meet targets in a learner's Education, Health and Care Plan, or an Individual Learning Plan (PSHE Association, 2020, p. 6). Planning the inclusion of the differentiated approaches is therefore imperative in schools.

PSHE differentiation in practice

As schools should design their own PSHE education curriculum in a way that reflects the needs of their pupils and communities, the programme will be a very varied one across all schools. While one size does not fit all, this variation and broad approach may result in students receiving very different experiences.

Vignette: A young teacher's experiences of the PSHE curriculum

A previous SENCo and School Leader writes of her personal experiences and opinions regarding this provision for PSHE:

When I started as a young teacher I had a somewhat utopian view of teaching PSHE. I saw it as an opportunity to reach children in a special way and make a true difference to each and every one of them. The reality was quite different and although many positive differences were made for the odd individual, it was not the groundbreaking change that most young teachers envisage. The greatest challenge for me was to differentiate broad topics for such a wide variety of children from such varied households. Interestingly one of the biggest challenges was delivering content to students with such different emotional intelligence and experiences. Some students were old beyond their years and others extremely naïve. The Nature vs. Nurture aspect of psychology became glaringly apparent and the children required different input according to their different environments. The schools that I have taught in have focused on differentiation, however this was based more on differentiating for vulnerable and under-privileged children as opposed to children with SEND. Considering that the content of the curriculum does include many areas that are affected by socio-economic differences, it does make sense to do so but without disadvantaging children with additional needs. I personally found that the provision for these children was considered an area for the SEND team to cover, and most of the time teachers were delivering the lessons as a tick box exercise 'required by Ofsted'. One school I taught in during my early years in teaching had a big drive in PSHE and employed a Head of Citizenship whose job was to design the curriculum and coach and manage a team of non-specialists (the tutors) to deliver the course. At that stage I was gaining experience in the SEND department as an assistant SENCo and remember becoming increasingly aware of a particular child in my tutor group who absolutely dreaded PSHE lessons and would become increasingly disruptive during the sessions. He had a diagnosis of ADHD and Asperger's and was teased mercilessly by the other students in the lesson. As PSHE lessons often require group discussions and students expressing opinions, his lack of understanding of many topics caused teasing, sniggering and laughing. Instead of helping him to integrate into the session, the structure of the course highlighted his differences and resulted in him requesting to be removed. Working with him and listening to his voice was a steep learning curve. I then ensured that my delivery was always clearly and properly differentiated but wondered if this was being mirrored by others teaching it. I asked some colleagues and many quite openly made comments such as 'I don't have time to plan PSHE – I just teach what is on the plan...' and 'most of the time I let the kids just chat about the topic ... it's only half an hour' and 'if they are so needy, then why is there not a TA in the lesson?'. While these comments were made flippantly to me and certainly are not opinions shared by all in the profession, it made me wonder how many did share these views. Where did the responsibility for ensuring these types of children are provided for lie?

(Smith, personal correspondence, undated)

The first author has discussed the current situation regarding provision for PSHE with a number of teachers employed in a different range of schools. From this, albeit limited, information, the picture appears to be variable and largely sporadic. Some teachers mirrored her own thoughts and experiences, however, others presented very different scenarios. The schools where good provision is seemingly taking place rely heavily on the input of the SENCo and his/her liaison with the PSHE curriculum lead teacher. An Assistant Head teacher from a small, relatively new maintained all-through school was particularly keen to share the good practice taking place at her school, recently awarded the Inclusion Mark. In discussion about how to ensure a full and inclusive PSHE education she commented:

> We have a robust quality assurance system. Every subject curriculum including PSHE is overseen and checked by the SENCo prior to delivery. Schemes of Work and lesson plans are created in liaison with the SENCo and in line with the school's policy on inclusion. PSHE lessons are included on the observation rota as are all subjects and differentiation is a key marker in all observations.
>
> (Smith, unpublished)

A second teacher, during discussion in an online PSHE group, stated that, as the SENCo, she was responsible for checking that the curriculum met the criteria of the children in her care. Again she mentioned the SENCo working alongside the PSHE lead teacher:

> Personally I think that this practice [SENCo-PSHE lead teacher collaboration] is commendable and should be taking place in all schools, however, being a SENCo myself – and understanding the task for any SENCo in a large maintained school – would it not be viable for PSHE leads to take on the onus of the preparation for all students with input from the SENCo in terms of quality assurance (QA) as opposed to the construction of him to integrate? It is important for them to understand and implement a creative approach to the curriculum which encompasses all learners without adding additional workload for the SEND team. Perhaps teachers should be all be trained to identify and deliver to meet the needs of children with additional needs? Surely this will ensure a more inclusive delivery?
>
> (Smith, unpublished)

Integrating differentiation into the PSHE curriculum

For a number of reasons – apart from the absolute need to respect the individuality and common humanity of all young people – it behoves us all to consider how the PSHE curriculum can and should be differentiated to take account of the needs of all young people, and to include them. The 2014 Children and Families Act has, for the first time, given children with special educational needs and disabilities the entitlement to an education that is not simply satisfactory, but can lead to the 'best possible' outcomes. The *Special Educational Needs and Disability Code of Practice: 0 to 25 Years* (DfE, 2015) makes it clear that the responsibility for the academic progress and welfare of learners in classrooms belongs, squarely, to the classroom teacher. The PSHE Association (2019c) has published what it calls ten evidence-based principles of PSHE Education, that are particularly relevant to considerations of differentiation:

1   Begin at the level of what learners can already do, say, know and understand, and involve them in lesson planning.

2 Build on what has gone before to introduce new learning, following the (1960) concept of the 'spiral curriculum'.

3 Be positive, avoid inducing guilt or shock, and focus on the positives: health, safety and the possibility of happy and fulfilling lives in the future.

4 Emphasize interactive learning with a variety of teaching approaches.

5 Offer realistic, relevant information that supports positive norms in society.

6 Encourage learners to reflect on new learning and ways in which it applies to other aspects of their lives.

7 Acknowledge that the PSHE curriculum is only one aspect of the ways in which schools can assist learners in their development, and make links to other school approaches and to families and the wider community.

8 Use the PSHE education as part of other school approaches to develop positive relationships with adults and support the most vulnerable learners.

9 Support learners to make decisions about their lives and to take responsibility for these.

10 Ensure the learning environment is safe and supportive so that learners have the confidence to ask questions, use their own experiences and challenge the information they are given.

(adapted from PSHE Association, 2019c)

The field of special educational needs and disabilities is very wide and covers a whole range of barriers to learning that, for the purpose of administrative convenience, as some might see it (Wearmouth, 2017), are grouped into four categories in the *Code of Practice* (DfE, 2015): communication and interaction, cognition and learning, social, emotional and mental health, and sensory and/or physical needs. Norwich and Lewis (2001), and a number of other educators interested in the SEND field, note how many learners with SEND, for example, those who experience cognitive difficulties at a mild level, may not need distinctively different teaching, but more time, more practice and more examples than others. Wearmouth (2019, p. 152), for example, discusses the case of 'George', a young man with cognitive issues whose needs were never really properly addressed in his mainstream secondary school. What would have helped him would in fact have helped a number of other learners in his class – in PSHE as well as other lessons. The tasks given to the class as a whole were often not achievable by him. The teacher often moved on too quickly, before he had a chance to think about what he had learnt. He would have benefited from a greater chance to handle concrete items and see visual representations such as pictures and diagrams rather than continuous teacher talk.

> He needed multiple examples of new concepts, carefully devised 'scaffolding' from a teacher, TA or peer with that scaffolding withdrawn as George became more confident with the task or concept at hand, lots of opportunities, certainly more than most of his peers, to practise newly learnt skills.
>
> (ibid., p. 152)

Self-audit for inclusive PSHE lessons: planning teaching, learning and support

An effective way to ensure that inclusive approaches to planning and teaching inclusive PSHE lessons and to assess the degree to which the learning environment predisposes to positive learning and behaviour is to self-audit lessons, or to ask a trusted colleague to carry out this activity. The authors of the Primary Strategy (DfES, 2006) developed a very useful inclusive teaching checklist to evaluate the extent to which pedagogy in classrooms is inclusive of all learners. It has been archived and is now available at http://webarchive.nationalarchives.gov.uk/20110202171650/http:/nationalstrategies.standards.dcsf.gov.uk/node/317753 (accessed 8 April 2020).

The Training and Development Agency for Schools (TDA) also archived a very useful framework for considering access strategies that are useful for a whole range of learners. This material is available at: https://webarchive.nationalarchives.gov.uk/20110212084529/https://nationalstrategies.standards.dcsf.gov.uk/

Including vulnerable learners

In terms of learners' vulnerability in PSHE lessons, we might take the example of those young people who experience social and emotional difficulties. There is considerable evidence now that young people's overall level of well-being influences their behaviour and engagement in school and their ability to make good academic progress (Gutman and Vorhaus, 2012).

Vignette: Application of 'mindfulness'

Numbers of in-class factors in PSHE, and other lessons, can influence learners' mental health and well-being. For example, the physical and social environment, including interpersonal relationships, may have profound effects on their physical, emotional and mental health as well as affecting their attainment. An example of a practical approach that increasing numbers of teachers use in schools to assist learners to become calmer and that can be incorporated into PSHE lessons, and others, is 'mindfulness'. This is a technique that emphasizes paying attention to the present moment in an accepting, non-judgemental manner. Increasingly, it is taught in many countries of the world, from the level of executives in corporations to children both at home and in school. Mindfulness-induced emotional and behavioral changes have been found to be related to functional and structural changes in the brain (Gotink et al. 2016). At each developmental stage, mindfulness can be a useful tool for decreasing anxiety and promoting happiness, but as with all powerful techniques of this sort, it should be used with care and in discussion with experienced colleagues.

Awareness of attachment issues

Relationships, learner-to-teacher and learner-to-learner, are a really important factor in learning in settings, schools and colleges. In recent years there has been a growing understanding of the extent to which the nature of a child's early attachment affects the way in which s/he behaves in relationships and interacts with other people into adulthood. As the National Research Council (US) Division of Behavioral and Social Sciences and Education (2001, p. 27) notes: 'Human relationships, and the effect of relationships on relationships, are the building blocks of healthy development.' It is crucial that teachers and other adults consider how to engage those with attachment difficulties, especially in lessons where the focus is on relationship-building. Bomber (2007, p. 39) offers some very important advice to staff in settings/schools/colleges in her reminder that, for many young people, their behaviour is a major means of communicating distress and that educational institutions should ensure that child welfare is high on their agenda:

> Please note that if a child is currently at risk, then their behaviour needs to be viewed as a communication expressing the danger they are in. Action needs to be taken, view their behaviour as a 'cry for help', and ensure you log concerns and follow your area's Child Protection guidelines.

Ensuring that PSHE teachers and others are aware of, and feel that they have the ability and skills to address, factors that can influence learners' mental health and well-being may be of prime importance for high-quality PSHE lessons. Where learners experience serious emotional and attachment issues, this might need to include access to specialist advice from external services such as educational psychology.

Conclusion

Offering a fair and even provision in any subject is imperative and personally the most important part of education. PSHE is the subject that assists young people in understanding the world around us and should ensure that all students despite differing backgrounds or barriers to learning are offered a fair path to adulthood. Schools are extremely influential to these young people as for many of them it is their only place of security and moral/ethical education. Only recently has the subject become statutory and hopefully this will ensure an improved and more standardized provision across schools nationally.

References

Bomber, L.M. (2007) *Inside I'm Hurting: Practical Strategies for Supporting Children with Attachment Difficulties in Schools*, Broadway: Worth Publishing.

DfE (Department for Education) (2015) *Special Educational Needs and Disability Code of Practice: 0 to 25 Years*, London: DfE.

DfE (Department for Education) (2020) *Guidance: Personal, Social, Health and Economic Education*. Available at: https://www.gov.uk/government/publications/personal-social-health-and-economic-education-pshe/personal-social-health-and-economic-pshe-education (accessed 25 January 2021).

DfES (Department for Education and Schools) (2006) *The National Strategies*, archived at http://webarchive.nationalarchives.gov.uk/20110202171650/http:/nationalstrategies.standards.dcsf.gov.uk/node/317753 (accessed 8 April 2020).

Gotink, R.A., Meijboom, R., Vernooij, M.W., Smits, M. and Hunink, M.G. (2016) '8-week Mindfulness Based Stress Reduction induces brain changes similar to traditional long-term meditation practice: A systematic review', *Brain and Cognition*, 108: 32–41.

Gutman, L.M. and Vorhaus, J. (2012) *The Impact of Pupil Behaviour and Wellbeing on Educational Outcomes*, London: Institute of Education/Department for Education.

National Research Council (US) Division of Behavioral and Social Sciences and Education (2001) *Early Childhood Development and Learning: New Knowledge for Policy*, Washington, DC: National Academies Press.

Norwich, B. and Lewis, A. (2001) 'Mapping a pedagogy for special educational needs', *British Educational Research Journal*, 27(3): 313–29.

Ofsted (Office for Standards in Education) (2013) 'Not yet good enough: personal, social, health and economic education in schools'. Available at: https://www.gov.uk/government/publications/not-yet-good-enough-personal-social-health-and-economic-education

Personal, Social, Health and Economic (PSHE) Association (2019a) 'Curriculum guidance'. Available at: https://www.pshe-association.org.uk/curriculum-and-resources/curriculum) (accessed 25 January 2021).

Personal, Social, Health and Economic (PSHE) Association (2019b) 'Programme of Study for PSHE Education Key Stages 1–5'. Available at: https://www.pshe-association.org.uk/curriculum-and-resources/resources/programme-study-pshe-education-key-stages-1-5 (accessed 25 January 2021).

PSHE Association (2019c) 'Ten principles of effective PSHE education'. Available at https://www.pshe-association.org.uk/curriculum-and-resources/resources/ten-principles-effective-pshe-education (accessed 25 January 2021).

Personal, Social, Health and Economic (PSHE) Association (2020) 'PSHE Education Planning Framework for pupils with SEND'. Available at: https://www.pshe-association.org.uk/curriculum-and-resources/resources/pshe-education-planning-framework-pupils-send-key (accessed 25 January 2021).

Wearmouth, J. (2017) 'Employing culturally responsive pedagogy to foster literacy learning in schools', *Cogent Education*, 4(1), doi:10.1080/2331186X.2017.1295824

Wearmouth, J. (2019) *Special Educational Needs and Disability: The Basics*, London: Routledge.

Index

Page numbers in italics are figures; with 'n' are notes.